Cycling The Netherlands, Belgium, and Luxembourg

Katherine and Jerry Widing

D1153492

BICYCLE  BOOKS

FROM

MBI Publishing Company

Dedication
To my father, who, when I was five years old, ran around the
backyard behind my bicycle and didn't tell me
he'd already let go.—*Kathy*

First published in 1998 by MBI Publishing Company, 729 Prospect
Avenue, PO Box 1, Osceola, WI 54020-0001 USA

MBI Publishing Company books are also available at discounts in
bulk quantity for industrial or sales-promotional use. For details write
to Special Sales Manager at Motorbooks International Wholesalers
& Distributors, 729 Prospect Avenue, Osceola WI 54020-0001 USA

Library of Congress Cataloging-in-Publication Data
Widing, Katherine.
        Cycling the Netherlands, Belgium &
Luxembourg/Katherine Widing and Jerry Widing.
                p. cm.--(Bicycle books)
        Includes index.
        ISBN 0-933201-91-5
        1. Cycling--Netherlands--Guidebooks. 2.
Cycling--Belgium-- Guidebooks. 3.
Cycling--Luxembourg--Guidebooks. 4. Netherlands-- Guidebooks. 5.
Belgium--Guidebooks. 6. Luxembourg--Guidebooks.
I. Widing, Jerry. II. Title. III. Series.
GV1046.N44W53   1998
914.9204'73--dc21   97-50237

On the front cover: The beautiful canals lend themselves perfectly
to scenic cycling.

On the back cover: Windmills are a familiar sight throughout
Northern Netherlands.

Printed in the United States of America

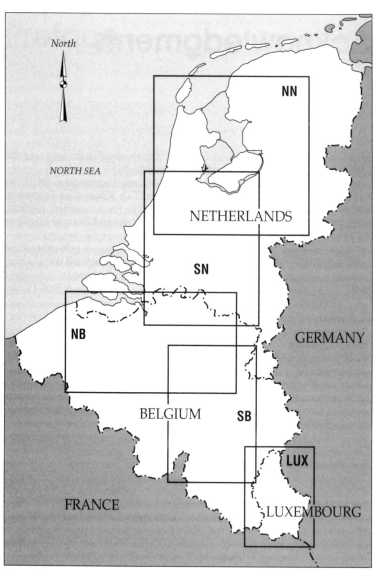

Map Key:
NN = Northern Netherlands Route
SN = Southern Netherlands Route
NB = Northern Belgium Route
SB = Southern Belgium Route
Lux = Luxembourg Route

Introduction

This book, written for both novices and experts, is designed for any person who wants to cycle in the Benelux and enjoy it, for just a day or for several weeks or months.

The first six chapters of the book introduce the cyclist to the Benelux and the practicalities of cycling in the three countries. If you are taking your own bicycle, there is information on preparation and planning.

The second part of the book is the route information. The routes can each be done in their entirety as a Grand Tour of the Benelux by linking all five routes, or simply as shorter routes, selecting a portion for a few days, or even as day trips, basing yourself in a place and doing a stage for the day. Note: the distance of each route is given in kilometers since all three countries follow the metric system and distance signs will reflect this system.

The routes are broken up into "stages" of varying lengths. Each stage begins and ends at a convenient point for sightseeing with a variety of accommodation and eating establishments. The majority of these locations are accessible by public transport for those wishing to rent bicycles, with information on bicycle rentals provided, and do a day or short tour. Some stages may be as short as 20 kilometers, while others are longer. A stage does not necessarily equal a day. For some people the 20 kilometers or so may be enough for a leisurely day's ride; for others a couple of stages may be completed in a day. Everyone rides differently; weather conditions vary; and some days there will be lots of sightseeing to shorten your distance. You are the best judge of your ability.

Each route provides directions plus any sights and points of interest along the way. At the end of each stage, whether it concludes in a city, town, or village, certain information is always listed. We begin with the sightseeing in the locale and the tourist office information, as this is your first and most valuable stop. Next the available accommodation choices are presented—hotels, bed and breakfasts, pensions, youth hostels, and campgrounds. (Note: The hotel listings provided are in economical and moderate price ranges. If the only option in a town is expensive, we have noted that fact.) At the stopping point for each stage, there will always be somewhere to find a meal, as well as shops or supermarkets for provisions. Where applicable, interesting areas to eat, or areas with lots of restaurants, are indicated, as well as regional food specialties worth seeking out and outdoor markets. Finally, one of the most important pieces of information mentioned in the practical information for each stage is the local bicycle shops and the possibility of bicycle rentals.

Each route in the book gives detailed directions and a series of associated maps. These maps are simply basic guides and are not intended to replace a proper, detailed map of the area. The more detail you have the better. A good map, such as those recommended at the start of each route, will help you plan the trip before you leave and help keep you on the right road while under way. Each day mark your proposed daily route and how far you intend to go. Be careful not to overestimate. You are here to experience the Benelux, so allow yourself the time to stop and smell the tulips, so to speak. Also, as you will learn early on in your trip, it is important to arrive at your destination early enough in the day to allow yourself time to settle in, relax, and enjoy.

By the way, if you're ever in doubt or feel you are lost, ask someone. People are friendly and willing to help.

One last thing. Even though this is a bicycle book, and we as authors are avid cyclists, we realize the need to put your bicycle away at certain times. You should consider rest days, and cities are often best explored on foot. Also, we have noted recreational areas where there is excellent hiking, and you may wish to take a break from your bicycle and don a daypack and your walking shoes.

Bon Voyage and Goede Reis!

Note

We have attempted to include the most complete and accurate information that will fit in a reasonably-sized book. We realize this will not include everything. Everyone plans differently, as everyone travels differently. Prices change, tourist offices move, hotels go out of business. All we can do is provide what we think is most important and carefully check the accuracy of what we have written. At the time of writing, we believe all of the information in this book to be correct. It is up to the reader to realize this not a static world.

Furthermore, although we can provide some specifics about safety in certain circumstances, the caution and common sense that should accompany every traveler is not purchased with a book. We hope that everyone who uses this publication as a tool will depart with a sense of adventure, the flexibility to go where the wind blows them, and the good sense to be as careful as possible.

Chapter 1

Why Travel by Bicycle?

Warning! Riding a bicycle is addictive, and touring by bicycle is an exciting and rewarding way to travel. The information contained within these pages may cause the reader to pack a bag and head to Europe.

Nothing is more invigorating than riding a bicycle along a dike in the Netherlands beside a field of tulips in full bloom or reaching the top of a hill in Belgium to be rewarded by the sight of a huge medieval abbey (with the thought of a picnic of the abbey's cheese, bread, and beer) or the sweeping view from a twelfth-century feudal castle towering above a spectacular river valley in Luxembourg.

Traveling by bicycle lends a totally different perspective to towns, country roads, sights, and life in general. While on two wheels, you have time to inhale and experience. Plus you are physically active and traveling as the locals do.

Europe is a premier cycling destination. Distances between villages are not great, making distances manageable for the novice. Bicycle shops in small towns offer repairs and rentals, and many railway stations rent bicycles. Plenty of bicycle paths can get you off the beaten track, and where there are no bicycle paths, there are numerous small country backroads. Best of all, Europeans are friendly to cyclists.

Touring by bicycle allows a choice of budget. Once you are in Europe, you have virtually no transportation costs. For the lower budget traveler, the bicycle offers an easy means of transporting camping equipment and personal gear, or should you choose to stay in hotels or bed and breakfasts, all you need to carry is your clothing and daily essentials.

While cycling, you are moving at a slower pace, giving you the opportunity to observe your surroundings and meet people. Locals will stop and chat with you and give you a piece of area information or folklore, and you will develop a camaraderie with other cyclists.

Even though you will be on a specific itinerary, you can be flexible. If you are told about something interesting in the vicinity, the bicycle allows for detours. With a bicycle, you don't have to miss out on a market or attraction in a village 10 kilometers away because no train or bus has a schedule that will work. There is always the car option. But if you rent a car and pay fuel costs, the car is an expensive option, and believe it or not, you can cover quite a distance on a bicycle with not too much effort.

Here is a perfect example of bicycle versus car that occurred in Luxembourg. The night before we had planned to cycle from Echternach to Grevenmacher we had met four Belgians who had driven to Luxembourg for a few days. The following morning we set off, and en route, while riding through a small town, the Belgians honked at us and stopped their car to chat. A short while later we were enjoying a picnic lunch on the banks of the Sûre River, and who should be strolling along the path, but the Belgians. Later in the evening, back in Echternach, we saw them again. After discussing what we had done during the day, we discovered that we had completed just as much in that day on our bicycles as they had in their car.

Some cycling days will be easy as you meander through quiet farmlands. Some days will be difficult as you battle a westerly wind or an enormous hill. The reward comes at the top of the hill or at the end of the day when you are both physically and mentally satisfied.

So, now that you've made the decision to bicycle . . .

Why Should You Choose the Benelux?

The choice of combining cycling in the three countries—the Netherlands, Belgium, and Luxembourg—is a natural. All three nations are extremely bicycle friendly, as most people cycle themselves. The people are welcoming, and language is not a big problem since English is widely spoken in the Netherlands and Luxembourg, and in Belgium most people know enough English to get by. Also, all three countries are well-endowed with bicycle shops and rental possibilities.

The marriage of these three countries is also perfect due to their diversity. The variety of terrain allows an obvious physical progression. The Netherlands makes an ideal starting point to begin building up your cycling strength with flat and extremely easy terrain; working your way south, there are gradual elevation gains from northern Belgium to the hills of southern Belgium that merge into the Ardennes Mountains. By the time you reach Luxembourg, you should be in great cycling condition for continuing into the Luxembourg Ardennes and the valleys of the Sûre and Eisch Rivers.

The Benelux is a microcosm of Europe. The three countries provide an interesting look at different cultures, histories, cuisine, architecture, and lifestyles—Dutch, Flemish, Walloon (Belgian French), and Luxembourgeois. Associated with this is a linguistic diversity, several languages being spoken in a relatively small area: Dutch, Flemish, French, German, and Letzeburgesch.

All things considered, touring the Benelux by bicycle will provide you with an unforgettable European experience, excellent cycling, interesting cultures, varied terrain, friendly people, and much more. Pack your panniers and find out!

Begin in the Netherlands

There is an old Dutch saying, "The Good Lord made the earth, and the Dutch made Holland." This of course refers to the elaborate land reclamation projects where the Dutch have added land to enlarge and protect their country. If a cyclist were to coin this phrase, it would have to be re-written as, "The Lord made the earth, and the Dutch made Holland heaven for cyclists." One can appreciate this after riding for as little as a few hours in this country where the cyclist has top priority in the hierarchy of vehicles on the road.

In the Netherlands, cyclists have privileges often not afforded to the motorist. One-way street signs, for example, often have a sign underneath with a picture of a bicycle and the word *uitgezonderd*, meaning "bicycles are excepted." Bicycle paths in rural areas are often in better paved condition than the gravel road for vehicles that runs right alongside. There are always bicycle parking facilities in the center of town where it can be impossible to park a car. Where traffic construction diverts cars many kilometers out of their way, the cyclist is hard-

It is not unusual to see bicycles parked on the sidewalk in front of houses in the Netherlands.

ly disrupted as special bicycle detour routes are normally set up through the construction site. In the Netherlands, as a cyclist, you will feel privileged with the incredible network of bicycle paths and special amenities for cyclists compared to other countries where cyclists are often viewed as a hindrance to cars. Queen Beatrix is known to be at her happiest when she is cycling around the Dutch countryside. Being a cyclist in Holland, you will feel safer and more comfortable than you could ever imagine, whether in rural areas or even in a big city like Amsterdam.

Holland is flat, except for a few hills in the southeast in the strip of land known as Limburg. The Netherlands does not have the instant dramatic beauty found, for example, in the Swiss Alps, but the country certainly does have its own beauty found in limitless skies, extensive horizons, lots of water—seas, canals, and rivers—and neat storybook villages.

The flat terrain makes the Netherlands an excellent choice for someone cycling in Europe, whether a novice or an experienced cyclist. It offers the novice a gentle introduction to foreign cycling yet offers the experienced cyclist the chance to utilize the extensive network of bicycle paths unique to this country. Another feature of cycling in the Netherlands is the feeling that it is "the thing to do." Everyone, it seems, rides a bicycle, from two year olds to grandmothers. It is a way of life. People use their bicycles to commute, shop, carry a load of vegetables or tools to a neighboring farm, or even to pull a windsurfer to a nearby lake. Most of the population owns a bicycle, and 40 percent of the population get into the saddle on a daily basis. The Dutch are a friendly group, and you quickly feel accepted as you pedal throughout the country.

On to Belgium

The Belgians are very fond of cycling, but more for short local trips rather than for long-distance bicycle touring. The one thing the Belgians are fanatical about is bicycle racing, and over the years Belgium has produced several recipients of international cycling trophies. The most famous, now regarded

under a tree, head for a café, or linger in a museum. If you are contending with several days of rain, try to reach an interesting town where you might be happy to sit out the storm for a day or so or judge whether you can persevere in spite of the rain. Whatever the case, don't allow yourself to get ill. Dry off at night, and if you're camping, consider splurging for a bed in a youth hostel or a bed and breakfast for a night or two. Chapter 4 has more information on weather in each individual country.

Resources

Learning about where you are going makes your trip more interesting. You should take advantage of the numerous resources. Each country, the Netherlands, Belgium, and Luxembourg, has National Tourist Offices all over the world. All are willing to send information, much of which is free. Be specific when contacting these offices, otherwise you may only receive general brochures when there is specific material available on cycling. Also check on the Internet for websites sponsored by these offices and for related material on other websites.

Books and maps are invaluable. This book offers basic sightseeing highlights for locales en route. However, for more depth information, consult specific publications such as the *Insight Guides* for background, the *Michelin Green Guide* and the *Norton Blue Guide* for a wealth of cultural and historic detail, and the *Rough Guide* as an all-around general guidebook. See appendix for more information. Maps are crucial for both planning and while traveling. Be sure to check bookstores and libraries.

Documents

First and foremost, check your passport. Nothing is worse than finding out that your passport is due to expire just before your departure date. If you do not have a passport, apply for one well in advance as the process can be time-consuming. Very few nationalities require visas for the Benelux countries, but check with your travel agent, airline, or specific consulate for more detailed information.

Some other cards you may wish to consider are Youth Hostel cards available directly from the Youth Hostel Offices, local youth hostels, agents in your country, or from most youth hostels in Europe. If you are a student, International Student Cards can be useful for discounts, especially on museum entrance fees. For campers, an optional document is a Camping Carnet. It can be used in place of a passport if the campground office requires you to leave one as a security, and some campgrounds offer discounts with the carnet. The Camping Carnet can be purchased in North America from the Family Campers and RVer's Association in Depew, New York, for U.S.$30, including their membership fee; however, it is also available in the Netherlands from major ANWB offices for approximately U.S.$15. (ANWB is the Royal Dutch Touring Club; see chapter 4 for more information.)

Personal Security and Safety

As much as we would like to hope "it won't happen to me," theft is something you need to be aware of, both before you leave, and on a daily basis while on the road.

Some of the most important items you are carrying are your documents. Once you have your passport in hand, it is a good idea to photocopy the pages that have your photo, passport number, and the date and place of issue. Make two copies, one to leave with someone you can contact from on the road and carry the other one with you, separate from your passport. This will be helpful for more efficient replacement should your passport be lost or stolen. The same procedure should also be considered for other important documents such as airline tickets and youth hostel cards. For traveler's checks and credit cards, take similar precautions; however, instead of photocopies, write the numbers down for security reasons.

To protect your valuables (passport, airline ticket, credit cards, traveler's checks, cash, etc.) wear a money belt or pouch. Both are worn concealed under your clothes, the belt around the waist or the pouch from your neck. Common sense dictates you should be conscious of your valuables at all times. While cycling, you may wish to take your pouch off and keep it in your handlebar bag, but as soon as you stop in a city or town or leave your bicycle, put it on!

Another personal safety consideration is health. Medical facilities in Europe are excellent. Check your health insurance policy prior to departure for international benefits and coverage. If you are not adequately covered, you may wish to consider additional travel insurance.

Money Matters

The most convenient way to take money on a trip is traveler's checks. These are readily converted into local currency at banks, exchange bureaus, and, in the Netherlands, at ANWB offices. Typically, you will be charged a small commission for the transaction. Check around as commissions vary. Be sure to write your traveler's check numbers down, cross them off after use, and keep them separate from your traveler's checks.

Credit cards are another way to deal with monetary matters. Credit cards are becoming more widely accepted in many countries, but there are some exceptions. Don't rely on credit cards in smaller family-run establishments or in smaller towns. Visa, Mastercard, and American Express are the most commonly used. Again, write down your credit card numbers and keep them in a separate place and also leave them with someone at home. Some credit cards allow you to withdraw cash at ATM machines, but be aware of the high interest rate plus additional charges levied by the bank for this international transaction. The same applies for a regular ATM card.

Plan ahead so that you are not short of cash for weekends and public holidays when banks are closed.

Planning Your Budget

The amount of money you spend is an individual decision. The major variations in cost depend on where you sleep and eat. The person on a higher budget will plan to stay in hotels and pensions and eat in restaurants, while the more economical traveler will stay in bed and breakfasts and youth hostels or camp, eating out occasionally and cooking for themselves.

Accommodation and food costs are a daily occurrence, but be prepared for some extras. Additional costs that you should take into account are sightseeing entrance fees (museums, castles, etc.), an unexpected bicycle repair, books or maps, laundry fees, souvenirs, and so on.

Your airline ticket to Europe will be one of your largest expenses; however, there are some other transport charges to consider. Allow for any connecting flights within Europe, as well as trains and ferries and, occasionally, public transport within a large city. Remember, there will be an additional charge for the bicycle on trains and some ferries.

Transporting Your Bicycle

Taking your bicycle to Europe requires a little planning. For international travel, some airlines allow your bicycle as a piece of checked baggage for no extra charge, while other airlines charge substantial fees. Airline regulations change often, so check these when purchasing your ticket.

If you do decide to take your bicycle, the first decision will be how to prepare it for travel. Although some airlines will accept your bicycle for shipment as is, most require a bicycle box. Most airlines will provide a bicycle box free of charge, and the box they provide is usually a simple cardboard box. With these, you need only remove the pedals, turn the handlebars sideways, deflate the tires somewhat, put it in the box, and tape it up. These boxes, however, are not very sturdy, and do little to protect your bicycle. A shipping carton obtained from a bicycle shop is sturdier but requires more disassembly of the bicycle to fit. Hard cases built specifically for bicycles are available and are the ultimate protection. They are, however, large, relatively expensive, and must be stored somehow at your destination.

Folding bicycles can make the shipping process simple. Several companies now produce good quality bicycles that fold and fit into hard cases that are within the airlines' allowance for regular baggage. You can simply check these as you would a normal bag. It's impossible to tell there's a bicycle inside this protective hard case. Bike Friday, made by Green Gear Cycling in Eugene, Oregon, is a good example. These bicycles are somewhat expensive but worth considering if you do a lot of traveling.

Fitting the bicycle into the box is not a complicated process but don't leave it until the last minute or wait until you arrive at the airport as it can take much longer than you might anticipate the first time you do it. You might not have a choice on your return, but you will have at least learned how it's done on the way over. You should pad the bicycle as well as you can, and the dead space in the box can be used for packing panniers (bicycle bags), sleeping bags, and other items. Do not leave any parts (pedals, for example) loose in the box as it is not uncommon for it to arrive at the other end with gaping holes in the cardboard.

Itinerary and Route Planning

The routes in this book are intended to guide you as you cycle through the Benelux. Time may allow you to choose all the routes, sections of some of them, or combine them with a larger tour of Europe. Whatever the case, you will need to do some research. Doing some basic reading and referring to some good maps will help you decide what suits you best. You can follow the tours or alter them to your needs and interests.

Maps are invaluable in planning, and you should try to obtain as many maps as possible prior to departure. The route maps in this book are simply guidelines and should be used with the maps suggested at the beginning of each route. More details on these maps can be found in the map sections specific to each country.

Consider your own time restrictions, and if part of a route or region interests you, cycle that portion then take a train and pick up the route in another area. The train system in Europe is extensive and bicycle friendly.

When planning the amount of time you will require for a specific itinerary, remember to allow yourself ample time for both the expected and the unexpected. With regard to sightseeing, there are some cities and towns where you may arrive in the afternoon, spend a few hours sightseeing, and feel satisfied to move on the next morning. Other towns or cities might deserve several days. Keep this in mind when you are making your plans.

It is also important to plan rest days into your itinerary, especially if you are planning a long tour. Rest days are easy to ignore, as you want to make the most of your time, but they are necessary, both physically and mentally. Furthermore, you will enjoy the trip more if you don't feel the pressure of being behind schedule. You should feel you have the flexibility to stay a bit longer than you had planned in a town or area that turns out to be much more interesting than you had anticipated. Stay an extra day when you discover a festival or special event, or make an interesting detour or side trip that you hear about while under way. Also, allow for less desirable delays such as bad weather, mechanical problems, or illness.

Bicycle touring gives you the independence to go where you like, when you like, but only if you give yourself that flexibility by allowing enough time.

How Far Should You Go Each Day?

Everyone is different! Ability, endurance, and interests are a completely individual matter. Some cyclists will ride greater distances and treat it as a challenge. Some people will choose to meander through the countryside at a much slower pace and cover less distance. Areas with many sights will decrease your day's overall mileage, and areas with less to see allow you to speed up. Don't be discouraged if you don't go far in a day as long as you've enjoyed what you've done.

Lingering over a picnic, touring an interesting museum, stopping at an inviting outdoor café, a headwind, cobblestones, a perfectly paved stretch, an extended hill, a tailwind, a picture postcard view, a downpour, a quaint village, or a field of tulips all contribute to your daily distance. You've come to Europe to enjoy but keep practicality in mind. Pace yourself comfortably, but plan to arrive at the end of the day in time to set up your tent, find lodging, buy supplies for the evening, or get to the tourist office before it closes.

Physical Conditioning

In order to complete the tours in this book, or any bicycle tour for that matter, you don't have to be a Tour de France contender. What you need is to be prepared both physically and mentally. It will not take you long to determine what levels you are comfortable with, and if you begin your tour with a reasonable fitness level, you will enjoy it all the more.

Some training is necessary before departure. If time doesn't allow extended rides, then do what you can—even an hour per day or every couple of days will suffice. Begin with short rides and build up. Then as departure approaches, add rear panniers with weight so that you can feel the difference and get used to them. If you are also using front panniers, do the same, noting that front panniers affect steering slightly.

If this is your first tour, take it step-by-step as suggested above. If you are camping and have never "cycle-camped" before, try a short practice weekend trip.

Once you arrive in Europe, don't push yourself too hard in the initial days. It can take up to a few days to get over jet lag and get used to full days of cycling. Avoid cycling the day you arrive. If you have not had a chance to do a lot of preparation, consider starting with day trips from a base city or cycling short days. The Netherlands and northern Belgium present a flatter terrain, a great area to begin. In the Benelux, go from north to south, that is, flat to gently undulating hills to the steeper terrain of the Ardennes Mountains.

Packing

Packing what you need or anticipate needing on your trip is obviously an important part of planning. Personal requirements vary. For the most part you will be dressed for cycling, but you may wish to take an outfit that you can wear out in the evening or when you may wish to wear something a little less casual than cycling gear.

For the most practical use of your garments, layer. This is particularly effective when you start out on a cool morning. You can peel off as the day warms up.

The most important thing to keep in mind is that everything you pack you will carry, so pack lightly and evaluate each item by asking, "Do I really need this?" You will find that you will require virtually the same amount of gear whether you are touring for two weeks or two months.

Be prepared to hand wash your small items on a regular basis and dry them overnight. Two useful items are tube soap and an expandable clothesline. From time to time you will need to stop at a self-service laundry. Many campgrounds have washing facilities as do some youth hostels. If you need to find a self-service laundry, the word in Dutch is *wassalon* and in French is *laverie*. Washing powder is usually available at the laundry in small packets, or you can purchase the smallest amount possible at a supermarket prior to visiting the laundry.

A tip on drying: If you have a wet or damp item, it is possible to dry it as you ride by tucking it under a bungee cord or by using the mesh outer pocket found on some panniers.

Once you have compiled your personal list, practice packing everything into your panniers. This is important for two reasons. First, you need to know that it all actually fits. Remember to leave a bit of room for food and additional items picked up along the way. Second, there is an art to packing panniers. Weight distribution is very important on a bicycle, and the time to figure what goes where is before you leave. Try to keep roughly equal weight in the left and right panniers. Cyclists disagree on the front and back weight ratio. Many feel that all your heavy items should be in the rear, while others feel it should be an almost equal distribution. Try it both ways on your bicycle to see which feels better to you. Unless you have waterproof panniers, you may wish to line your panniers with large plastic bags for extra protection. Also, remember not to overpack your handlebar bag.

The lists below are suggested packing lists and will vary with individual needs.

Clothing
- 1 rain jacket
- 1 pair rain pants
- 1 fleece jacket or 1 sweatshirt
- 1 long sleeve
  (capilene-type fabric) top
- 3 T-shirts (or cycling jerseys)
- 2 pairs padded cycling shorts
- 1 pair regular shorts
  and/or 1 skirt
- 1 pair jeans or other long pants
- 1 pair long cycling pants
- 1 bathing suit
- underwear (for women include
  2 sports bras)
- 3 pairs socks
- shoes: cycling shoes (optional),
  walking or tennis shoes,
  thongs (for showering)
- hat or cap
- bandanna or scarf

Personal
- toiletries kit
  (include any prescription drugs
  and refills)
- first aid kit
- 1 towel (Packtowl brand folds
  compactly and dries quickly)
- soap
- toilet paper
- towelettes (great when no water is
  available to wash dirty hands)
- dental floss (not just for teeth,
  handy for tying and repairing
  things, even serves as an extra
  clothes line)
- expandable clothesline
- tube detergent
- sunglasses (spare glasses or
  contact lenses, if applicable)
- sunscreen
- insect repellent

Miscellaneous
- camera and film
  (film is expensive in Europe)
- Swiss Army knife or similar
- bungee cords
- spare batteries
- scissors
- sewing kit
- journal and pen
- Ziploc bags
- garbage bags (for picnicking on
  damp grass, or extra ground
  cover when camping)
- travel alarm clock
- security pouch
- small address book
- guidebook/maps
- phrase book or small dictionary
- headlamp or flashlight (detachable
  front bicycle light works)
- daypack (small, folds up easily)
- extra passport photos
- automobile club card (such as
  AAA or RAC, if you wish to use
  the services of the ANWB)

Chapter 3

Equipment

Types of Bicycles

Recommending a bicycle to someone is like recommending a pair of shoes. You can tell them that boots will work better than ballet slippers for a certain task, but the exact brand, style, and fit that is perfect for one person may not work at all for another. The way the bicycle fits is in fact more important than the type of bicycle. A good quality bicycle of any type, as long as it fits and is comfortable, will work for touring. Things you should be looking for in any type of bicycle you choose include a sturdy frame, a wide range of gears, good brakes, sealed hub bearings, a comfortable saddle, the right tires for touring, fenders, and, again, the proper fit for you.

If you are purchasing a new bicycle for the trip, you will find your choices will fall into three main categories: touring (or road) bicycles, mountain bikes, and hybrid (or cross bicycles). Each have their own advantages and disadvantages, and any of them might suit you best.

The "true" touring bicycle, also called a road bicycle, is designed for maximum speed and efficiency on paved surfaces. It has a stiff, lightweight frame, a longer wheelbase for a smoother ride, and often lighter rims and components. The handlebars are the drop style, giving the rider numerous hand positions and good leverage for climbing. For those who don't ride much at home or those who are used to the straight handlebar, these may seem less comfortable, but you will be happy to have them the first time you hit a steep hill or stiff headwind. The frame geometry of this type of bicycle ensures maximum efficiency and comfort on paved roads, but it is not the most maneuverable when off paved surfaces. Also, prices tend to be high and selection limited due to the limited demand for this type of bicycle.

Mountain bikes are designed for mountains. They are designed to be extremely rugged, able to take the constant pounding of trail riding. Some even have suspension systems to help absorb shocks. The frame geometry is designed for maximum ground clearance, giving you a higher center of gravity; this is useful on a trail but is not optimal for touring. They normally have wide, high-volume "knobby" tires to help absorb the shock and provide maximum stability on loose or slippery surfaces. While the mountain bike is extremely comfortable on short rides, it is actually your worst choice for touring. It is certainly possible, and many people do tour with their mountain bikes. If you do choose to do so, the bare minimum you must do is change to narrower, slicker tires. Whereas the geometry of this type of bike will be just slightly less efficient, the "knobby" tires will slow you tremendously and drive you crazy with the constant vibration and noise.

There is a compromise between these two types of bicycles. Called a cross, hybrid, or sometimes a fitness bike, it combines the best of both worlds. A quality cross bicycle will have a frame geometry closer to that of a road bicycle, the straight handlebars and more upright seating style of a mountain bike, and tires halfway between the two. It will never match a road bicycle for speed, nor will it follow a mountain bike on a rough trail, but it is an excellent choice for a rider who doesn't want a bicycle for either extreme but does want a bicycle that will competently handle any condition encountered on a touring trip. It is a much better choice for a long ride than a mountain bike, and you needn't be as afraid of the odd patch of gravel or dirt road as you might be with a touring bicycle. A large range of cross bicycles is available. Most will have the straight handlebars, but those can be switched for the drop style if you wish. Some will have 26-inch wheels like a mountain bike, others will have the slightly larger 700-millimeter wheels of a road bicycle. Although the smaller wheels are also a bit more rugged, the larger 700-millimeter wheels are more efficient for distance.

If convenience of traveling with your bicycle is important, you might also want to consider another option—the folding bicycle. A number of companies manufacture bicycles that actually fold into a custom-fitted suitcase. The less expensive of this variety tend to be inferior bicycles good only for basic transportation once you arrive at your destination, but a few quality designs are available, such as the Bike Friday manufactured by Green Gear of Eugene, Oregon. Unfortunately, the better folding bicycles do tend to be fairly expensive, but if you travel a lot, you could save a substantial amount of money on excess baggage charges with some airlines, not to mention less worry about how your bicycle will be handled by the airlines in a cardboard box.

There is a great deal of overlap in bicycle design, and there is no substitute for shopping around. It is important to test ride a variety of styles and brands. Good, logical arguments can be made for each type of bicycle, and 10 bicycle shop professionals will give you 11 opinions; some of them will argue passionately and convincingly. Go to several shops, try a variety of bicycles, take notes, and make your decision later.

Also, remember that you need not stick to any bicycle exactly as it is presented in the shop. Any bicycle, new or old, can be customized or personalized for the trip. For example, a comfortable saddle is important on a long trip. A number of new saddle styles are available with high-tech padding or gels. Consider trying a new saddle on your old bicycle or upgrading to a better saddle if you are buying a new bicycle. Most dealers will give you credit toward the upgraded saddle if you do so at the time of purchase. Handlebars can also be switched on virtually any bicycle. If you find the right bicycle but want drop handlebars instead of straight, talk to your dealer. Most sport bicycles today are sold without fenders. This is fine at home where you can simply choose never to ride in foul weather, but it is an absolute necessity on a long trip in Europe to have fenders. Tires can be switched. Also remember to add a kickstand. Although it may not hold up a fully-loaded bicycle while en route, it is handy once you have taken your panniers off.

Touring Gear

Once the bicycle is chosen, you will find you've only just begun. Outfitting the bicycle with touring gear and accessories can be just as time-consuming, not to mention just as expensive, as the bicycle itself.

First, you need a rack or racks. A rear rack is essential. Whether or not you need a front rack depends on what type of touring you will be doing. If you are camping, there is no question—you will need both front and rear. If you are doing light touring, you might be able to manage with just rear panniers and a handlebar bag. Even so, we recommend both. They give you more flexibility and better balance, and no cyclist ever complains of having too much room in their panniers.

Any good rear rack will work. Ask your bicycle shop to recommend one for your bicycle. You will have two options for the front rack. One style is similar to a rear rack but shorter; the other is a "low rider" rack. We recommend a low rider, as the lower weight distribution gives you far superior handling.

There are many panniers (bicycle bags) to choose from. Look for a larger pair for the rear and a smaller pair for the front. They need not be the same brand or style. In fact, it can be an advantage to have different styles. It is worth paying a bit more for good quality panniers. Most will be weather resistant, but you will want to pack everything in plastic bags. The only truly waterproof panniers we are aware of are made in Germany by Ortlieb. They are available worldwide, although it might take some searching. It is nice to have at least one pair of completely waterproof bags.

There are also many good choices in handlebar bags. Again, it comes down to personal choice. Two things to keep in mind, though, are the importance of a good, waterproof map holder, and the fact that a bigger handlebar bag is not necessarily better. Too much weight in the handlebar bag can make the bicycle hard to maneuver.

Accessories

A number of accessories are suggested for both safety and comfort. Some are necessary, some very much optional. Some of the more necessary include a helmet, water bottles, bell, lights, pump, and lock. Most Europeans you see on bicycles will not be wearing helmets. You might decide to forego your helmet in some cases, such as on an auto-free bicycle path in Holland. You will need it, though, when you ride along a busy highway, or on the hilly, twisting rural roads of the Ardennes, for example. You will notice that the hard-core sports cyclists in Europe do tend to wear helmets now. Take your cue from them. Regardless of what the locals are doing, play it safe and wear a helmet.

A bell might not seem important to you, but the reason it is included in the necessary category is that it is required by law in many European countries, including all three Benelux countries. The same is true of a light, even if you are not planning on riding at night.

We recommend having two bottle cages mounted to the bicycle. It is important to drink constantly, even if you don't feel thirsty, to avoid dehydration.

A bicycle lock, although it adds a good deal of weight, is an unfortunate necessity.

A pump that fits the type of valve on your tires is essential. Some excellent "mini-pumps" are available today that do a good job yet take up very little room and weigh next to nothing. There is, of course, the full-size, bicycle-mounted pump, but that generally uses space on the frame that could be used for a bottle cage.

The number of optional accessories is endless. Some you might want to consider are a bicycle computer, compass, rearview mirror, bungee cords, and saddle cover. The computer will let you know how far you've ridden, which can help with navigation, and how fast, which can help with planning. A compass can also help with navigation. Some bicycle bells available in Europe actually incorporate a compass. A small handle-mounted rearview mirror can allow you to monitor traffic (or your cycling partner) behind you without constantly turning your head, which could cause you to veer unsteadily. Bungee cords allow you to strap almost anything onto your racks. A water-proof saddle cover will keep the saddle dry when you leave the bicycle out-side, although a plastic bag will also work.

Tools/Repairs

One advantage to cycling in the Netherlands, Belgium, and Luxembourg is that you will never be too far from a bicycle shop. The popularity of bicycles both as sport and transportation in all three countries ensures that even most small towns will have a bicycle shop. Therefore, an elaborate array of tools is not necessary. If a major problem arises, you are never too far from help. Basic items are still a good idea. These include:

- spare tube
- tube repair kit
- tire levers
- spare spokes (taped to frame)
- spoke wrench
- Phillips and regular screwdrivers
- adjustable wrench
- Allen wrenches
- lubricant
- pliers
- duct tape
- waterless hand cleaner

This might seem like a long list, but many companies make combination tools that include most or all of the basics in extremely compact packages. These can be an excellent choice. Check with several dealers to get an idea of variety and price.

In addition, you might choose to carry extra brake pads and cables, a chain link removal tool, and a freewheel tool, but these should not be necessary and should be considered only if you are planning an extremely long tour and are an avid bicycle mechanic.

Camping Gear

If you will be camping on your trip, considerable thought must be given as to how much equipment you will need. Little more than a tent and sleeping bag are absolutely necessary. Beyond that you face the classic cyclist's dilemma—the tradeoff between comfort and weight. Ask yourself exactly what kind of camping you really want to do. How self-sufficient do you want to be? Do you really want to cook for yourself every day, or will you eat out most of the time? Our suggestion is to start with the bare minimum you feel you can survive with. If you find you need more, it is not difficult to find camping supply shops in Europe. The following is a basic list of camping supplies that should get you through:

- tent
- sleeping bag
- insulated sleeping mat
- flashlight (or headlamp)
- stove (Make sure your stove is compatible with canisters available in Europe. GAZ brand is the most widespread. Note: The gas canister cannot be taken on the plane.)
- matches or lighter
- small cooking pot
- plate (frisbee can be used as plate or dish), cup, knife/fork/spoon set
- Swiss Army knife or similar
- can opener and corkscrew
- dishcloth, scourer, detergent

Chapter 4

Country Information

The Netherlands

Which is correct, the Netherlands or Holland? It seems today that the two are used interchangeably. In fact, "Holland" refers to two of the provinces on the western side of the country, namely North Holland and South Holland. When translated into Dutch, Netherlands, or Nederland, means "low land." In French the country is known as Pays Bas, again translated literally as "low land." The Netherlands is clearly low with a good percentage of the country being below sea level. The correct name, therefore, is the Netherlands, but the Dutch are generally accepting of either name.

The stereotypical view of the Netherlands is that of windmills, tulips, wooden clogs, and canals. Yes, these symbols do exist, but the Netherlands is more than these cute images. The country is one of the most progressive countries in Europe, both culturally and socially. The Dutch government subsidizes several types of educational, artistic, and social programs resulting in a well-educated population with an awareness of their background and the value of historical monuments and architecture. All corners of the country are rich in museums, galleries, and exhibitions.

The Dutch influence through history can be found all over the world. They exerted their power both at home and abroad leaving their legacy in art and exploration, especially during the Golden Age. Water is obviously a great Dutch forté, whether it be pumping it out, enclosing it, or sailing on it. The Dutch were great seafarers and colonized Indonesia, parts of the Caribbean, and parts of Africa. Their huge trading influence is especially evident through the exploits of the Dutch East India Company. The strong Dutch influence in the art world is displayed through masters such as Rembrandt and van Gogh and is still in evidence today with modern artists such as Jopie Huisman and M. C. Escher.

The Dutch are definitely "flower people." The tulip has become the national symbol with the country producing 650 varieties of the bulb and exporting 780 billion flowers and bulbs annually. Tulips, surprisingly, were not native to Holland but arrived from Turkey in 1550 and flourished in the damp lowland soil. Each year from late March through early May the country is ablaze with flowers and flower festivals. Throughout the year, flower markets abound, and the Dutch take pride in their own gardens.

The Dutch have been battling the sea for centuries. Much of the country is below sea level and prone to flooding. The windmills you see are not just symbols for the tourist. In earlier days these behemoths were used to drain lakes and keep the *polders* (reclaimed land) dry. They were strategically placed along canals and were the difference between swamp and fertile, usable land. Today many working windmills have been retired, and most are kept as beautiful and graceful antiquities or for demonstrations, but all in all the romance and utility of the classic windmills have been replaced with modern sleek aerodynamic windmills, or pumps. Note: Some windmills were also used to grind grains; some of these can still be found in use throughout the country. Another feat of Dutch engineering is the Afsluitdijk, the 30-kilometer dike that turned the saltwater Zuiderzee into a fresh water lake, allowing for a great deal of land reclamation.

VVV (Tourist Information Office)

The VVV, or Tourist Information Office, will become your most cherished resource while in the Netherlands. VVV stands for *Vereniging Voor Vreemdelingenverkeer,* which literally translates as Association for Foreign Traffic, but the abbreviation VVV is affectionately used by all. You will become accustomed to searching out the VVV (pronounced like a cross between Vay Vay Vay and Fay Fay Fay) when arriving in a new town. The VVV symbol is clearly designated as three white Vs in a triangular format on a royal blue background. The offices are usually centrally located, often in a building with historical significance. You will be amazed how widespread the locations of the VVV offices are, even being located in tiny towns where you would least expect one.

Staff members are very helpful and organized, with lots of information at their fingertips. They provide sightseeing information, often free literature, sell books and maps, reserve accommodations (sometimes for a small fee), and can assist with directions and local information. Generally, VVV personnel are willing to spend time with you to ensure that you have a good stay in their area or town. However, in heavily touristed areas, staff may seem a little harried if lines are long. If this is the case, have your questions ready and have an idea what brochures, maps, and sightseeing and accommodation information you might need, so as to make your time, and theirs, more efficient.

Museum Card

VVVs sell the *Museum Jaar Kaart* (Museum Year Card). If you intend to visit at least a half dozen or so museums during your stay in the Netherlands (especially the Rijksmuseum and Van Gogh Museum in Amsterdam, probably the two most expensive in the country), then consider purchasing the Museum Jaar Kaart. It is good for entry into all municipal and state museums, of which there are hundreds, and it is valid for one year from the date of issue. Take a passport size photo with you as the card requires one. In 1998 the cards cost Dfl 55.00 per adult. The cards are also available at most museums. Adult admission prices for museums vary from Dfl 3 to Dfl 10.

ANWB Offices

Another excellent resource is the ANWB, or Royal Dutch Touring Club. This is the equivalent of the American AAA or British RAC. Membership to your country's automobile association entitles you to use their services, which includes everything from books and outstanding maps (used in the route section) to travel accessories and even collapsible bicycles, plus free maps and other literature. They also offer currency exchange services, often with rates as good as banks, and very low commission levels.

The history of the ANWB is an interesting one, especially when it comes to bicycle trivia. ANWB stands for *Algemene Nederlandsche Wielrijders Bond,* which translates as General Dutch Cyclist's Association. Note the similarity of

The knee high ANWB "mushrooms" provide directions for cyclists and hikers all over the Netherlands.

the word *Wielrijders* to the English wheel + riders (= cyclists). The ANWB existed well before the car and was, at its inception over 100 years ago, a cyclist's club. Today it caters to both the driver and the cyclist.

The ANWB is also the organization in charge of providing the signposting around the country for cyclists. These include the red and white directional signs, various route signs, and the little ANWB *paddestoelen*, or "mushrooms," knee-high directional signs for cyclists and hikers that look like large mushrooms.

Weather

The warmest and sunniest months are June through September. It is possible, however, to get an exceptional week or two in May when the spring weather rivals the most perfect summer day. Average summer temperatures are around 20–21 degrees Celsius (low 70s Fahrenheit) and ideal for cycling. Remember that because most of the Netherlands is below sea level, it can be damp. (This is an important consideration when camping.) The weather is changeable, and rain tends to be drizzle rather than heavy downpours.

The main season for viewing the flower fields for which Holland is so famous is from the end of March to early May. This will vary a little from year to year. Even outside of this season there are plenty of flowers and gardens to be viewed.

The winds whistling through the country can be your friend (wind behind you) or your enemy (wind against you). Since the country is so flat, there is nowhere to hide from the wind. The wind is not constant, and there are still days, but you may encounter several windy days in a row.

Currency, Banks, and Credit Cards

The unit of currency in Holland is the guilder (or florin). (U.S.$1 = approximately Dfl 1.70.) The guilder is abbreviated Dfl or Fl, stemming from the old word florin. The guilder is divided into 100 cents. Compare banks and exchange places as rates and commissions vary for both traveler's checks and cash. Banks are open Monday through Friday 9 A.M.–4 P.M. or 5 P.M. Be sure to change money for the weekend. Some exchange places are open longer hours and on weekends, but don't rely on this outside of big cities. Also, it is possible to use a bank machine card, but expect a fee for each transaction when you get home.

Credit cards are not widely used in family-owned small shops (including village bicycle shops), small hotels, pensions, bed and breakfasts, and are rarely accepted in campgrounds. Larger hotels and stores will take credit cards. Supermarkets don't usually accept credit cards, and acceptance in restaurants varies. However, things are changing, and credit cards are more widely accepted each year.

Business Hours

The Dutch love their weekends. Shops begin closing anytime after lunch on Saturday, and many do not reopen until Monday at 1 P.M. To compensate for this, sometimes shops are open late on either Thursday or Friday evenings. Most shops open from 9 A.M. to 5 P.M. or 6 P.M., but some larger chain supermarkets are open until 8 P.M. in bigger towns. In some small towns, a shop may be closed one weekday afternoon per week.

Museums and monuments are normally open from 10 A.M. to 5 P.M. daily, except many are closed on Mondays.

Telephones

The country code for the Netherlands is 31.

There are two types of public phones. One is the traditional type that takes coins. The other style of phone takes only a phone card. Phone cards are available at train stations, post offices, and some VVV offices and can be purchased in various denominations, usually starting at Dfl 10. Local calls cost 25 cents for approximately 3–5 minutes. Coin phones take coins of Dfl 0.25, Dfl 1, and Dfl 2.50.

Important note: The Dutch totally revamped their phone number area codes and prefixes within the country in October 1995. We have used the updated phone numbers within this book, but be aware that some publications and brochures printed prior to October 1995 will have the old numbers and need to be checked.

Post Offices

Post offices are open Monday–Friday 8:30 A.M.–5 P.M.; some are open Saturday 8:30 A.M.–noon. Larger post offices offer *poste restante* and currency exchange. To send mail out of the country, put it in the slot marked *overige*.

Public Holidays and Special Events

On official public holidays, shops and businesses will be closed; however, some museums and restaurants will be open.

The major public holidays are as follows:

January 1 (New Year's Day); Easter (Good Friday, Easter Sunday, and Easter Monday); Ascension Day; Whit Sunday and Whit Monday (Pinksteren which occurs 40 days after Easter); Koninginnedag (Queen's Day), celebrated with parades and other festivities every April 30 when Amsterdam becomes the site of a huge party (more goes on in Amsterdam than in the rest of country. If you enjoy crowds, join in. Otherwise, steer clear until the party's over); December 25 (Christmas Day) and December 26 (Boxing Day).

There are two "unofficial" holidays. Both of the "unofficial" holidays are "Remembrance Days," and even though neither of these days are official holidays, some shops and services may be closed. Both these days are associated with World War II. May 4 is a memorial day honoring those who died, and May 5 acknowledges Liberation Day.

Carnival (Mardi Gras), the week prior to Ash Wednesday, is celebrated only in the predominantly Catholic provinces of North Brabant and Limburg.

During May is National Bicycle Day with races and cycling events throughout the country.

In May and June is the Eleven Cities Bicycle Race (see Hindeloopen).

Language

The official language is Dutch.

Friesland is a bilingual province. In Friesland, everybody speaks Dutch, and about 75 percent of the population speaks Friesian (Fryske), an ancient Germanic language. Road signs in this part of the country are in both languages.

When the language genes were handed out, it seems that the Dutch won the lottery. The linguistic ability of the Dutch is quite astonishing. Apart from their own language, most people you meet speak English like natives, plus many are proficient in German and French. You will easily get by with English in the Netherlands, but a sure way to bring a smile to a Dutch person's face is to be able to use some basic Dutch.

A small dictionary or phrase book is recommended for that menu item that is eluding you or the sign that might be important to translate.

Belgium

When you visit Belgium, it's like getting a "two for one" deal, two countries for the price of one. You enter Belgium, but in fact, you are going to be enchanted by two completely different "Belgiums": Flemish Belgium, or Flanders, and French Belgium, known as Wallonia. You will encounter differences in culture, language, architecture, politics, and history. And just for some more variety, there is a small enclave of German-speaking Belgians in the east around Eupen.

As well as the cultural and linguistic division, there is a difference in terrain. The line of demarcation almost follows the linguistic boundary, separating the flat lands and culturally rich north from the hills and scenically beautiful south. This offers great variation within a small area. In the level north, the population is the most dense; the cities and towns are closer together, and the area boasts some impressive medieval cities. In the south, the hilly terrain dictates that distances between towns are greater. This area, including the Belgian Ardennes, is more scenically dramatic than the north.

Even with these differences, the country is united, so much so that Brussels, an area unto itself (not part of Flanders or Wallonia), is home to the European Commission, where most decisions affecting the European Union are made. Belgians as a whole, even though divided in their Northern Flemish and Southern Walloon ways, are very supportive of a united Europe.

Belgium is bordered to the north by the Netherlands and to the west by France. Germany is to the east, and Luxembourg tucks itself into the southeast edge. Due to its central location, Belgium, like Luxembourg, has been vulnerable to occupation and invading armies. Over time Belgium has been ruled by the Romans, French, Spanish, Austrians, and Germans. Belgium has hosted its fair share of battles, one of the most famous being Waterloo. Belgium was a battleground in the two World Wars, the famous Battle of the Bulge being fought in the Ardennes area of Belgium and Luxembourg.

Belgians are proud of their country and its native sons. They have a long list of talents such as van Dyck, Brueghel, Rubens, and more recently, Magritte. Belgians have proved their artistic prowess in areas other than on the canvas. Well-loved Hergé was creator of the world famous cartoon *Tintin*, and Maigret was the character developed by prolific author Georges Simenon. In other areas, Belgians are renowned for their beautiful tapestries and lace work.

Today, Belgian cuisine is famous the world over. Gourmets consider Brussels one of the great "food" cities of the world, and restaurants all over the country maintain a high standard. The Belgians brew over 350 varieties of beer, from Pilsner to Trappist, and as a result, they lead the world in beer consumption. Belgium is a mecca for connoisseurs of chocolate, producing some of the finest quality chocolate in the world. Taste a Léonidas or Neuhaus chocolate, and Belgium's outstanding reputation for chocolate is confirmed.

Tourist Information Offices

The Tourist Information Office will supply you with all types of brochures, maps, and other information, as well as help you with accommodations. You will find that the words for tourist office vary in Belgium. In Flanders you will see it written as VVV (as in the Netherlands) or *Dienst voor Toerisme*. In Wallonia, the two terms used are *Office du Tourisme* and *Syndicat d'Initiative*, which is often abbreviated as SI.

Weather

The north and west of Flanders have a maritime climate. The prevailing winds are westerly and can at times be strong across the northern flatlands. As you head east, the weather tends to be better, with there being slightly less rainfall overall. Traveling south, the wind is less frequent and not as strong. However, less wind is due to the hills, which lend themselves to slightly higher temperatures in the warmer months and cooler temperatures in winter, especially in the Ardennes.

The driest months are April and May, and of course, the warmest months are June, July, and August, with an average high temperature around 22 or 23 degrees Celsius (mid-70s Fahrenheit). September and October can be pleasant, both the weather and lack of crowds. Autumn can be particularly beautiful due to the varying and changing colors of the leaves, especially in the forests of the south and the tree-lined canals of the north.

Currency, Banks, and Credit Cards

The unit of Belgian currency is the Belgian franc, abbreviated BEF. (U.S.$1 = approximately BEF 30.) Compare banks and exchange places since exchange rates and commissions vary. Rates also vary between traveler's checks and cash. Banks are open Monday through Friday 9 A.M.–4 P.M. (some close for the noon hour). Be sure to change money for the weekend. Some exchange places are open longer hours and on weekends, but don't rely on this outside of big cities.

Credit cards are widely used in Belgium; however, some small shops and businesses and small family-run lodgings are not set up for credit cards. Some campgrounds and youth hostels even take credit cards. Larger hotels and bigger stores accept them, but at present, supermarkets do not. Restaurants vary.

Note: Belgian francs can be used interchangeably with Luxembourg francs in Luxembourg, but not vice versa.

Business Hours

Shops are open Monday through Saturday 9 A.M. or 10 A.M.–6 P.M., and some are open later on Friday evenings. Some bakeries, supermarkets, and small shops are open on Sunday. Some shops close for lunch.

Museums are usually open 10 A.M.–5 P.M. daily, and many are closed on Monday.

Telephones

The country code for Belgium is 32.

You will find very few coin-operated phones left in Belgium. If you do, they will typically be at the train station, or, if there is a group of phones in a city, one may be coin operated. Rumors have it that there has been a lot of phone card fraud, and coin phones may be on the way back. Otherwise, you will find a lot of phones that take the phone cards. Phone cards are available at train stations and newsstands and can be purchased in denominations of BEF 200 and up. Local calls cost BEF 20. Coin phones take coins of BEF 20 and BEF 50.

Post Offices
Open Monday–Friday 9 A.M.–5 P.M. Larger post offices offer *poste restante* and currency exchange.

Public Holidays
On official public holidays, shops and businesses will be closed; however, some museums and restaurants will be open.

The major public holidays are as follows:

January 1 (New Year's Day); Easter (Good Friday, Easter Sunday, and Easter Monday); Ascension Day (sixth Thursday after Easter); Whit Sunday and Whit Monday (seventh Monday after Easter); May 1 (Labor Day); July 21 (Belgian National Day); August 15 (Assumption Day); November 1 (All Saints' Day); December 25 (Christmas Day) and December 26 (Boxing Day).

November 15 is the King's Birthday; however, most shops and banks are open.

Language
Official languages are Flemish (Dutch dialect), spoken in the north, French in the south, and German in a small area on the eastern border. The "linguistic divide" separates the country almost in half linguistically, culturally, and geographically.

Belgians are not as willing to speak English as the Dutch, as many are not as proficient as the Dutch and thus are a little embarrassed. Many older people are reluctant to speak English at all. You have a better chance with people under 50, and it would be helpful to learn some basic Dutch and French to get by.

A small dictionary or phrase book is recommended, especially for rural areas.

Note: Be aware that often a town's name will be signposted in Flemish and French. Some examples are: Antwerpen/Anvers, Brussel/Bruxelles, Ghent/Gand, Luik/Liège, Leuven/Louvain, Namur/Namen.

Luxembourg
Luxembourg is a small and very compact country. It is unfortunately often left off the traveler's itinerary. For those who do visit, the rewards are great. Crammed into the smallest country in the European Union, with only 999 square miles and only 400,000 residents, is an amazing array of sights, including museums and castles. The varied landscape of hills, valleys, rivers, and pastoral lands lends itself to a variety of outdoor activities.

Luxembourg divides itself geographically into two regions. The hilly Ardennes of the north, known as Oesling, and the fertile farmlands of the south, Bon Pays or Gutland (Good Land). Most of Luxembourg's heavy industry, namely steel, is situated in a small pocket in the southwest. The rest of the country is left "green," and the heaviest production is grapes from the vineyards that drape the sides of the Moselle River in the southeast and produce from rural farmlands that dot the rest of the south. Other than the Moselle River, the spectacular Sûre River cuts through the country from west to east, and the pristine Our River forms a border with Germany on the northeast. Numerous other rivers and streams cover the country.

Luxembourg is surrounded by Belgium, France, and Germany and has had a tumultuous past with a harsh history of invasions and occupations. The Celts, Romans, Gauls, and Germans have all occupied Luxembourg. Those interested in World War II history will find an abundance of battle sites, monuments, and museums dedicated to the Battle of the Bulge which raged in the Luxembourg Ardennes. Despite it all, the people of Luxembourg are charming, have a lot of integrity, and are very proud of their nation. This is evident in their National motto: *Wir wölle bleiwe wat mir sin* (We wish to remain what we are). This, of course, is a great way to be in a country that today boasts one of the highest living standards and educational levels in the world and some of the lowest taxes in Europe.

Two-thirds of the population lives in the capital and the industrial south, leaving the rest of the country uncrowded and excellent for cycle touring. Even Luxembourg City, the largest urban area, has less than 80,000 inhabitants and is one of the most dramatically situated capital cities in Europe. Far from flat, the country has some challenging hills for the cyclist; great rewards await.

Tourist Information Offices

Luxembourg has an efficient network of tourist offices. They are located in most major cities and towns of interest to tourists. They are indicated by the words *Office de Tourisme* and sometimes, *Syndicat d'Initiative.*

Weather

Luxembourg has a moderate climate and is slightly drier than Belgium and Holland; however, temperatures are a touch lower. May and June are the driest, and thus sunniest, months, with the warmest months being June, July, and August, which boast average temperatures of around 20–22 degrees Celsius (low 70s Fahrenheit). Autumn is a gorgeous time to be in Luxembourg, with cool, crisp days and incredible color variations in the forest foliage. Winter is colder than its neighboring Benelux countries, due to the altitude. The Ardennes can be under a blanket of snow for a good part of the winter, thus cycling is not recommended.

Currency, Banks, and Credit Cards

The currency, Luxembourg francs, are denoted as LUF. (U.S.$1 = approximately LUF 30.) Luxembourg does mint its own money, which has exactly the same value and denominations as the Belgian franc. The Luxembourg and Belgian franc are interchangeable within Luxembourg. Note, however, that Luxembourg francs are not accepted in Belgium. If you will be traveling to Belgium after your stay in Luxembourg, when you exchange money at any bank in Luxembourg, you can ask for Belgian francs rather than Luxembourg francs.

Compare banks and exchange places as exchange rates and commissions vary. Rates also vary between traveler's checks and cash. Banks are open Monday through Friday 9 A.M.–noon, 1 P.M.–4 P.M. or 4.30 P.M. Be sure to change money for the weekend. In Luxembourg City you will find a few currency exchange places, but don't go searching these out anywhere else in the country. You can use your bank machine card, but expect a fee for each transaction when you get home.

Use of credit cards varies. As with most of Europe, large establishments accept credit cards, but smaller shops and family-run accommodations may not. As a country that lists tourism and international banking as two of its major industries, though, credit cards are more widely accepted here than many countries.

Business Hours

Regular business hours are Monday–Friday 9 A.M.–5:30 P.M., with some shops opening at noon on Mondays. Some shops close for lunch. Shops are open half or full day on Saturdays and closed on Sundays.

Telephones

The country code for Luxembourg is 352.

There are two types of public phones in Luxembourg, the traditional coin-operated style plus the newer type that takes a pre-purchased phone card. Phone cards are only available at the post office, the cheapest being LUF 250, so unless you'll be in Luxembourg for a long time or plan to make lots of calls, stick to coins.

Local calls cost LUF 5 with no time limit.

Note: There are no area codes within Luxembourg.

Post Offices

Post offices are open Monday–Friday 9 A.M.–5.30 P.M. Larger post offices, such as in Luxembourg City, offer *poste restante*. To send mail in Luxembourg, go to the post office or use the ubiquitous yellow mail boxes strategically placed on the walls of many public buildings.

Public Holidays and Special Events

On official public holidays, shops and businesses will be closed; however, some museums and restaurants will be open.

The major public holidays are as follows:

January 1 (New Year's Day); Easter (Good Friday, Easter Sunday, and Easter Monday); Ascension Day; Whit Sunday and Whit Monday (40 days after Easter); May 1 (Labor Day); June 23 (National Day); approximately August 15 (Assumption Day); November 1 (All Saints' Day); December 25 (Christmas Day) and December 26 (St. Etienne Day).

"Unofficial" holidays may see some businesses closed. Such days are Carnival (Mardi Gras) around Shrove Tuesday. Festivities and parades abound. During the year festivals are held throughout the country, especially in the Moselle Valley during the wine harvest. Check with local tourist offices.

Language

Official languages are Letzeburgesch and French.

You can almost expect most Luxembourgeois to be trilingual. The native language is Letzeburgesch, spoken by most of the native population. It is a Germanic-style language unique to Luxembourg. Most residents of Lux-embourg also speak either French, German, or both, and many will speak English.

In Luxembourg, on entering a town you will notice the signs are written in two languages, the commonly used name and Letzeburgesch. For example: Dillingen/Deiljen, Echternach/Eechternoach, Hoesdorf/Heischdréf.

Chapter 5

Lodging and Eating

A Bed for the Night

Night falls at the end of every day, and you will face the important question of where to sleep. For some people, flexibility is paramount, and this is a decision that will be made each day. For others it is something that is planned in advance. Europe has a range of lodging types, and your own level of comfort and budget will determine where you rest your head each night. Throughout the routes, accommodations such as hotels, pensions, bed and breakfasts, youth hostels, and campgrounds are listed to help you plan.

If you are a person who needs to know that your bed awaits every evening, you can reserve anything from a hotel to a campground in advance, either before you leave or while on the road. Extensive accommodation listings are available from tourist offices, travel agents, and various guidebooks. Planning in advance lends a sense of security. However, your routes must be set, and you must cycle the determined distance daily. This limits your ability to detour and linger in an area you are enjoying.

Some people determine lodging on a day-to-day basis. This offers more freedom and flexibility, but this is not for everyone. If you choose this style of travel, there are certain things to bear in mind. You should arrive early enough to locate lodging before rooms fill up and to seek the advice of the tourist office before it closes. Bear in mind busy tourist times and local festivals where towns can be crowded and rooms scarce. On the other hand, an advantage to flexibility is that you can stop en route at an unexpected locale, such as a cozy inn, farm, or private campground.

Hotels and Pensions

Hotels are the most familiar and abundant of lodgings. They range from the very cheap and simple hotel to the luxurious. Cities have a selection in all price ranges, but if you're trying to stay within a budget, be warned that some small towns have only one or two hotels, and you may have to pay a little more. Large cities tend to be more expensive, yet in some well-visited towns where hotels vie for tourist dollars, competition keeps the rates affordable.

A good alternative, in both cities and towns, is the *pension*. Pensions are commonplace in Europe and are a smaller family-run establishment, often cheaper than a hotel. The word *auberge* (inn) is often used in place of pension in the French-speaking parts of Belgium and in Luxembourg.

In both hotels and pensions, you will often have the option of a private or shared bath. Be sure to ask about this when checking the room price. Also ask whether breakfast is included. In most cases it is. Don't be afraid to ask to see the room, and determine whether there is a place off the street to keep your bicycle overnight. You will find listings of hotels and pensions in the route section of this book. The ones listed are in lower to moderate budget levels, as these are often harder to locate and fill up more quickly than higher priced establishments.

Bed and Breakfasts

The bed and breakfast in a private home offers a friendly atmosphere and a cultural experience as you are welcomed into the family home. Bed and breakfasts are often an excellent value. Breakfast is included, and there is usually a place for your bicycle in the backyard, garage, or shed.

As a general rule, you will be able to find bed and breakfasts throughout the Netherlands. If you have your heart set on staying in a bed and breakfast, try to get to the town you will be overnighting in early enough to get to the tourist office before it closes. They will book you a room and give you directions, but remember, most tourist offices close at 5 P.M., and many close at lunchtime on Saturday and are closed on Sunday. In the Netherlands, bed and breakfast is *logie met ontbijt*, but in Friesland you will see it written in the local Fries language as *bed en brochje*.

In Belgium and Luxembourg bed and breakfasts are not as widespread as in other European countries, although the concept is growing. Some families open their homes as a bed and breakfast during the main tourist season. Check with the local tourist office for bed and breakfast possibilities in the area. In the north of Belgium (Flanders), ask for *logie met ontbijt* as you would in the Netherlands; while in the south of Belgium (Wallonia) and Luxembourg, use the French term *chambre d'hôte*.

Throughout the routes, towns where bed and breakfasts are available are indicated. As this form of lodging is often seasonal, we have not listed addresses and phone numbers. Check with local tourist offices for up-to-date information.

Youth Hostels

The International Youth Hostel Federation (IYHF) provides accommodations open to people of all ages. In Europe, they are an economical form of accommodation. Many hostels are centrally located, but some can be on the outskirts of towns. Some are regular buildings, while others are converted castles, farms, or historical homes. To stay in a hostel you need to be a member, but nonmembers can usually stay by paying a small supplement, or you can join the first time you stay. Most hostels have single sex dormitory rooms with shared bathrooms, but some have family rooms, where a family or husband and wife can share the room. Many hostels have curfews and require a sleep sheet. Youth hostels are a great alternative, especially for the camper on a rainy evening.

Youth hostels often provide meals, and some have kitchens and laundry facilities available for members. There are youth hostels spread throughout the Benelux. Listings are available from the hostels themselves, from the *Youth Hostel Handbook*, and tourist offices. In this book, youth hostels convenient to the routes have been listed.

Be aware some places may call themselves "unofficial hostels." Often they do not maintain the same standards as IYHF. In an IYHF hostel the cost varies between U.S.$12 and $20 per person for a bed, usually including a basic breakfast.

Note: In Dutch, the word for youth hostel is *jeugdherberg* and in French *auberge de jeunesse*.

Camping

Camping offers the most flexibility of any means of accommodation. You are literally carrying your bedroom and kitchen with you, and this generally allows you to stretch your money and time. With official campgrounds in the Netherlands numbering over 2,000, Belgium over 500, and Luxembourg over 100, campers are never far from a place to pitch their tent. If you are camping, remember to plan for the extra weight. Camping equipment will add substantial weight to your load and may slow your daily pace.

Facilities in official campgrounds vary. You will always find bathing facilities plus amenities ranging from a small shop, restaurant, swimming pool, and playground to washers and dryers. Some campgrounds also provide basic wooden huts with a couple of bunk beds and a gas burner for cooking plus a place for your bicycle. All you need is your sleeping bag. These huts are known as *trekkershuts* or *blokhuts*. The huts cost about Dfl 52 or BEF 1,000 and sleep four. Be warned, huts are popular and require reservations in the summer and on weekends.

In addition to larger campgrounds, there is what is called "mini-camping," which is a small private campground often on a farm. It is also known as "camping on the farm," *camping bij de boer* (Dutch), or *camping à la ferme* (French).

In the Netherlands you can also camp on castle grounds through an association called Nederlanse Landgoed en Kasteel Campings. More rustic is *natuurkamping,* an association of Dutch campgrounds, usually found in forest settings and natural areas. (A small membership fee is required with memberships available from ANWB offices.)

Facilities also vary for these smaller campgrounds. All have showers and toilets (except some *natuurkamping* that may not have showers). Some have a communal room with tables and chairs and often provide a refrigerator for use. The amenities that these smaller campgrounds do not provide are more than compensated for by the ambiance. They are more intimate, less crowded, and often in a lovely rural setting where you can get a feel for farm or country life.

The hosts are welcoming as they see their camping area as an extension of their home, sometimes offering farm produce of fresh eggs, milk, potatoes, etc., for sale to their guests.

When you reach the Benelux, head to a tourist office, ANWB office (Holland), or bookshop and purchase one of the many books on camping, such as *Kleine Campings* (Small Campgrounds) or the *Trekkershut Guide*. In the Netherlands, also available at VVVs or ANWB Offices is a campground location map, *Kamperplaatsen in Nederland*, divided into areas with addresses and phone numbers.

The Belgian Tourist Office provides two free brochures of campground listings, one for Flanders, and one for Wallonia. Ask at a tourist office, but take note, you're unlikely to find the Wallonia campground guide in Flanders, and vice versa. You will need to wait until you're in a large tourist office in the vicinity in order to pick up the appropriate guide.

In Luxembourg the tourist office can provide you with a brochure listing the approximately 100 official campgrounds.

Note: With all three countries, you are likely to come across a sign on the road directing you to small, private campgrounds not listed in the brochures and books. Also, don't forget to ask at the local tourist office. Remember, many campgrounds are open all year, but some only open from April until sometime in October.

Gîtes

Gîtes d'étapes are large hostel-like buildings found throughout Belgium. Sometimes they are only open to groups, but some are open to individuals. *Gîtes ruraux* are weekly house rentals, typically found in the countryside.

Time to Eat

Food is your body's fuel. As a cyclist, you owe it to yourself to eat regular, healthy meals. You can satisfy almost any appetite in the Benelux with a variety of food and cuisine from around the world as well as regional specialties.

For picnics and supplies, bakeries, cheese shops, delicatessens, and supermarkets abound. Don't forget outdoor markets. As well as fresh produce and local products, they offer great atmosphere. Supermarkets are always convenient. In the Netherlands chains include Albert Hein, De Boer, and Edah. In Belgium the chains are Nopri, Super, and GB, while in Luxembourg, supermarkets at this stage tend to still be individually owned. In Holland a great picnic snack available at most bakeries is a *broodje*, a croissant-like pastry filled with cheese, ham, or a spicy *saté* filling and served warm.

Food and food styles vary from country to country. The Dutch begin their day with a hearty breakfast consisting of several varieties of bread, butter, jam, cheese, ham, a boiled egg, and coffee or tea. In Belgium breakfasts vary from north to south. In the north it is more like the Dutch style, while in the south it is more French with bread, butter, jam, and coffee or tea. In Luxembourg breakfasts vary from the basic French style to something more like the Dutch breakfast.

There is a wide variety of cuisine available in the Netherlands. Dutch food itself is basic and hearty. The Dutch vary their meals and eat a lot of fish and seafood plus meat and poultry. The Dutch dairy products and cheese, such as *Gouda, Edam,* and *Leiden,* are excellent. Specialties include a thick pea soup (*erwtensoep*), mussels (*mosselen*), herring (*haring*), eel (*paling*), french fries with mayonnaise (*frites*), pancakes (*pannekoeken*—large and a meal on their own, served with savory or sweet accompaniments), sweet mini-pancakes (*poffertjes*), and small hard waffles glued together with syrup (*stroopwaffel*).

From the days when the Dutch colonized Indonesia, they have developed a taste for delicious Indonesian cuisine, and this has almost become the Dutch national food. For a veritable Indonesian feast try *rijstaffel* (literally translates as rice table) where you will be treated to a table full of Indonesian delicacies and taste sensations such as *gado-gado* (a vegetable salad with peanut sauce), *saté*, curries, rice and noodle dishes, some being quite spicy. A *rijstaffel* costs anywhere from Dfl 30 to Dfl 50, and every visitor to Holland should experience this feast at least once. A few words of advice: come hungry; there is a lot of food, and you will finish your meal bloated and with a smile on your face. You can also order many of these dishes individually. There are Indonesian (*Indisch*) restaurants, but you will often see a Chinese-Indonesian (*Chinees-Indisch*) combination.

The Dutch brew a good strong cup of coffee. Meeting for coffee with friends is a favorite pastime. You will see ubiquitous signs advertising *Koffie is Klaar* (Coffee is Ready) and *Koffie en Appel Geback* (Coffee and Apple Pie [or in season, another fruit]). This is a nice afternoon treat at an outdoor café. On the alcoholic side, try one of the varieties of Dutch beer (Heineken, Amstel, Oranjeboom) and *jenever* (gin).

Many people say that if French cuisine is the best in the world, Belgian is right behind. Of course Belgians wouldn't agree, they would rate their cuisine as number one! Belgians have a discerning palate and are particular about the quality of their food. The farther south you go, the more similarities you see to French food. Meals can vary from the widespread steak and frites to innovative meals with rich sauces and unusual flavors.

Two words that you will be quick to learn in the Belgian snack department are *frites* and *waffels* (*gauffres* in French). The Belgians love their *frites* (french fries). They are traditionally served in a paper cone topped with sauces such as mayonnaise, ketchup, or spicy sauces like *Andalouse*. You will find the ubiquitous Belgian waffle served by street vendors, at market stands, and in cafés and restaurants. Sprinkled with powdered sugar, they are also served with fruits that are in season.

Some Belgian specialties to look for are mussels (*mosselen* or *moules*), rabbit in beer sauce (*lapin à la bière*), eels in green sauce (*paling in 't groen*), Belgian endive (*witloof*, often served wrapped in ham and baked in a cheese sauce), and *waterzooi* (a rich chicken or fish stew).

If you are a chocoholic, Belgium is the place. The Belgians make some of the world's finest chocolate, everything from chocolate filled with fresh cream (*crème fraiche*) and pralines to truffles and block chocolate. Look for chocolatiers such as Léonidas, Neuhaus, and Godiva as well as brands such as Côte D'or and Callebaut.

Belgium is also the home of some of the best and most unusual beers in the world. Trappist monks have been producing outstanding beers in Belgian monasteries for almost a thousand years. Some of the more widely distributed Trappist beers to try are Leffe, Grimbergen, and Chimay, but many others are available only in the areas in which they are produced. Other unusual beers are the cherry-flavored *kriek* beers, or raspberry-flavored *framboise*. Overall, Belgium produces almost 500 different beers—more than any other country in the world.

While dining in Luxembourg you are treated to French quality and German quantity. Luxembourg cuisine has French overtones; however, there is a definite German influence, especially along the eastern border. The Luxembourgeois have a French attitude to dining and take their time to savor their meals.

Like their northern neighbors, you will find the Luxembourgeois, too, have a penchant for mussels. Ardennes ham is a specialty, as are pastries and local fish such as trout. The wines of the Moselle are served with pride as are locally brewed beers such as Diekirch and Mousel.

Throughout all the routes you will find mention of some very regionalized specialties we think are worth seeking out.

Chapter 6

Bicycling in the Benelux—Everything You Need to Know & Won't Have to Ask

Bicycle Shops

Holland is probably the easiest country in the world in which to find a bicycle shop. Virtually every city, town, and village has one, with more than 5,000 shops in this small country. As you cycle through towns, you will be quite amazed to see so many bicycle shops. In Belgium and Luxembourg they are almost as prevalent. In some cases the retailer will be a combined bicycle/motorcycle business. Most shops will be able to handle repairs and carry spares and parts, although measurements for tires will often be metric. Some shops may rent bicycles.

Throughout the routes we have listed bicycle shops, but you can also check with the tourist office or with the ANWB in Holland. If you need to look up a shop in the telephone book look under *Rijwielen*, *Tweewiel*, or *Fiets* in Holland and Flanders, and under *Vélos* or *Bicyclettes* in Wallonia and Luxembourg.

An important thing to note about Dutch bicycle shops (and shops in general) is that they close on Saturday afternoon and do not reopen until 1 P.M. on Monday. If you need repairs in that time period, remember, most train stations have a bicycle shop, and these are usually open seven days a week. In Belgium and Luxembourg you will have an easier time finding a shop open on a Saturday afternoon or a Monday morning, but most are closed on Sundays.

If you are looking for anything to do with bicycle accessories, look no further than a Dutch bicycle shop. An incredible selection of clothing, panniers, bells, and racks is available. You will want to take all sorts of new "toys" home. If you find something you like, purchase it, ask for a box, and ship it home. The Dutch have the most extensive collection of commuting and shopping panniers in the world, available in a wide variety of colors, fabrics, and styles. There is an amazing variety of bicycle bells available. If you come across one with a compass, treat yourself to one and take some home as gifts for your cyclist friends. They're a great gift.

Bicycle Rental

In Holland, many bicycle shops rent bicycles. Some 80 train stations all over the country also rent bicycles. A reduced rate applies if you have a valid rail ticket or pass. Pick up the booklet *Fiets en Trein* (Bike and Train) on arrival in Holland. It lists all the stations with rentals. You can pick up a bicycle at one station and drop it back at another designated station. In heavy tourist areas or at peak tourist times it is advisable to reserve ahead for both bicycle shop and railway rentals.

Railway stations tend to rent the basic Dutch "sit up and beg" bicycles. These practical and very solid bicycles are usually of good quality and often come with a rack and a lock. If you would like more variety, such as a mountain bike or tandem, your best bet is a bicycle shop offering *fietsverhuur* (bicycles for hire). A yellow brochure entitled *ANWB-erkende fietsverhuurders* is a comprehensive listing, updated annually, of such bicycle shops. It includes the types of bicycles they rent and the charges and is available free from the ANWB if you are a member of an automobile association in your home country. (Be sure to take your card.) Note: Some railway stations have tandems. Wherever you rent you will have to leave a deposit of between Dfl 100 and Dfl 200. Daily bicycle rentals run approximately Dfl 8.

In Belgium, some bicycle shops in larger urban centers rent bicycles, but the largest percentage of bicycle rentals is through the Belgian Railways. You can rent bicycles at 35 stations throughout the country, and the bicycle can be returned to the same location or one of the designated "return" stations, thus allowing you to do a one-way journey. If you are doing a combination train and bicycle trip, there are reduced rates for passengers holding a train ticket or Eurail-type pass.

Bicycles can be rented on a daily basis or for longer periods. If you are renting from the station, be sure to pick up the brochure *Train + Vélo* or *Trein + Fiets*. The daily rental fee is approximately BEF 325. You will have to leave a deposit for the bicycle, which can run you as much as BEF 1,500.

In Luxembourg, unlike Belgium and Holland, the railway station is not the main source for bicycle rental. Bicycle shops tend to sell, service, and rent bicycles, especially in the main tourist and recreational areas such as Luxembourg City, Echternach, and Vianden. Sometimes bicycles can be rented from campgrounds. Bicycles can be rented by the half-day, day, or week, and the cost is approximately LUF 400 per day.

Transporting Your Bicycle by Train

In Holland, the booklet *Fiets en Trein* has all the information regarding transportation of your bicycle on the train both within the country and internationally. This is great if you can understand Dutch, but if not, we have listed the necessary basic information.

The Dutch Railways, *Nederlandse Spoorwagen* (NS), is an efficient system, and they make it very easy to take your bicycle on the train. Most trains, except a tiny local *stoptrein*, will accept a bicycle, although some very heavily traveled routes will not allow bicycles during peak times. Some trains only have capacity for four or five bicycles, and in summer the capacity may be filled, especially on weekends, which means you may have to wait for the next train. Try to avoid traveling at peak times so it is easier to deal with loading and unloading your bicycle, and so the bicycle capacity isn't filled.

Purchase a ticket for your bicycle at the same time as you purchase your own ticket. Loop the ticket for your bicycle in a visible place on your handlebar and seal it with the adhesive edge. Load and unload your bicycle into a special "bicycle car" which is part of a regular car, usually in the middle of the train. The bicycle area is a special wide section with pull-down seats so you can sit next to your bicycle. You need not take your panniers off.

Basically the same procedure applies for international travel. Some international trains do not allow for bicycles, so check ahead to avoid disappointment. If you change trains en route, you may have to follow a similar procedure listed below for Belgium and Luxembourg.

Should you wish to take your bicycle on the train in Belgium, the Belgian National Railways (Societé de Chemins de Fer Belgique or SNCB) do not make it as easy as in Holland or Luxembourg. You must check whether the train allows bicycles to be carried as accompanied luggage. You need to take off all your panniers and load the bicycle into the luggage compartment. If the compartment is full, then you will need to wait for the next train. (Often station attendants will be able to inform you of this ahead of time.) If you need to change trains, you will need to unload your own bicycle from the train and take it to the connection to reload it.

When you purchase your train ticket, you need to purchase a ticket for your bicycle (for all segments if you are changing trains). You purchase your own ticket from the regular window but need to obtain the bicycle's ticket from the luggage office. If you are traveling within Belgium, all you need is your ticket and the one for your bicycle, but if you are crossing a border, you will also need a customs form.

Once you have your appropriate documentation, head to the platform. It is possible to ask if you can be escorted across the tracks (much easier than stairs) by a railway official. Some Belgian railway stations allow this, others do not. See if you can find out where the luggage compartment of the train stops so that once on the platform you can position yourself properly. Once the train arrives you often have only a minute or two to load your bicycle and then find your carriage. The bicycle will either be hung on a bicycle hook or leaned against a wall. Do not use your lock in case the bicycle needs to be moved en route. Make sure the guard knows at which station you are getting off. It may help speed up the unloading process.

The Luxembourg Railways (Chemins de Fer Luxembourgeois or CFL) is extremely bicycle-friendly and encourages cyclists to take bicycles on trains within the country. The easiest and most economical way to purchase a ticket is to buy a *carnet* (a set of 10 tickets). No matter where you go within Luxembourg, the bicycle uses one ticket, LUF 40 (approximately U.S.$1.40), any time, any day. As an example, an adult will use three tickets of the *carnet* to travel from Luxembourg City to Ettelbruck. You must validate the tickets you will use before boarding the train. Check with the ticket office as to how many tickets you will need, then add one for the bicycle.

Every domestic train has a carriage equipped to carry bicycles. This carriage has bicycle hooks but also has plenty of room to lean your bicycle against the wall. Seats are provided in the carriage so that you can remain with your bicycle. If the train is crowded and you have to hang your bicycle on the hook, you will be required to take your panniers off. Otherwise you can usually just take your bicycle on as is.

For an international journey, it is slightly different. Most trains allow the bicycles to be carried as accompanied luggage, but check ahead of time just to be sure. You will need to take off all your panniers and load the bicycle into the luggage compartment. If you need to change trains at a point on your trip, you will need to unload your own bicycle from the train and take it to the connection to reload it. You need to purchase a train ticket for yourself and one for your bicycle for all segments of the trip.

Once you have purchased your *carnet* or ticket, make your way to the platform. In Luxembourg City some parts of the station can be accessed by elevators. Otherwise, some tracks need to be reached by stairs. At stations other than Luxembourg City you can ask a railway official if you can be escorted across the tracks.

Transporting Your Bicycle by Ferry

In Holland, ferries are a way of life and come in all shapes and sizes. They are an extension of the road system, and the Dutch have determined they are more cost-effective than building hundreds of small or large bridges (although there are many bridges to be found). Ferries will transport you across rivers, waterways, and sea. They can be a tiny ferry that only handles bicycles and pedestrians or a slightly larger barge type that carries cars as well. Some of the very small ferries are operated by a pulley, while others are motorized. The biggest ferries are the huge variety that run between the mainland and the Wadden Islands.

You will pay a nominal fee on the small ferries which run on demand (when they have a few passengers, they leave). Sometimes they will take you across on your own. A higher ticket price is required on the large ferries which run on set schedules. Try to keep small change handy if you will be riding on a route using a small ferry. There is nothing worse than handing over Dfl 50 when all you need is Dfl 0.75 for the short ride. Some ferries do not charge at all.

Maps

The Netherlands

The Dutch have a penchant for detail, as is evidenced by the meticulously signposted roads and *fietspads* (bicycle paths). This spills over to their fine maps. Dutch cartography is the cyclist's dream. Many excellent maps are available when you reach the Netherlands.

Before you leave home, a good planning map is the Michelin 1:400,000 (orange) series, Map #408, but this map is not sufficiently detailed for cycling. Two Michelin maps in the 1:200,000 (yellow) series cover the entire country and are the best cycling maps available outside Holland. Michelin Map #210 titled *Nederland/Pays-Bas (Amsterdam-Groningen)* covers the northern half of the country. Michelin Map #211 titled *Nederland/Pays-Bas (Rotterdam-Apeldoorn-Maastricht)* covers the southern half of the country. Another overlap map worth considering is Michelin Map #212, titled *Nederland/Belgique (Brugge-Rotterdam-Antwerpen)*. It covers the north of Belgium, the province of Dutch Limburg, and a portion of southern Holland. The 1:200,000 series provides a lot of valuable information for the cyclist. These maps indicate even the tiniest roads, major inclines, scenic roads, distances, unpaved roads, some bicycle paths, and plenty of tourist information.

Once you enter the Netherlands, visit an ANWB office or a VVV office, and you will have numerous map choices. For the purposes of the routes used in this

Typical directional signs for bicycles found all over the Netherlands.

book, we used a map series co-produced by the ANWB and the VVV. This "green" *Toeristenkaart* series is scaled at 1:100,000 and is ideal for cycling. The maps are readily available for Dfl 11.95 per map. Each map is designed with the cyclist in mind and is beautifully clear. They show incredible detail, including bicycle paths (*fietspads*), ANWB "mushrooms" with numbers, plus tourist information such as location of windmills, bulb fields, campgrounds, youth hostels, castles, forests, sand dunes, and much more.

There are 12 maps in the series, one for each province of the Netherlands, and which maps are used for each route is indicated. The 12 provinces are Friesland, Groningen, Drenthe, Utrecht, Flevoland, Gelderland, Overijssel, North Holland, South Holland, Zeeland, North Brabant, and Limburg. If you intend to buy these maps, our routes cover all the provinces except Groningen, Flevoland, and Zeeland, and only a tiny section of the northern route touches the western corner of Drenthe (and some of the province of Drenthe overlaps with the Overijssel map).

Note: The Zeeland, North Brabant, and Limburg maps cover part of the north of Belgium and are worth carrying to guide you through northern Belgium where map resources are not as good as in Holland.

If you are a map aficionado, you're in the right country. Both the VVV and ANWB produce their own individual map series. The ANWB has yet another series at the scale 1:100,000, and the VVV has a series with a 1:50,000 scale if you prefer even more detail. Other provincial maps are also available from individual VVVs offering cycle paths within their immediate area plus regional ANWB circular tour maps such as the Bollenstreek Route in the region between Haarlem and Leiden where the bulb fields are located.

Belgium

Maps in Belgium are a disappointment. The best maps to be found can actually be purchased in any country, so don't feel that resources will be better when you arrive. The Michelin 1:350,000 (orange) series, Map #409, which covers all of Belgium and Luxembourg, is an excellent planning map but not detailed enough for cycling.

Three Michelin maps in the 1:200,000 (yellow) series cover the entire country and are the best cycling maps available. Map #212, titled *Nederland/Belgique (Brugge-Rotterdam-Antwerpen)*, covers the north of Flanders, Limburg province, and a portion of southern Holland. Map #213, *Belgique (Bruxelles-Oostende-Liège)*, covers almost all of Flanders, i.e., northern Belgium. Map #214, *Belgique (Mons-Dinant-Luxembourg)*, covers Wallonia, i.e., southern Belgium, as well as a good portion of Luxembourg.

The 1:200,000 series provide a lot of valuable information for the cyclist. It shows tiny roads, inclines, scenic roads, distances, unpaved roads, some bicycle paths, and includes plenty of tourist information.

After searching for maps in numerous bookstores in Belgium, we determined that the Michelin maps are the way to go for the cyclist. Sales staff and Belgian cyclists we discussed this with agreed. We searched for a good 1:100,000 map but were not completely satisfied. This was made all the more frustrating having come from Holland where there are several superb 1:100,000 series available.

If you would like something a little more detailed than the Michelin 1:200,000 series, a Belgian company called Geocart produces a series of nine maps with a scale of 1:100,000. The nine maps cover each of the nine provinces, and the series is titled *Fietskaart/Carte Cycliste* and subtitled with the name of the province. The Belgian provinces are Brabant, Limburg, Antwerpen, Oost-Vlaanderen, West-Vlaanderen, Hainaut, Namur, Luxembourg, and Liège. If you wish to buy the Geocart maps, our routes do not enter the provinces of Hainaut and Liège. These are reasonable maps but not as clear as the Michelin maps. All the roads are marked in gray and can be at times confusing. The best thing about these maps is that most of the *fietspads* (bicycle paths) are indicated, showing whether they are separated from the roadway, adjacent to it, etc. These maps are available from most major bookstores in Belgium, such as the FNAC chain, as well as the Belgian Automobile Association.

Note: The ANWB/VVV *Toeristenkaart* maps (see above) of the Dutch provinces of Zeeland, North Brabant, and Limburg, the three southern provinces of the Netherlands, cover part of the north of Belgium, and are worth carrying to guide you through northern Belgium where map resources are not as good as in the Netherlands. Purchase these in the Netherlands as they are not readily available in Belgium.

Luxembourg

Luxembourg is a small country, and the two maps of choice are both Michelin. Both are in the Michelin yellow series, the first being Map #215, *Grand-Duché de Luxembourg*, which covers the entire country, its scale being 1:150,000. The second is Map #214, *Belgique (Mons-Dinant-Luxembourg)*, covering Wallonia, i.e., southern Belgium, as well as all of Luxembourg north of Luxembourg City, with a scale of 1:200,000.

Map #215 is an excellent cycling map with good detail. For the purposes of the routes in the book, Map #214 is an adequate reference because none of our routes venture south of Luxembourg City. It is also the map to use if cycling Wallonia, thus it becomes a dual-purpose map. Should you wish to pick up Map #215 once you reach Luxembourg, it is readily available in book shops in Luxembourg City and other cities. The Michelin maps supply tourist information plus indicate small backroads, inclines, scenic roads, distances, and unpaved roads; some of bicycle paths are marked.

A worthwhile stop in Luxembourg City is the tourist office at the station. This tourist office services the entire country (as opposed to the tourist office at Place d'Armes which specializes in Luxembourg City only). Pick up the 14-page booklet *Cycle Tracks* which gives basic information on the cycle routes throughout Luxembourg. As they are constantly adding routes, the booklet may be updated. Ask for the English version. The tourist office at Place d'Armes does not carry this booklet.

Bicycle Parking

In Holland there are two types of bicycle parking to be considered. The first is the ubiquitous bicycle rack found outside supermarkets, shops, restaurants, at bus stops, outside the VVV, and anywhere you might need to leave your bicycle. These racks appear in various forms, as a free-standing rack, as concrete slots in the pavement, as small covered shelters, or as metal attachments connected to the side of buildings. Be sure to lock your bicycle up when you leave it. Do not leave valuables on your bicycle unattended.

The other type of parking is called a *fietsenstalling* (bicycle storage). These are like bicycle parking garages and can be found in many cities and larger towns. These are usually privately owned, and for a small fee your bicycle will be parked in its own spot and watched over by an attendant. These are great if you are coming into a city or town for the day and want to sightsee on foot for several hours. The other place where you can almost always find a fietsenstalling is the town's main railway station. Many railway stations have fietsenstalling, and the booklet *Fiets en Trein* (see Bicycle Rental above) has a list of the stations in the back under *bewaakte fietsenstalling*. You can always check with the VVV for a fietsenstalling when you enter a town.

In Belgium and Luxembourg, you may find the occasional fietsenstalling-type setup; however, most parking will be bicycle racks.

Whichever country you are in, at night, make sure your bicycle is put in a secure place and off the street. Of course, lock it up.

Bicycle Security

In general people are honest, and Europe is typically safe. Unfortunately, a few precautionary warnings are necessary.

In big cities, it is not safe to leave your bicycle locked on the street. Bicycle theft in larger cities is rampant, and if you've brought your own bicycle from home, it will stand out from the solid European leviathans and could be tempting to the would-be bicycle thief. If you have a rental bicycle, then it is less conspicuous, but still be sure to lock it and remove all valuables.

Never leave full panniers unattended on the bicycle. You are carrying your personal belongings and if camping, your "home" and your bed. If you are visiting a city for a long period of time, either use the fietsenstalling or check into your accommodation or campground, leave the bicycle there, and walk around on foot. In small towns and villages life is much safer, and we felt comfortable leaving unloaded bicycles locked up while shopping, wandering around, or visiting a museum. If you are traveling with another person, use two locks and lock the bicycles together, as well as onto a rack, tree, pole, or something immovable. If traveling alone, two locks are advisable.

Use your own discretion, but *never* leave the bicycles locked up when loaded unless you can watch them from a restaurant, café, or through the bakery window. Also, remember to take off your bicycle computer and handlebar bag when you leave your bicycle. *Never* leave your passport, money, and other valuables on the bicycle unattended. Carry them on your person in a money pouch or belt. (If two people are traveling together and all you need is a brief visit to a bakery or supermarket, it is sometimes quicker to have one person run in while the other waits with the bicycles.)

These words may sound like the voice of doom, but you know that old saying "better safe than sorry," and you don't want your trip spoiled because you left temptation in somebody's way.

Bicycle Paths and Roads

It will not take long before you recognize the words *fietspad* and *piste cyclable*. These are the words in Dutch and French for "bicycle path." In Holland approximately 10,000 kilometers of these fietspads crisscross the country making it a pleasure to cycle safely and comfortably. In the majority of cases these fietspads are smooth and well maintained. You will quickly learn to appreciate the Dutch fietspads used by commuters and recreational cyclists alike as a superb way to cycle.

Finding your way on Dutch fietspads is not difficult. There are numerous bicycle route signs. The directional signs specifically for cyclists are white signs with red lettering giving the town's name and distance and are painted with a little red bicycle. The tip of these signs is shaped to a point indicating the direction. These will be located at turns or intersections. Sometimes these signs are in green denoting alternative scenic routes. There are also a number of bicycle route signs provided by the ANWB. These include regional route signs taking you on scenic loops or to points of local interest. Maps of these routes are available from VVV and ANWB offices in the area.

There is also a system of longer routes, called LF Routes (Landelijke Fietsroutes). This network includes more than 6,000 kilometers. Booklets covering these routes, and an LF network map, can also be purchased from VVV or ANWB offices. These routes are well marked with signs indicating the LF route number and name. From time to time our routes will follow portions of these.

Another signpost, the most easily missed by those not used to them, are the ANWB *paddestoelen*, or "mushrooms"; they are four-sided, knee-high markers roughly in the shape of a mushroom. These are specifically for hikers and cyclists, and each one is numbered to correspond with the applicable ANWB map. (See phot page 26.)

As mentioned, cycle paths are of great importance to the Dutch. Therefore, when a fietspad crosses a freeway or major intersection, instead of forcing the cyclist to deal with the traffic obstacles, there will usually be a tunnel under the roadway or a special bridge or overpass that the cyclist can use. In the case of a roundabout there are special lanes for the cyclist around the edge. These are marked by broken white lines. Large bridges crossing a canal or river will have a bicycle lane.

Holland is the one country in the world where roads are of no real concern to cyclists because a cyclist hardly ever uses the road except on adjoining cycle paths. Occasionally in rural areas, there are no cycle paths on quiet farm roads. Here the cyclist uses the road, staying close to the right or on the right shoulder. If you do need to ride on a road in Holland, there is little to worry about as cars are very aware of cyclists and treat cyclists with respect.

Belgium doesn't have nearly as many bicycle paths as Holland. In fact, you will find them scattered throughout Flanders but lose them as you head south into the Ardennes where there is less traffic and the roads are quieter. The one exception is the province of Limburg where the quantity and quality of fietspads resembles Holland more than the rest of Belgium. The Belgian fietspads vary from smooth to cracked and bumpy.

Belgium has one of the highest percentages of motor vehicles per

The network of bicycle paths throughout Luxembourg are well signposted.

square kilometer in Europe and along with this, some very heavy traffic, especially on major routes. For a cyclist, the best solution is to stay on the small backroads or use designated *fietspads/pistes cyclables* (bicycle paths) whenever possible. Road surfaces on most roads are good. Sometimes, though, the bicycle paths on the edge of the road can be bumpy. Then there are cobblestones, known as *pavé* or *cailloux*. You will run into these in the older parts of some towns and even in the rural north of Belgium. This is just part of cycling in Belgium. Sometimes the choice is a quiet cobblestone road or a smooth, but busy, highway.

Luxembourg is a small country, and traffic is not hectic, thus cycling without bicycle paths is not a problem. Luxembourg, however, is making a concerted effort to promote the bicycle and currently has approximately 400 kilometers of bicycle paths with the number of kilometers due to reach 600 by the year 2000. Most of these bicycle paths are in immaculate condition, and a good portion of them are off-road through forests and valleys, skirting farmlands and following the old, and now unused, railway tracks. For the small size of Luxembourg, this is a huge amount of paths and an extremely adventurous program.

The roads in the Grand Duchy are some of the most well maintained in Europe. Luxembourg offers the cyclist an abundance of minor roads, denoted by CR, which are quiet country roads with fine cycling. Several of the larger N roads are not heavily trafficked, and by using the CR and N roads, one can pretty much avoid the busy E roads, which carry the highest volume of traffic.

Signposting is excellent. A fine feature found in Luxembourg is very clever town signposting. As expected, when you enter a town there is a yellow sign with the town's name. When you leave the town, there is a sign with the town's name with a diagonal red line through it and above is the name of the next town to which you will come on that road.

Whichever of the three Benelux countries you are in, you will find several types of bicycle paths. Many run alongside the roadway, sometimes indicated by a simple white line or sometimes completely separated by a ridge of concrete or a grass strip. Most bicycle paths are blacktop; however, some are indicated by special red paving bricks. Or the surface, instead of blacktop, is a reddish color. Bicycle paths can be either one-way, two-way, bicycle only, or can be shared with pedestrians, mopeds, small motorcycles, or equestrians. One thing to be especially careful of on those paths shared with mopeds, or *bromfietsen*, is that they will expect you to stay to the right side of the path, allowing them to pass. Although they always have a bell or horn, they expect the noise of the motor itself—very loud—should be enough warning for cyclists. It is dangerous to ignore this fietspad hazard, as they only seem to go one speed—as fast as they can.

Many bicycle paths crisscross the countryside and take you away from the main roads. These make the most idyllic cycling. Many go from village to village, and the distance is often shorter than using the paths along the roads. They are optional; however, we have used them whenever possible. They go alongside dikes and rivers, edge farmers' fields, and pass by forests, through sand dunes, or along the coast. They are used by locals for commuting, but many of them are used for recreational purposes and have benches and picnic tables strategically placed. These off-road fietspads are the ideal place to have that quiet picnic lunch.

In all three countries bicycle paths are often repaved unused railway tracks, usually taking an off-road, car-free course through the countryside.

Along canals in Belgium and Holland some of the bicycle paths are the old towpaths, known as *jaagpads*. These are the paths along the canals that were used prior to motorized barges for horses to pull the loads. Today, these are often multipurpose service roads, used by cyclists, pedestrians, and sometimes cars. In Holland and northern Belgium you will also find many bicycle paths adjacent to, or on top of, the dikes.

Other obstacles to watch out for while cycling are tram lines and train tracks (especially when wet), cattle grids, and in some rural areas, the cattle themselves. Rural paths will often pass through grazing areas.

Some Basic Rules for Bicycle Paths

1. When a bicycle path is provided, it is compulsory to use it. Even where the road surface seems to be smoother, you are required to stay on the bicycle path.
2. Bicycle paths are "bicycle roads," so adhere to basic traffic rules. Overtake on the left, don't block the path, and if you need to stop, pull over to the side in order to keep the path clear.
3. In the Benelux each bicycle must be fitted with a bell. This is essential for overtaking. Lights are also required.
4. Be aware of signs such as *Fietsers Oversteken* (translates as Cyclists Cross Over) indicating the bicycle path is ending on the side you are on and will cross the road and continue on the other side. Other signs indicating that a bicycle path is ending often say *Einde Fietspad*.
5. Only ride two abreast if it is not hindering other traffic on the path. Try to ride single file if bicycle traffic is heavy, if it is a two-way bicycle path, or if you know someone is about to overtake.
6. Unless it is otherwise marked, always assume cars have the right of way when a bicycle path crosses a road. Often (almost always in Holland) white triangles will be painted on the path or roadway indicating whether you or the cars should yield, in addition to the traditional triangular yield sign. Drivers tend to have a great deal of respect for cyclists in these countries, but always err on the side of caution.
7. Although this is a rule for roads as well as bicycle paths, do not forget to signal your intention to turn with an outstretched right or left arm.

Chapter 7

Route 1— Northern Netherlands Route

Total Distance:	709 kilometers (440 miles)
Terrain:	Flat, a few gentle hills in the Hoge Veluwe
Maps:	Michelin Maps 210 and 211 (1:200,000), ANWB Maps—North Holland, Friesland, Overijssel, Gelderland, and Utrecht (1:100,000)
Connecting Route:	Route 2—Southern Netherlands

Northern Netherlands is primarily flat and easy to cycle. Despite the flat terrain, there is a lot of variation within this part of the country. You will follow some beautiful coastline, meander through sand dunes, cross over one of the world's great feats of engineering, spend time on an island, and cycle through idyllic farmlands and along storybook canals.

This part of the country allows you to explore Giethoorn, a village where no cars are allowed, discover the ancient Hanseatic and fortress towns of Zwolle and Deventer, visit the picturesque "cheese towns" of Edam and Alkmaar, and, of course, begin in one of the great cities of the world, Amsterdam. You will travel through the province of Friesland where the people speak their own language and have a cultural pride all their own. You will spend time in the Hoge Veluwe National Park with a terrain very different to anything else in the Netherlands. Its museum is hailed as one of the nation's treasures.

Amsterdam

Amsterdam is a city for everyone. This magical city is a world of contrasts. It is cosmopolitan, yet quaint. It is elegant, yet offbeat. It is a city of history, yet it is progressive. It is dotted with busy squares and gathering places, yet has quiet canal promenades and parks. It is a big city, yet its intimate neighborhoods give it the feel of a small town. It is a city of culture, housing some of the world's great museums, yet it is a city where the bicycle reigns, and everyone from students to businesspersons are at home on a bicycle.

You can explore Amsterdam by bicycle, by foot, or view it from the canals. It is a compact city and easy to find your way around. It is built on a pattern of concentric circles of canals, crossed by a strategic network of roads, interwoven with winding streets and alleys, market places, and squares. You can visit museums, galleries, and churches, frequent sophisticated or charming restaurants, casual bars, or congenial brown cafés, cross hundreds of bridges, admire the architecture of the gabled houses, and by night, check out the famed Red Light District.

What to See in Amsterdam

There is so much to see and do in Amsterdam that it could fill the rest of the book. A good way to get your bearings and get a different perspective is to take a canal boat. One good option for a canal tour is the Amsterdam Museumboot, which makes a canal circuit, stopping at several points and allowing you to get on and off near most of the major museums. The ticket entitles you to a discount on museum entrance fees as well. It leaves from opposite Centraal Station, where several companies offer canal tours.

Amsterdam deserves at least a few days. Some of the world's best museums are located here. Top billing goes to the three museums near the Museumplein. The striking building of neo-Renaissance architecture here is the Rijksmuseum (National Museum). It

The stately fourteenth-century Waag (weigh house) in Alkmaar.

houses a fine collection of Northern European paintings, especially Dutch masters, including Rembrandt's *The Night Watch*. Allow plenty of time for this 150-room museum (closed Monday). Almost next door is the Van Gogh Museum with its superb permanent collection of hundreds of paintings and drawings plus exhibits reflecting on the artist's life and development as a painter (open daily). Right next door is the Stedelijk Museum (Municipal Museum), a collection of contemporary art with changing exhibits. The sculpture garden is free. Use the separate entrance facing Museumplein (open daily).

Some other museums to consider are the Amsterdam Historisch Museum (Amsterdam Museum of History) where you can learn the history of the city from its origins as a fishing village to the global trading empire of the eighteenth century (open daily, Kalverstraat 92). The Tropenmuseum (Museum of the Tropics), originally devoted to the cultures of Holland's former colonies in the East and West Indies, now focuses on peoples and cultures of third world countries (open daily, Linnaeusstraat 2). The Joods Historisch Museum (Jewish History Museum) traces the history of Jewish people in the Netherlands and the impact the Holocaust had on the Jewish community of Amsterdam (open daily, Daniel Meijerplein 2-4). Across the road is the Portuguese Synagogue. Built in 1675, it was the largest in the world, and today the interior is still intact (closed Saturday). The Verzetsmuseum (Resistance Museum) tells the story of resistance fighters during World War II, focusing on espionage, sabotage, and underground communication (closed Monday, Lekstraat 63).

One of Amsterdam's most visited sites is Anne Frankhuis (Anne Frank's House). The famous young Dutch girl lived in hiding with her Jewish family during World War II in the attic of this house. Her story became famous because of her eloquently written diary. Plan to stand in line in the summer months (open daily, Prinsengracht 263). Another well-known house is Rembrandthuis (Rembrandt's House), the home of seventeenth-century Dutch artist Rembrandt van Rijn. Etchings and furniture are on view (open daily, Jodenbreestraat 4-6).

The most famous square in Amsterdam is Damplein (Dam Square), the site of the original dam that crossed the Amstel River. On the square is the Koninklijk Paleis (Royal Palace), not a residence, but used for official functions; De Nieuwe Kerk (New Church), constructed around 1500; and the National Monument, erected in 1956 in honor of those who perished in World War II.

Behind the palace and a few blocks west is Westermarkt and the Westerkerk (West Church), completed in 1631. The church's beautiful 85-meter (275-foot) tower is the highest in the city. Climb it (in summer only) for a view over the city. Rembrandt is buried here. Also of note in Westermarkt is house #6 where the philosopher Descartes, of "I think, therefore I am" fame, lived for a short time. Keep going a little farther to the Jordaan area. This area has become the bohemian quarter, with lots of artists taking up residence, as well as lots of cafés and unusual shops.

Another lively area is Muntplein (Mint Square) with the impressive fifteenth-century Munttoren (Mint tower) where coins were once minted. The structure is left over from one of the old city wall gates.

Markets abound in Amsterdam. Waterlooplein is known for its flea market, Albert Cuypstraat (between Van Woustraat and Ferdinand Bolstraat) is home to the Albert Cuyp Markt, the city's largest street market as well as one of Europe's biggest, where everything is sold from shellfish to shampoo, fabrics to film. On Saturday, head to Noorderplein for the Bird Market, while the

Bloemenmarkt (Flower Market) is a daily occurrence on Singel Canal. A bit farther afield, on the outskirts of Amsterdam, is Aalsmeer, where you will find a huge warehouse complex with flowers as far as the eye can see. The Netherlands is the largest exporter of flowers in the world. Fifty percent of exported flowers are purchased by international buyers from this market (open daily, 7:30 A.M.–11 A.M., except weekends).

Wander down Utrechtsestraat with its intimate restaurants and unusual shops. Be sure to visit the "Street of Seven Bridges" at the intersection of Reguliersgracht and Herengracht a bit south of Rembrandtsplein. Look north and south on Reguliersgracht and east and west on Herengracht; you are surrounded by at least a dozen bridges. At night the bridges are lit, and it is a superb sight. There are also some good restaurants in this area.

If you are interested in beer, tour the Heineken Brewery (closed Sunday, Stadhoudererskade 78). And for some tranquillity, the Begijinhof is a pleasant haven in the city. The tiny houses and garden were established in the fourteenth century. The house at #34 is the oldest preserved "wooden" house in Amsterdam, dating to 1475. Also visit Vondelpark, an area of 120 acres that in the summer features outdoor concerts and performers and offers a place to relax.

At night Amsterdam is a city of lamplit canals and the awakening of the Red Light District. Be careful in this area at all times as pickpockets stalk the area.

A note about bicycles. It is easy to get around Amsterdam by bicycle, but do not, under any circumstances, leave your bicycle out in Amsterdam, even if it is locked. Bicycle theft is rampant in the city. You also need to be extremely careful riding in Amsterdam. Bicycle paths abound, but you need to watch out, not only for cars and other cyclists, but also for pedestrians, trams, and tram tracks. You will notice local cyclists disregarding virtually every traffic regulation in Amsterdam. Do NOT follow them through red lights and stop signs. They know the traffic patterns and what they can get away with. You don't. Be careful.

Tourist Information

The VVV has three locations in Amsterdam. Note: These are probably the busiest of all the VVVs in Holland.

Stationsplein 10, to left and across from Centraal Station, phone 06 034 340 66, inside Centraal Station (downstairs), and Leidesplein 1.

ANWB Office, Museumplein 5. Phone 020 673 08 44.

The ANWB sells travel books, maps, and resources, but another useful address is:

American Book Center, Kalverstraat 185 (near Heiligeweg). Phone 020 625 55 37. Maps and guide books are available here, as well as books and magazines in English.

Schiphol Airport

For directions to the airport from Amsterdam, see the Southern Netherlands Route.

From the moment you arrive at Amsterdam's Schiphol Airport, you know you're in a bicycle country. Where else would you have two great options to get into town? You can put your bicycle on the train at the station downstairs in the terminal building or go outside and get directly onto a designated bicycle path that begins just a few steps from the terminal building.

By train—The railway station for *Nederlandse Spoorwagen* (NS) is downstairs in Terminal 3. Buy your tickets one level above the train station on the arrival level. The fare for an adult is Dfl 6.00 and Dfl 10.00 for bicycles. You will need to use the bicycle carriage indicated by the bicycle symbol above the door. Trains run between 5:30 A.M. and midnight with approximately four to five trains per hour for the 20-minute ride to Amsterdam's Centraal Station.

To ride—Most international arrivals come into Terminal 3. From the arrivals level go to the end of the terminal where the car rental companies are located. Go out the door and turn right. At the end of the covered area is the start of your first Dutch fietspad (bicycle path) indicated by a round blue sign with a white bicycle. You will notice a bicycle parking area at the beginning of the bicycle path.

Take this bicycle path, which will take you through a tunnel then along a farm road until it reaches the N232 highway at Badhoevedorp on the north end of the airport grounds. Turn right along the N232 and follow it a couple hundred meters until you see a bicycle sign for Amsterdam indicating you turn left. Follow the signs through Badhoevedorp. On the northeast side of town you will spot your first Dutch windmill on your left (Molen van Sloten). Continue past the windmill, and you will shortly join a bicycle path along the canal that will take you all the way to Vondelpark. Follow the directional signs for Amsterdam or Amsterdam Centrum. Ride through Vondelpark, and you are already on the southwest end of Amsterdam Centrum.

Accommodations

Amsterdam has lodgings to suit every price level. The VVV can assist you with reservations. If you are flying into Amsterdam and want a day or two to acclimatize and get over jet lag, you may want to pre-book a hotel. Make sure wherever you stay they have a place for your bicycle inside.

A couple of hotel suggestions to get you started follow:

Hotel De Harmonie, Prinsengracht 816. Phone 020 625 01 74. Dfl 120–150 Dbl. Historic building located on canal in residential area. Close to Rembrandt-splein, Utrechtsestraat, and museums. Place for bicycles on landing.

Hotel Seven Bridges, Reguliersgracht 31. Phone 020 623 13 29. Dfl 120–180 Dbl. Pleasant, older style hotel, well located in the bridges area, convenient to restaurants, museums, etc.

Youth Hostel Vondelpark, Zandpad 5. Phone 020 683 17 44. Located across from Vondelpark.

Youth Hostel Stadsdoelen, Kloveniersburgwal 97. Phone 020 624 68 32. Central location.

Bob's Youth Hostel, Nieuwe Zijds Voorburgwal 92. Phone 020 623 00 63. Not far from Centraal Station. "Unofficial" hostel with large dorm rooms. Very crowded.

Camping Vliegenbos, Meeuwenlaan 138. Phone 020 636 88 55. Closest campground to Centraal Station.

Camping Zeeburg, Zuider Ijdijk 44. Phone 020 694 44 30. Quite a way east of the city. Very large.

Camping Gaasper, Looosdrechtdreef 7. Phone 020 696 73 26. Farther out in Gaasper Park.

Where to Eat

In Amsterdam, almost every nationality's cuisine is represented. You will have no trouble finding excellent Indonesian food, Italian, Middle Eastern,

Suriname, traditional Dutch, vegetarian, and the list goes on. There are bars, brown cafés (local cafés that take their name from the brown woodwork), take out, and if you're camping, small markets and supermarkets. There is an eclectic selection of restaurants on Utrechtsestraat, around Leidesplein, at Reguliersgracht, and countless brown cafés, and cozy neighborhood restaurants and bars can be found on small side streets as you wind your way through the maze of canals and streets of Amsterdam.

Bicycle Shops/Rentals

Amsterdam Centraal Station Bicycle Shop and Rental, known as Take-A-Bike. Exit station, turn left, and after 20 meters or so go down the stairs or ramp. Phone 020 624 83 91. Open from 6 A.M. to 11 P.M., depending on day of week and season. This is important if you need repairs on Sunday, late evening hours, and Monday mornings. Fietsenstalling also available.

Holland Rent-A-Bike, Damrak 247. Phone 020 622 32 07. Centrally located, near Beursplein.

Amsterdam to Edam: 26 Kilometers

From just behind the Centraal Station, take the IJ ferry (IJveer) across the river. When you get off the ferry, you will notice an immediate transformation from big city to village. Follow the signs for Durgerdam and Marken, which will take the scenic route through several villages along the water to Durgerdam. There are several bed and breakfasts here. After Durgerdam the fietspad goes up onto the dike along the IJmeer. This is a beautiful ride with the IJmeer to your right and lovely rural coastal scenery to your left. You will pass

through a couple of very tiny villages with nothing but a few houses and a café. There are no shops or hotels; however, there are a few bed and breakfasts. Continue north along the coast, always following the signs to Marken. The road to Marken will veer to the right, going east across a spit of land until it reaches the unique town of Marken.

Marken, once an island, is now joined to the mainland by a causeway built in 1957. Although Marken gets its share of tourists, it still maintains a certain charm with its clusters of traditional green and black houses built on stilts and its small, picturesque harbor. Take a walk or ride through the town, getting away from the touristy harbor for a while, and you will get a sense of the identity of this fishing community and the island's past. Visit the Marken Museum at Kerkbuurt 44 and get a glimpse of the lifestyle in Marken (open daily, Easter–November).

At the harbor, take the Marken/Volendam Express, a 25-minute ferry across the water to Volendam. Cost is Dfl 8 for an adult with a bicycle. It leaves every 30 to 45 minutes depending on the season.

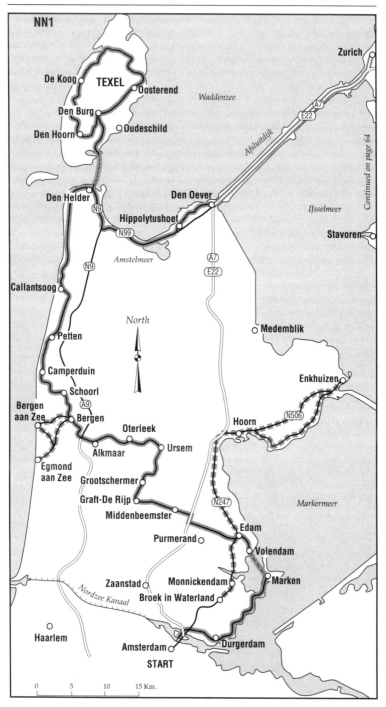

NN1

De Koog

TEXEL

Oosterend

Waddenzee

Den Burg

Den Hoorn

Oudeschild

Zurich

A7

E22

Afsluitdijk

Den Helder

N9

Den Oever

Hippolytushoef

N99

IJsselmeer

Stavoren

Amstelmeer

A7

E22

N9

Callantsoog

North

Medemblik

Petten

Camperduin

Enkhuizen

Schoorl

A9

Bergen aan Zee

Bergen

Oterleek

Hoorn

N506

Alkmaar

Ursem

Egmond aan Zee

Grootschermer

Graft-De Rijp

Middenbeemster

N247

Markermeer

Purmerand

Edam

Zaanstad

Monnickendam

Volendam

Marken

Nordzee Kanaal

Broek in Waterland

Haarlem

Amsterdam

START

Durgerdam

Continued on page 64

0   5   10   15 Km.

You will arrive in the scenic harbor of Volendam, a bit larger and very different in character to Marken. Lots of seafood restaurants and cafés line the harbor area and hotels and campgrounds are in the vicinity.

Leave Volendam and follow the signs another 3 kilometers to the gorgeous cheese town of Edam.

Edam is the archetypal Dutch town with bridges crisscrossing canals, quaint gabled houses, the ubiquitous Stadhuis (Town Hall), Kaasmarkt (Cheese Market), and church; the town has remained relatively unspoiled. Wander around, beginning at the VVV in the eighteenth-century Stadhuis on the main square. Stand on the bridge for a view of the Speeltoren, the remnant of a fifteenth-century church that has one of the oldest carillons in the country from 1561. Cross the bridge to the Edam Museum. It is located in Edam's oldest house, built in 1530, decorated in period style, and containing an amazing floating cellar (open daily). Visit the Waag (Weigh House) on the Kaasmarkt where a market is held on Wednesday mornings in July and August. The fifteenth century Grote Kerk, or Nicholaaskerk, is famous for its stained glass. Although cheese is no longer made in Edam, check with the VVV for cheese factories in the area.

Edam also makes a great base for a side trip to Broek in Waterland and Monnickendam, or follow the coast farther to Hoorn and Enkhuizen.

Tourist Information
VVV Edam, Stadhuis, Damplein 1. Phone 0299 37 17 27.

Accommodations
There are a few hotels, and there is a list of approximately a dozen bed and breakfasts available from the VVV.
Pension de Harmonie, Voorhaven 92. Phone 0299 37 16 64. Dfl 80 Dbl. Small hotel.
Hotel Fortuna, Spuistraat 3. Phone 0299 37 16 71. Dfl 130 Dbl. On a pretty canal. A collection of five renovated seventeenth-century houses.
Camping Strandbad, Zeevangszeedijk 7A. Phone 0299 37 19 94.

Where to Eat
There are several restaurants and cafés in Edam, and Volendam, just 3 kilometers away, has many restaurants, especially on the harbor.

Bicycle Shops/Rentals
Ronald Schot, Kleine Kerkstraat 9-11. Phone 0299 37 15 33.
Ton Tweewielers, Schepmackersdijk 6. Phone 0299 37 19 22.

Side Trip: Monnickendam and Broek in Waterland
Round Trip: 18 Kilometers
An easy ride on the fietspad along the N247 will take you to these two picturesque towns. Monnickendam's VVV is located in the fifteenth-century Grote Kerk. On the main square of the town is De Waag, the colorful old Weigh House that was built around 1600 and is now a restaurant. The sixteenth-century Speeltoren, the gracious bell tower in the center, still chimes on the quarter hour. Visit the small harbor and cycle through the narrow streets viewing houses with their attractive facades.

Head south, continuing on the N247 to Broek in Waterland. It is a real surprise to find such a quaint village so close to Amsterdam. Turn right into the center. As the road veers to the left, you find yourself at the pride of Broek in Waterland, the Dutch Reformed Church. Originally built in 1573 but burned by the Spanish, it was rebuilt in 1628 with later additions and renovations. Inside, the ceiling has been restored to the original (six coats of paint were removed to do this). The chandeliers are from 1650. What looks like marble at the front, and above the windows, is actually painted wood. The artist cleverly painted his own face into the grain of the faux marble. See if you can spot it near the farthest forward window on the right side. (There should be a docent to help you find it.) There are carved wooden lions on each pew. This is an extremely interesting church. Do take the time to visit if it is open (daily May–September, except Sunday).

Continue by riding along the canals and tiny streets beyond the church, noticing the wooden houses, some from the seventeenth century. The canals of Broek in Waterland were the setting for the 1865 story, *Hans Brinker* or *The Silver Skates*. Return to Edam via N247.

Optional Route: Edam to Enkhuizen via Hoorn
One Way: 43 Kilometers

Leave Edam following the green bicycle signs (to Hoorn), which indicate the scenic route along the dike. The dike will be on your right, obscuring your view of the water, but you'll have lovely rural landscape to your left. Just as you reach the tiny town of Warder, you will notice some stairs climbing the dike. Stop here, go through the gate, and climb to the top of the dike. In addition to the view over the Markermeer, you'll get a good look at how the water level of the Markermeer is higher than that of surrounding countryside, including the road you are riding on. Approximately 10 kilometers from Edam you will come to the tiny town of Schardam where there is a campground on the shore of the Markermeer. Continue on into Hoorn.

Hoorn was once a prosperous harbor on the Zuiderzee, but that all changed with the building of the Afsluitdijk in 1932. Now a port on the freshwater Markermeer, the picturesque harbor area is still maintained mainly for pleasure boats. The many old buildings and mansions reflect the rich life of merchants and traders of bygone days. The Rode Steen, a picturesque square, is surrounded by restaurants and shops. Set in amongst these are the 1609 Waag, now a restaurant, and the West Fries Museum, located in a magnificent old building. In the center is the statue of Jan Pieterszoon Coen, founder of the Dutch East India Company. Other sights in town include the Stadhuis and the Hoofdtoren, originally a watchtower for the harbor.

The Hoorn VVV is on Veemarkt 4, phone 06 340 310 55 and can provide information on hotels (priced at Dfl 100 plus Dbl). There is a youth hostel in town. Two campgrounds are south of town in a poor location near a freeway. Cycling to these you see that Hoorn is a sizable town, and the suburban sprawl detracts a little from its pleasant center. The bicycle shop and rental is at Hoorn Railway Station, Ruiter Rijwielshop, phone 0229 21 70 96

Hoorn makes an interesting stop, but for an overnight stop you will be rewarded if you ride on to Enkhuizen.

There are two ways to go to Enkhuizen. The most direct, but not the most scenic, is to head straight up the N506. There is a fietspad along the road for most of the 17 kilometers. If time allows, the coastal route is worth the extra few kilometers. For the coastal route leave from Rode Steen, follow Grote Oost (street), which begins directly across from the West Fries Museum. The street turns into Kleine Oost and then Willemsweg. A fietspad starts at Willemsweg. About 50 meters after joining the fietspad, you will veer off to the right onto Schellinkhouterdijk. There are ANWB route signs pointing you this way for both the Zuiderzee and Koggen routes. They are easy to miss though. Both route signs are on your left.

This takes you up onto the dike, with the water on your right. After approximately 4 kilometers you will come to the thatched Schellinkhout windmill on your left. Approximately 1 kilometer later, at the town of Schellinkhout, is a nice waterfront park, ideal for picnics. About 4 kilometers farther on is a campground on the beach at Wijdenes. Continue until the dike road ends, and you will veer right joining the main road into Enkhuizen.

Enkhuizen is the gem of the former Zuiderzee. This quaint port town oozes charm and ambiance. It is about one-third the size of Hoorn and makes a wonderful stopping point. The cobblestone streets lined with rows and rows of restored gabled houses, many with gorgeous facades, make you feel like you are walking through a storybook town. Add to this a pretty harbor and some interesting sights, such as the Dromedarius Tower with its carillon and view from the top, the Stadhuis, the old Gevangenis (jail), and the main attraction of the town, the Zuiderzee Museum.

The Zuiderzee Museum is actually two museums, the Buiten (outdoor) and the Binnen (indoor). Although some may be skeptical of these re-created outdoor museums, this one is so well done that it dispels all fears of kitsch. It preserves the history of the Zuiderzee with actual houses, shops, workshops, and various other buildings transported and reconstructed from the villages in the vicinity of the Zuiderzee. (The Zuiderzee was the sea that was contained by a masterful Dutch engineering feat in 1932, the Afsluitdijk, a 30-kilometer dike across the northern entrance creating the freshwater IJsselmeer. For more information, see Den Oever to Workum stage.) The indoor museum across the road has interesting maritime exhibits, period rooms, intricate models of boats, and memorabilia from the Dutch East India Trading Company all housed in the 300-year-old warehouse used by the Dutch East India Company. The Buitenmuseum is open daily from April through October, and the Binnenmuseum is open daily, all year round.

Tourist Information
VVV Enkhuizen, Tussen 2, Havens 1. Phone 0228 31 31 64. Across the road from the railway station.

Accommodations
For a small town, Enkhuizen is well-endowed with lodgings. There are six hotels and several bed and breakfasts. These are conveniently listed on the VVV door for after-hours.
Hotel 't Centrum, Westerstraat 153. Phone 0228 31 89 86. Dfl 100 Dbl. In center.
Het Wapen van Enkhuizen, Breedstraat 59. Phone 0228 31 34 34. Dfl 85–110 Dbl. Near Zuiderzee Museums.
Camping Enkhuizer Zand, Kooizandweg 4. Phone 0228 31 72 89. North of town.
Camping de Vest, Noorderweg 31. Phone 0228 32 12 21. North of town.

Where to Eat
There are several restaurants of all price ranges in town, several with a lovely setting on the harbor. Fish is a specialty.

Bicycle Shops/Rentals

Dekker Tweewielers, Nieuwstraat 2-6. Phone 0228 31 29 61. Or Westerstraat 222. Phone 0228 31 24 90.

Route Options from Enkhuizen

From Enkhuizen there are several alternatives. You can retrace the route back to Edam and continue on to Alkmaar or head due west directly to Alkmaar. If you are heading to Friesland, you can either take the ferry that leaves three times daily to Stavoren and join the route there or head north to Den Oever and then cross the Afsluitdijk.

Edam to Alkmaar: 39 Kilometers

Continue out of Edam in the direction of Alkmaar. The fietspad will follow a dike directly east. When you come to the town of Kwadijk, do not follow the Alkmaar sign and cross the bridge over the dike. Continue straight for another couple of kilometers. You'll then take a right and very shortly another left in the direction of Middenbeemster.

You will enter the town of Middenbeemster along a lovely tree-lined road. The route will take you straight on through town, but at the main intersection (the only one with a traffic light), you might want to turn right and ride a couple hundred meters to see the lovely homes along the canal, then return to the route. Stop in at the bakery a few doors from the intersection and turn the clock back a century or so. The shop is called Bakker Bakker, showing that the family Bakker has been in the bakery (*bakker*) business for some time. The route continues straight on through town.

Just over 4 kilometers farther you will climb up onto a dike. Turn left, then almost immediately turn right across a small bridge to enter the town of De Rijp. Notice the great old houses on both sides of the narrow road. Continue into the center of town, which will be very obvious as you come to the VVV located in the Stadhuis built in 1630. The ground floor, which once housed the Waag, is now the VVV. Turn left over the bridge and visit the Gothic church, noted for its seventeenth-century stained glass windows. Visit the Museum In 't Houten Huis (Museum in the Wooden House) for a history of the town and area (open weekends only, except July and August). As you head back to the Stadhuis and the main road, turn right next to the church and ride along the canal to view the backs of the houses that you saw as you rode into town. Head back to the Stadhuis and continue east. The present town, which was once two separate villages, Graft and De Rijp, merged in 1970 to become one long, narrow town that stretches for 2 kilometers. As you reach the end of town, you turn right, following the sign toward Schermerhorn. Just after you turn, notice the beautiful house on your right, formerly the city hall of the separate village of Graft.

Heading north, you will pass through the village of Noordeinde after just a kilometer. Turn right, continuing to Grootschermer 2 kilometers farther. Turn left there and head straight north 4 kilometers until you reach the intersection at the N243, easily identified by the group of three windmills on your left. One of these windmills houses the Museummolen Schermerhorn (Schermerhorn Windmill Museum). This is well worth a visit to learn the function of windmills in Holland and how they work. This is one of the 11 remaining working windmills of the 50 original working mills of the Schermer area (open daily, April through October).

From Schermerhorn, continue north to Ursem, approximately 3 kilometers, then Rustenburg, another 2 kilometers. Leave town in the direction of Oterleek, 3 kilometers farther. There are about 7 windmills along this stretch, not counting the 3 in Schermerhorn. Although few are still operational as windmills, most still serve as homes. As you ride this part of the route, note how the water level in the canals is higher than the surrounding farmland. The water of the *polder* (reclaimed land) has been pumped up to canal level and flows out to the sea. In earlier days, this was the job of the windmills. Today, modern pumping stations do the work.

Pass through the tiny town of Oterleek. Notice the statue of otters just outside the shop on the corner. A fietspad starts here and continues the 8 kilometers into Alkmaar. Follow the signs to Alkmaar Centrum.

The town of Alkmaar is best known for its traditional cheese market held Friday mornings through the summer. Held in the square next to the ornate fourteenth-century Waag, the spectacle showcases the cheese-carriers who transport brightly colored sleds piled with cheeses from the auction ring to the Waag. Today the market is kept alive in Alkmaar for tourists, who arrive on market day by the busload from Amsterdam. Almost every guidebook on the Netherlands mentions the cheese market, but most virtually ignore the town itself, which is a pity. It is an attractive and historic town in its own right. The old center is surrounded by moats and canals, and the streets are filled with stunning houses dating from as far back as the fourteenth century.

Among the highlights are the Waag and the Kaasmuseum (Cheese Museum) located inside (open April through October, closed Sunday); the sixteenth-century Vismarkt (Fish Market); the Grote Kerk and Stadhuis, both built in the fifteenth and sixteenth centuries; and an eighteenth-century windmill, the Molen van Piet, which is still in use as a flour mill and is open for visits. Other museums in town include the Stedelijk Museum, the National Beer Museum, and the Hans Brinker Museum, dedicated to the famous story of the silver skates.

Tourist Information

VVV Alkmaar, Waagplein 2. Phone 072 511 42 84. In the Waag.
ANWB Office, Kennemerstraatweg 12. Phone 072 511 90 41.

Accommodations

Hotel De Nachtegaal, Langestraat 100. Phone 072 511 28 94. Dfl 110 Dbl. Opposite the Stadhuis.
There are several bed and breakfasts, and the VVV will book them for a fee.
Bed and Breakfast Netty and Jacques Dekker, Noodervaart 97, Stompeltoren. Phone 072 503 93 68. Dfl 90 Dbl. Excellent lodging, friendly hosts, 5 kilometers out of Alkmaar.
Camping Alkmaar, Bergerweg 201. Phone 072 511 69 24. West of Alkmaar on road to Bergen.
Camping Molengroet, Molengroet 1, Noord Scharwoude. Phone 022 69 34 44. Six kilometers north of Alkmaar.

Where to Eat

There are many restaurants in town with plenty of local and ethnic variety. You will find a few on the Waagplein and canals and streets leading away from it. For wonderful Dutch pancakes try the Pancake Bakery at Hof van Sonoy, an old almshouse on Nieuwesloot.

Bicycle Shops/Rentals
Alkmaar Railway Station. Phone 072 511 79 07.

Alkmaar to Den Helder: 46 Kilometers

From Alkmaar, follow the signs to Bergen 4 kilometers away. Bergen is a lively resort town with several galleries stemming from the Bergen School of Art and is still home to many artists. In Bergen and beach towns in the vicinity, there is an abundance of hotels and restaurants plus plenty of camping. In Bergen, a bicycle shop, Busker, is at Kerkstraat 1, phone 072 589 51 96. There is also a youth hostel in Egmond.

VVV Bergen is not as cooperative as most because they are used to dealing with hoards of tourists in the summer months. They charge for everything, including a map of the town and have a higher than normal booking fee. VVV Bergen is located in the center of town at Plein 1, phone 072 581 31 00. You can also find a VVV in Bergen aan Zee and Egmond aan Zee.

Here you are on the edge of the Noordhollands Duinreservaat (North Holland Sand Dune Reserve). You will ride through some of this on the continuation of the route, but if you want to see more and the small seaside towns around, you can make a short side trip out of Bergen. There are several bicycle paths through the Dune Area.

Optional Side Trip to the Coast
Round Trip: 23 Kilometers

Go south to Egmond a/d Hof. Follow the signs to Egmond. You will begin by riding through the residential area of Bergen, which has lovely houses. About 2 kilometers from the VVV you will start on a fietspad through a gorgeous forest. This continues until Egmond a/d Hof. Turn right here, following signs to Egmond aan Zee, a typical small seaside tourist resort. There are a couple of museums, and you can follow some of the routes through the dunes if you wish.

Return to Egmond a/d Hof and head back toward Bergen. Approximately 2.6 kilometers from the information sign, a fietspad through the dunes veers off to the left. It is directly across from the guesthouse Gasterij 't Woud. There is an automated ticket machine where you must stop to buy a daycard to enter the Dune Reserve. Proceed along the path, and 4.3 kilometers later you will arrive in Bergen aan Zee, another heavily touristed seaside resort. From there it is 5 kilometers back to Bergen. (Note: If you are doing the Texel side trip later, you will see similar dunes there.)

To continue to Den Helder from Bergen, follow the signs north to Schoorl. This is a pleasant road with a fietspad, taking you through a forest area on the edge of the dunes. You will reach Schoorl in approximately 4.5 kilometers. Turn left just past the VVV onto the main street and continue along the fietspad which will enter the Dune Reserve. Follow signs toward Camperduin, clearly marked on several ANWB mushroom signs. Continue north along the fietspad. You will be on the edge of the dunes the whole way to Den Helder. There will be a lot of gentle ups and downs, as opposed to the usual flat in Holland. The dunes will be on your left, and on your right will be farmland, much of it used for tulip and daffodil bulbs. If you are here in the spring, you will see lots of color. You will pass through several small towns, such as Petten and Callantsoog. There are plenty of campgrounds along the way. Much of the route runs along the road with signs for Den Helder. Another good indication is the LF1b fietspad signs.

About 5 kilometers before Den Helder, you'll see ANWB mushroom signs for Den Helder pointing in a different direction to signs for the Texel ferry. Following the fietspad route directly to the ferry will take you along the coast where you will continue through the dunes, a more pleasant ride than through the city streets. About 1.5 kilometers before the ferry you will see a sign on the right to Centrum (of Den Helder). It is just a couple hundred meters to the shopping area. It has a VVV (Bernhardplein 18, phone 0223 62 55 44) and ANWB office (Bernhardplein 75, phone 0223 61 48 02), as well as shops and restaurants, but it is not an exceptional city to stop in. It is a naval base, and there is a Marine Museum detailing the history of the Dutch navy.

To take the ferry to Texel, continue straight to the ferry terminal. Follow the bicycle signs, and enter the terminal through the door on the left marked *Tweewieler*. Purchase your ticket there. The cost will be about Dfl 16 round trip for an adult with a bicycle. The ferry crossing is approximately 20 minutes, and ferries leave every hour until about 9 P.M.

The Island of Texel
Suggested Circle Route: 46 Kilometers

After you leave the ferry, head to the main town of Den Burg about 7 kilometers away. It is an easy ride along the fietspad and well marked. As you follow the signs off the main road into Den Burg, the VVV will be on your left. The staff is extremely helpful, and they have a lot of information on Texel, including an excellent bicycle route map/information card (in English) with four tours of the island. It is well worth the Dfl 3.50.

Texel is the largest of the Wadden Islands. The island is mainly rural. Pastures of contented cows and sheep, along with fields of brightly colored flowers, dot the island. There is an impressive group of dunes on the west side, many of these leading to lovely white sand beaches.

Don't miss the western route from Monnikenweg north to De Slufter. Begin just north of Den Burg along Pontweg. After approximately 1 kilometer you will turn left toward the coast. You will cycle along Monnikenweg through a cool forest. Shortly after the dunes begin you'll see the signs for EcoMare, a sanctuary for birds and seals as well as a natural history museum. This entire area along the dunes is a series of nature reserves and home to over 300 species of birds. Thus, this area provides great bird watching.

Proceed north to De Koog. The dunes continue beyond the heavily touristed town of De Koog to De Slufter. In July and August, notice the gorgeous purple wildflower known as Sea Lavender covering the dunes. If you are interested in birds or natural areas, stop at De Muy, a nature area in the dunes.

Crossing over to the eastern side of the island, you will go through the Eierland Polder, reclaimed land that was not naturally part of the island. Ride along Oorsprongweg, and when you reach the east side of the island, ride south along the dike from Stuilweg. The dike was built as a barrier against the sea. The area is a breeding ground for waterfowl, birds, and Brent geese. You will pass a very scenic windmill, Het Norden, used to keep the polder drained. Just past the windmill, turn to the right and into the tiny old village of Oost. Continue on to Oosterend, a somewhat larger village that still retains the old Dutch charm of yesteryear. Note the traditional Texel architecture in the town, the houses with dark green aprons and white trim, and the lovely old restored church, the oldest church on the island.

Continue on to De Waal. Ride through the village, which has not changed much in the last century, and then on to Den Burg. You can explore the island in another direction or head back to the ferry. To return by ferry to Den Helder, you just ride on. There is no fare collected in this direction.

Tourist Information
VVV Den Burg, Emmalaan 66. Phone 0222 31 28 47.

Accommodations
There are plenty of accommodations on the island, especially in Den Burg, the largest town and island center, and De Koog (west), plus some of the other villages. It is most crowded in July and August and on weekends.

Hotel de Merel, Warmoestraat 22, Den Burg. Phone 0222 31 31 32. Dfl 120 Dbl. In town center.

Hotel 't Koogerend, Kogerstraat 94, Den Burg. Phone 0222 31 33 01. Dfl 120 Dbl. In town center.

Youth Hostel Panorama, Schansweg 7, Den Burg. Phone 0222 31 54 41.

Youth Hostel De Eyercoogh, Pontweg 106, Den Burg. Phone 0222 31 54 41.

Camping: There are 14 regular campgrounds, plus 9 *camping bij de boer* (camping on a farm). Most of the campgrounds are located between Den Burg and De Koog on the west side of the island. The VVV has a list.

Camping De Koorn-aar, Grensweg 388. Phone 0222 31 29 31. En route from Den Burg to west side.

Camping bij de boer, Fam. Snoey-Bakker, Waalderweg 120. Phone 0222 31 24 68. Camping on farm. Halfway between Den Burg and De Waal.

Bicycle Shops/Rentals
F. Zegel, Parkstraat 14, Den Burg. Phone 0222 31 21 50.
There are also bicycle shops in De Koog.

Den Helder to Den Oever: 27 Kilometers

Less than 1 kilometer from the ferry terminal, you'll see signs for Centrum and also for Alkmaar/Leeuwarden. If you don't wish to go into town for any reason, take the latter to skirt the city along the waterfront. The center of town is only 1 kilometer farther.

Leaving Den Helder, take the fietspad in the direction of Leeuwarden, which follows the N250. Follow this for approximately 6 kilometers. As you reach the Bethlehem service station, take note of the directional signs. You will turn right here and take the overpass to join the N99. Make sure you do not continue straight past the service station, which puts you on the N9. Follow the N99 with the Balgzand Kanaal on your left and flower fields on your right (depending on season either tulips or lilies). Notice some of the newer houses with the traditional thatched roofs. After another 6 kilometers, you will reach an intersection.

Continue in the direction of Den Oever, crossing the canal, staying along the N99. On the right you will see the Amstelmeer, a large lake, popular with windsurfers when weather permits. Continue for 7 kilometers to the town of Hippolytushoef. At the Bistro Café Brammetje, turn right and take the underpass which takes you into the town. Proceed to the main square. It's a small town, so just head for the church steeple. Follow the signs out of town toward Den Oever, which is approximately 7 kilometers east. Do not go back to the main road but take the more scenic route, which passes through the charming towns of Stroe and Oosterland and along some pretty tree-lined, shady lanes. This is part of the LF10, so you will have ANWB route signs to follow. Stroe is 4 kilometers from Hippolytushoef. Oosterland is another 1 kilometer, and Den Oever 2 kilometers more. As you leave Oosterland, notice the field filled with modern art sculptures.

Den Oever is a tiny town. The VVV is located in a café on the harbor. There is an excellent campground in town, a hotel, a youth hostel, a few restaurants, a supermarket, and several shops.

Accommodations

Hotel Zomerdijk. Zwinstraat 5. Phone 0227 51 12 06. Dfl 100 Dbl. Pleasant hotel in center of town.

Den Oever Youth Hostel, Gemeenelandsweg 116. Phone 0227 51 12 72.

Camping de Gest, Gesterweg 17-19. Phone 0227 51 12 83.

Camping 't Wiringherlant, Noord Stroeerweg 5. Phone 0227 51 14 23. En route in Stroe/Hippolytushoef.

Den Oever to Workum: 53 Kilometers

Leave Den Oever in the direction of Leeuwarden. This will take you immediately to the start of the Afsluitdijk. This 30-kilometer dike was built in 1932 to close off the IJsselmeer from the sea. At the beginning of the dike is a statue in honor of Lely, the engineer. 6 kilometers from Den Oever you reach a stopping point. There is a monument commemorating the completion of the dike, as the last stone was laid here, along with an explanation of

this amazing feat of engineering. The tower, which affords a panorama over the IJsselmeer and Waddenzee, has the inscription, "A living nation builds for its future." There is another point halfway across where you can stop for drinks or snacks. Then it is straight on to the other side.

When you leave Den Oever, be prepared to do the full 30 kilometers. Take the weather into consideration. With the wind at your back, it's an easy ride. When facing a stiff wind, it can be a long trip.

Crossing the Afsluitdijk you will enter the province of Friesland with its verdant green pasturelands dotted with characteristic black and white Friesian cows. The Friesians are extremely proud of their province and have their own language. You will notice town and road signs in two languages, Dutch and Friesian. The first town on the Friesland side is the tiny town of Zurich. If you can't make it any farther after the ride over the Afsluitdijk, it does have a hotel and some bed and breakfasts, but there is not much else to the town.

Follow the bicycle sign to Bolsward, which will take you south from Zurich and along the A7 motorway. Signs will point the direction to Makkum. Follow these 9 kilometers to Makkum. This is a neat little town with a busy working harbor. The town is famous for ceramics, which rival Delftware. The Fries Aardwerkmuseum (Ceramics Museum) is open daily and is located in the Waag, the lower floor of which also houses the VVV. You can also see the Makkumware in several shops in town such as Tichelaar on the Markt. The town has a couple of hotels and bed and breakfasts, and several eateries.

Leave town to the south in the direction of Piaam, Gaast, and Workum. It is 5 kilometers to Gaast. (You will pass the tiny village of Piaam en route.) Workum is 6 kilometers past Gaast. For most of the way the coastal dike will be on your right side with gentle rural landscape on your left.

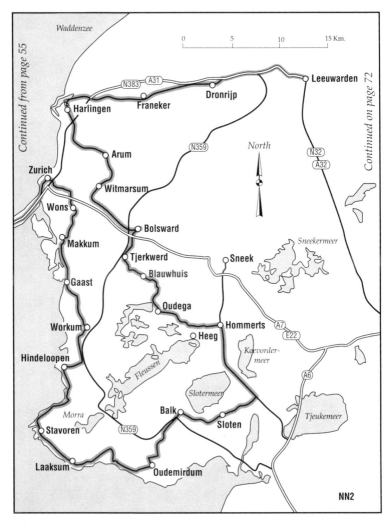

When you arrive in Workum, turn left after the bridge. The town, which stretches for 2 kilometers along the main street, lies before you. The hub of the town is the Merk (Main Square) where you find the fifteenth-century Stadhuis, the huge sixteenth-century Gothic St. Gertrudiskerk, and many other houses of architectural interest. Across the Merk, the VVV is in the seventeenth-century Waag. The town is the home of the artist Jopie Huisman, and a few doors down from the Merk is the museum of the same name. The entire museum is devoted to the remarkable art of this man who was a junk man and with no formal training began painting his wares. Some of his most famous and brilliant works are of old shoes, rags, worn clothing, and the like (open daily).

Tourist Information
VVV Workum, Waag, Noard 5. Phone 0515 54 13 00.

Accommodations
Hotel De Gulden Leeuw, Merk 2. Phone 0515 54 23 41. Dfl 92.50 Dbl. Center of town.
Bed and Breakfast Op de Hoek Van de Stal, Sud 154. Phone 0515 54 29 62. Dfl 70 Dbl. Working farm 2-minute ride from Merk.

Bicycle Shops/Rentals
Jan Visser, Merk 27. Phone 0515 54 13 58.

For overnight lodgings Hindeloopen, 5 kilometers farther, is an alternative to Workum. Hindeloopen has two hotels and six bed and breakfasts at approximately Dfl 70 Dbl (list available from the VVV) as well as two campgrounds.
Camping Hindeloopen, Westerdijk 9. Phone 0514 52 14 52.
Camping Schuilenburg, Schuilenburg 2. Phone 0514 52 12 60.

Workum to Stavoren: 13 Kilometers

Return to the south end of Workum where you originally entered town. Take the road in the direction of Hindeloopen. In 2 kilometers join the fietspad, turning right; continue another 3 kilometers into Hindeloopen. This charming little town on the banks of the IJsselmeer is riddled with canals and wooden footbridges. It is a picturesque town and deserves time just to wander around the narrow streets and harbor and admire the quaint houses and the impressive church steeple. The VVV is at Nieuwstad 26, phone 0514 52 25 50. In days gone by, Hindeloopen was famous for its wooden painted furniture, examples of which can be seen in the Hidde Nijland Stichting Museum on Dijkweg 1 (open daily, March through October). Hindeloopen is home to the Schaats Museum (Skating Museum), a converted shop that has memorabilia from the Elfstedentocht.

Hindeloopen is one of the towns of the Elfstedentocht (Eleven Towns Race). This skating marathon, on frozen canals, is a tradition that began in 1909 and can only be held in years when the weather conditions are perfect. The 200-kilometer skating race connects 11 historic towns in Friesland and begins well before the sun comes up. The decision to run the race can only be made at the last minute when it has been determined that the ice is at least 15 centimeters (6 inches) thick for the entire route. The whole country is glued to the event, either watching it on television or actually being at the race. Often there is a break of several years between races. The last race was January 1997 with 16,000 participants. The winner's time was an unbelievable 6 hours, 49 minutes. The previous race was 11 years earlier in 1986.

The Elfstedentocht is now more than a skating race. In the spring there is an 11-cities bicycle race that attracts over 15,000 participants and is slightly longer at 230 kilometers. The 11 towns are Leeuwarden, Bolsward, Sneek, IJlst, Sloten, Stavoren, Hindeloopen, Workum, Harlingen, Franeker, and Dokkum. An ANWB Elfsteden cycling Route Map is available.

Leave Hindeloopen and follow the dike road south in the direction of Stavoren. Approximately 4.5 kilometers out of Hindeloopen, the road turns left. Do not veer left with the road. Continue straight ahead through a gate. There is a large blue fietspad sign to assure you this is indeed the correct way. You will go through a series of three gates on this path, as you are sharing the area with grazing animals. Approximately 3.5 kilometers farther, you will enter Stavoren, a little port town.

Stavoren has a small, but quaint, harbor. The ferry to Enkhuizen (Dfl 10.50/adult, Dfl 5.75/bicycle one way), leaves three times daily in summer, approximately every four hours. The crossing duration is approximately 90 minutes. There is only one hotel in town, De Drouwe van Stavoren, located on the harbor at Havenweg 1 (phone 0514 68 12 02, Dfl 90 Dbl), and a campground, Camping Sudemer, on the way out of town on the left. The VVV is at the ferry terminal (phone 0514 68 16 16), and there is a bicycle shop with rentals, P. Bakker at Smidstraat 14 (phone 0514 68 12 88).

Stavoren to Balk: 24 Kilometers

From the ferry terminal, head across the bridge into the main part of town and follow the canal. Cross another bridge across the Johan Friso-kanaal, past the marina, hugging the coast. Do not take the left turn to Warns. About 2.5 kilometers out of town there is a memorial, a large rock, Rode Klif. The view is great, and it makes a lovely picnic spot. Approximately 1.5 kilometers farther is the tiny village of Laaksum. Just past the town the road follows along the top of the dike for a while, giving you sweeping views of the IJsselmeer.

After another 2.5 kilometers you will reach an intersection outside the tiny village of Mirns. This village is not on all maps. Go straight, up a hill 1.1 kilometers farther to an intersection with a sign to Camping Witte Burch pointing left, and a picnic bench located near the sign. Somewhat hidden, a fietspad off to the right starts here. ANWB mushroom #20944 indicates the direction along the fietspad to Mirns and Rijsterbos. You will ride almost 2 kilometers on a dream fietspad. The path, which is slightly downhill much of the way, takes you through a forest with a fern-covered floor. It is somewhat like going through a long, cool, shady tunnel. You will come out into an open pasture area next to a farm. Shortly after, you will come to a road. Turn left. You will see an information map for Het Rijsterbos (Forest of the Rijs Area). Continue on this road, again following the coast with the IJsselmeer on your right.

A rather unique memorial is on your right about 3.5 kilometers from the information map. It is a large empty frame with a small sign saying "Friesian Farm." As you stand in front of it, you realize it is framing an actual farm in the background. There is a poem on separate signs, on the left in Dutch and on the right in Friesian. It is a clever idea and a good photo opportunity.

A couple hundred meters farther on you enter the very small town of Oudemirdum. The center is comprised of a couple hotels, a few shops, and several restaurants. If you wish to stop here, there are at least five camping areas within a kilometer of town. It is a pleasant area with a nearby sandy beach and forests.

Your next landmark is one of the camping areas, Camping de Waps. Signs from the center of town direct you to all of the different campgrounds. Follow the sign to Camping de Waps, 0.5 kilometer out of town. The fietspad to Balk starts right at the entrance to the campground. It is 6.4 kilometers from this point to Balk. It starts on a pleasant trail through the forest. After 1.7 kilometers, you take a right turn over a bridge, cross a road, turn left, and join a fietspad again. It is marked, but this is an easy turn to miss. Continue into Balk following the signs.

Balk is a small, ordinary town, except that it does have a really beautiful Stadhuis and some nice old building facades from the eighteenth century along the canal. The VVV is in the Stadhuis. The area is known for water sports on the many lakes and for hiking in the forest areas. Just 1 kilometer northeast of Balk is the lake, Slotermeer.

Accommodations
Hotel Teernstra, Van Swinderenstraat 69. Phone 0514 60 20 20. Dfl 90 Dbl.
Bed and Breakfast, H. Wagenaar, Wijckeldijk 12. Phone 0514 60 25 39. Dfl 65 Dbl.
Camping Marswal, Tsjamkedykje 6. Phone 0514 60 38 00. One kilometer
    northeast on Slotermeer, on the opposite side of the canal from the yacht
    harbor. Leave town staying on the left side of the canal.

Bicycle Shops/Rentals
Rijwiel Gaasterland, Van Swinderenstraat 45. Phone 0514 60 22 84.

Balk to Bolsward: 38 Kilometers

From the Stadhuis leave town in the direction of Wijckel and Sloten. Just 3 kilometers along is Wijckel, a village on the edge of a nature reserve. It has a nice campground located in the reserve, Camping 't Hop. This is on the west end of town, about 300 meters down a lane, well signposted. There is not much in the village itself, so if you are not using it as a camping stop, continue by turning left just past the church in the direction of Sloten. A fietspad starts about 100 meters from this intersection, following the road. The sign in Wijckel says 1 kilometer to Sloten, but it is actually about 2 kilometers to the center of town.

As you reach Sloten, veer right off the main road and take the narrow lane through town for a few hundred meters. You will come to a picturesque tree-lined canal that runs through town. The VVV is on the far end of town opposite a small supermarket. There is no hotel, but there is one pension and a campground and some restaurants and cafés.

Sloten is the smallest of the so-called 11 cities of Friesland, the Elfsteden. It is a pretty, moated town but somewhat touristy, frequented by boaters moored on the nearby lake, Slotermeer, and day-trippers. There is a windmill located by the old water-gate (Lemsterpoort), a small yacht harbor, quaint seventeenth- and eighteenth-century houses, and you can still walk part of the old city wall.

Leave town in the direction of Sneek and Tjerkgaast. In about 2 kilometers you will pass through the tiny farming village of Tjerkgaast. Blink and you'll miss this town, even on a bicycle.

A view of Bolsward from the main square, with its beautiful Stadhuis (town hall) in the background.

Four kilometers out of Sloten is the N354 highway. Turn left (northwest), following the sign to Sneek and Woudsend. You can't miss this intersection as it is dominated by a huge telecommunications tower that you can see all the way from Sloten. Follow this road 9 kilometers to the town of Hommerts.

Turn left as you enter Hommerts but before you reach the center of town. You will be turning left at the intersection with a large Indonesian restaurant called Jelte State. There are bicycle signs pointing to Heeg and Oudega. You will be on a fietspad for the first couple of kilometers until it turns off toward Heeg. Don't turn toward Heeg unless you want to head to the campground or youth hostel on the lake. Continue on a small farm road with little traffic to the town of Oudega, 7.5 kilometers from Hommerts.

Oudega is a lovely, quiet, surprisingly charming town in the middle of nowhere with pretty houses lining its small canal. If you need supplies, there is a small but well-stocked supermarket. If you'd like to stay in this inviting little town, there is a hotel and a campground plus a couple of places to eat.

To leave, continue on the main road through town in the direction of Blauwhuis. Again you will be on a small farm road for the 4.5 kilometers to the town of Blauwhuis. As you enter the town, you will be struck by the magnificent church steeple with its blue, red, and gold clock. This is the Catholic Church of St. Vitus, built in 1868, and it dominates the main street of this otherwise ordinary town. The church is worth a stop before you continue on.

Four kilometers past Blauwhuis, you arrive at Tjerkwerd. Here you will find a fietspad right along the canal into Bolsward, or another option is the service road alongside the N359 highway. Although the fietspad is more scenic, it is a very bumpy ride, and we recommend the less scenic but smoother and more comfortable ride on the service road. Go about 3.5 kilometers to the center of Bolsward, following the signs.

Bolsward is a delightful town with a charming and very lively shopping street with several restaurants lining both sides of the main canal through town. It has one of the most impressive town halls in the Netherlands. This Stadhuis built in 1614 also houses the Oudeheidkamer (Museum of Antiquities), which displays silverware, costumes, and local artifacts. Also of interest is the Martinikerk, a large fifteenth-century Gothic Church. Bolsward, small in size, is a very pleasant and manageable town with lots of atmosphere. We highly recommend it as a stopping point.

Tourist Information
VVV Bolsward, Marktplein 1. Phone 0515 57 27 27.

The VVV is now located at Marktplein 1 in the center of town across from the Hotel de Wijnberg. Some maps and information will have it at its old address of Broereplein 1. Warning: you will pass the VVV just about the time you get your first glimpse of the Stadhuis, which could cause you to miss it.

Accommodations

Hotel de Wijnberg, Marktplein 5. Phone 0515 57 22 20. Dfl 120 Dbl. Classy hotel in center of town.

Hotel de Posthoorn, Marktplein 6. Phone 0515 57 23 64. Dfl 80 Dbl. Right next door to Hotel de Winjnberg. Basic lodgings.

Bed and breakfast. Family Van Wijk, Kleine Dijlakker 45. Phone 0515 57 75 76. Dfl 60 Dbl. Walking distance to center.

Camping: The tiny campground (18 places) is located behind the bus station and is part of the swimming pool complex. It is on Sneekerstraat. Ask at the VVV for directions. It is on the east edge of town.

Bicycle Shops/Rentals

Koopmans Tweewielers, Grote Dijlakker 58. Phone 0515 57 27 17.

Bolsward to Harlingen: 20 Kilometers

Leave Bolsward by heading west, crossing the N359, and following the fietspad alongside the large A7 freeway for the first part, following signs for Den Helder. 5.3 kilometers out of town the fietspad ends briefly, and you will need to join a small farm road in the direction of Witmarsum. Just 1 kilometer farther you will rejoin a fietspad along the main road, turning right. You will reach the town of Witmarsum 8 kilometers from Bolsward. You can either stay on the main road and skirt Witmarsum or veer right where you see the camping sign and go through the town, which has several shops and a restaurant. Going through town does not add much distance, as you loop right back to the main road. There is not much to see, but the town does have a unique church steeple.

Either way, continue on in the direction of Harlingen, passing through the small town of Arum along the way. You will enter the seaport of Harlingen on Kimswerderweg. Follow this road under the N31 freeway until the road ends at Stationsweg. Turn left and follow this road until you see the sign for the VVV. Turn right, and a short block brings you to the Zuiderhaven (South Harbor), one of two harbors in town, the other being Noorderhaven (North Harbor). Following signs to the VVV will take you through streets filled with gabled houses. Down Voorstraat, the main tree-lined shopping street, you will find the elegant eighteenth-century Stadhuis and the Gemeentemuseum het Hannemahuis (Town Museum) with its maritime, whaling, and seafaring exhibits.

Harlingen is also the jumping-off point for the islands of Terschelling and Vlieland with three daily ferries to each island. These are two more of the Wadden Islands. Both islands offer beaches, nature trails, bird watching, and a quiet pace. The islands are popular summer getaways and can be crowded on weekends. Vlieland is the more tranquil of the two, with no cars allowed, except for a few owned by residents. Either island is great for cycling. Both have limited hotels and several campgrounds, and Terschelling has a youth hostel. There is a VVV on each island plus bicycle shops and rentals.

Tourist Information

VVV Harlingen, Voorstraat 34. Phone 0517 41 72 22.

Accommodations

There are four hotels and eight pensions in town. (Check with VVV for updated pension listings.)

Hotel Anna Casparii, Noorderhaven 67-69. Phone 0517 41 20 65. Dfl 125 Dbl. Charming hotel on harbor.

Hotel Het Heerenlogement, Franekereind 23. Phone 0517 41 58 46. Dfl 110
    Dbl. Near Voorstraat.
Pension Arends, Noorderhaven 63. Phone 0517 41 50 88. Dfl 80 Dbl.
Pension Lehman, Zuiderhaven 15. Phone 0517 41 87 10. Dfl 70 Dbl.
Camping De Zeehoeve, Westerzeedijk 45. Phone 0517 41 34 65.

Where to Eat
    Voorstraat and surrounding streets have several restaurants and cafés.
Fish is a specialty, as Harlingen is right on the water. There is a lively market
along Voorstraat on Saturday mornings.

Bicycle Shops/Rentals
Huizer, Lanen 20. Phone 0517 41 22 01.

Harlingen to Leeuwarden: 30 Kilometers
    Follow Voorstraat down to the harbor and leave town past the ferry ter-
minal, following signs toward Midlum. As you reach the town of Midlum just
a couple of kilometers out of town, you will see signs for Franeker. This route
will take you on fietspads all the way, going under the big A31 freeway and
following the smaller road to Franeker via the small town of Herbaijum. You
will reach Franeker in just over 10 kilometers.
    There are only two reasons to stop in Franeker, and they are conveniently
located right across the road from each other. One is the splendid Stadhuis, and
the second is the Planetarium. There is another small museum next door to the
VVV at Voorstraat 51, which you will pass on your way to the other two sights.
    The sixteenth-century Stadhuis on Raadhuisplein is a stately building
with a wonderful exterior. You can visit the council chambers on the main
floor (closed weekends). Across the canal from the Stadhuis is the Planetarium. Now a museum, it is the old home of Eise Eisinga, an eighteenth-century wool-comber and self-educated astronomer. Eisinga spent seven years,
from 1774 to 1781, creating an ingenious and incredibly accurate planetarium
on his living room ceiling. The museum offers a video in English, and you can
also visit the attic to see the actual workings, made of oak and metal, which
are still moving the celestial bodies around Eisinga's living room.
    Leave Franeker to the east in the direction of Leeuwarden. There is a fi-
etspad the entire way. For some reason the distance is not well documented.
Sometimes the signs indicate it is several kilometers farther than the previous
sign, and the first sign from Franeker stating 13 kilometers is overly optimistic.
It is in fact about 18 kilometers from Franeker to the center of Leeuwarden. You
will follow the A31 freeway most of the way. You will notice that Leeuwarden
is a fairly large city as you ride for quite a while through the suburbs before arriving at the town's center.
    Leeuwarden, the capital of Friesland, is a much underrated and under-
visited city. It has a most agreeable center with historic areas, canals, lovely
parks, and lots of quiet, architecturally interesting streets to wander through.
    The two museums that dominate most of the tourist literature on
Leeuwarden are the magnificent Museum Het Princeshof at Grote Kerkstraat
11 (open daily) and the Fries Museum at Turfmarkt 11 (closed Monday). Museum Het Princeshof, located in a seventeenth-century palace, has one of the most
comprehensive collections of ceramics in the world. There are four floors of displays including antique tiles from Turkey, Spain, North Africa, and Holland, ce-

ramics from Asia and Europe and much more. The Fries Museum is devoted to the history of the province of Friesland, containing arts, crafts, costumes, and archaeological finds. The top floor is a Verzetsmuseum (Resistance Museum) outlining the activities of the Friesian resistance during World War II, the role played by Friesland, and the plight of Jews in the area during the Holocaust.

One of Leeuwarden's most famous citizens was Mata Hari, the World War I spy and exotic dancer. Her statue is on Korfmakersstraat where it meets Over de Kelders. Her house is now the Friesian Literary Museum on Grote Kerkstraat 212 (closed weekends), which contains Mata Hari memorabilia and Friesian documents.

At the far end of Grote Kerkstraat is the Grote Kerk or Jacob's Church. Also of interest is the huge, incomplete Gothic tower Oldehove (closed Monday). It is possible to ascend the tower, although not on windy days, as the tower is actually leaning. Near Oldehove in the center of a traffic circle is Us Mem, which translates as "Our Mother," a statue of a cow representing Friesian prosperity.

Tourist Information
Friesland/Leeuwarden VVV, Stationsplein 1. Phone 06 32 02 40 60.
ANWB Office, Zaaliand 112. Phone 058 213 39 55.

Accommodations
There are at least six hotels in town and about the same number of bed and breakfasts, which can be booked at the VVV for approximately Dfl 60–70 Dbl. We were lucky enough to stay with Mrs. de Haan, a wonderful lady whose house on Spanjaardslaan is a 10-minute walk from the center. Check with VVV for availability.

Hotel de Pauw, Stationsweg 10. Phone 058 212 36 51. Dfl 80 Dbl. Across from station.
Hotel 't Anker. Eewal 69-75. Phone 058 212 52 16. Dfl 80 Dbl. Centrally located.
Camping Martena State, Swarte Singel 2, Cornjum. Phone 058 257 25 38. Four
    kilometers north of Leeuwarden.
Camping Lyts Tjaard, Tjaarderdijk 5a, Wirdum. Phone 058 255 26 49. Five
    kilometers south of Leeuwarden.

Where to Eat
There are several restaurants lining Nieuwestad, as well as a variety throughout the city from The Pancake Boat to cozy cafés.

Bicycle Shops/Rentals
Leeuwarden Railway Station.
    Phone 058 213 98 00.
    There are three bicycle shops (no rentals) clustered together on Naauw Kelders, not far from the Mata Hari statue.

Leeuwarden to Heerenveen: 33 Kilometers

From the main railway station, right in front of the VVV, there is a set of bicycle direction signs. Take the fietspad east in the direction of Heerenveen. Go one block

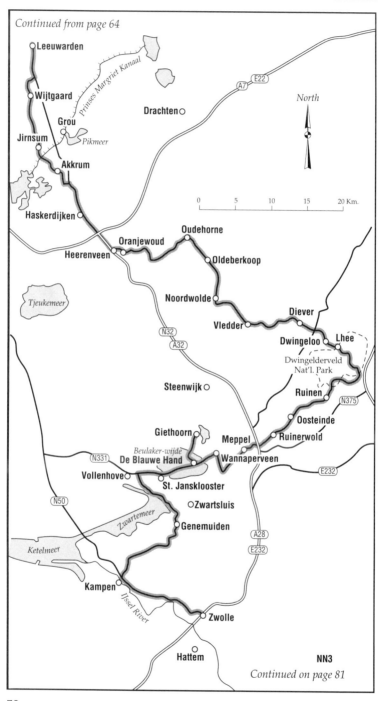

Continued from page 64

Leeuwarden

Wijtgaard

Grou

Jirnsum

Prinses Margriet Kanaal

Drachten

Pikmeer

Akkrum

North

Haskerdijken

0   5   10   15   20 Km.

Oudehorne

Oranjewoud

Heerenveen

Oldeberkoop

Tjeukemeer

Noordwolde

Diever

Vledder

Dwingeloo

Lhee

N32

A32

Dwingelderveld Nat'l. Park

Steenwijk

Ruinen

N375

Giethoorn

Oosteinde

Meppel

Ruinerwold

Beulaker-wijde

N331

De Blauwe Hand

Wannaperveen

Vollenhove

E232

St. Jansklooster

N50

Zwartsluis

Zwartemeer

Genemuiden

A28

Ketelmeer

E232

Kampen

IJssel River

Zwolle

NN3

Hattem

Continued on page 81

then follow signs to the right over the railway tracks. Continue south for 7.5 kilometers through the small town of Wytgaard. Continue south another 7.5 kilometers through Jirnsum.

Just south of Jirnsum you cross the very large Princess Margriet Kanaal. You can stop at the restaurant on the south shore and watch the parade of boats. Go across the bridge and take the first left to reach the restaurant on the canal. Otherwise continue straight on to Akkrum, approximately 4.5 kilometers farther on.

As you enter Akkrum, notice Coopersburg on the left, a grand series of attached buildings dating back to 1900. These were originally built as residences for the impoverished and unwell. They were donated by a local, wealthy citizen, F. H. Kuipers, returning to Akkrum after making his fortune in the United States. Just beyond Coopersburg approximately 300 meters is the VVV.

Akkrum is a small town with a pleasant ambiance. There are hotels, bed and breakfasts, camping facilities, and restaurants. It makes a more pleasant overnight point than Heerenveen, if you need to stop in this area.

To reach Heerenveen, continue south approximately 12 kilometers on the fietspad, which follows the N32. Pass through the two tiny adjoining villages of Haskerdijken and Nieuwebrug. Shortly thereafter you will start seeing the suburbs of Heerenveen. Notice the houseboats in the canal to your right. The fietspad takes you under the A7 motorway and follows the canal to the center of Heerenveen. Follow the signs to the VVV. The VVV and ANWB share the same office, which is located just before you reach the center of town. Heerenveen is quite an ordinary town with several traditional old houses alongside a lot of newer buildings.

Akkrum Information
Tourist Information
The tiny Akkrum VVV is located on Ljouwerterdijk a few hundred meters beyond Coopersburg on the same side of the road.

Accommodations
There are a couple of hotels and three bed and breakfasts (approximately Dfl 60 Dbl), some of which are posted on the VVV door.

Hotel De Oude Schouw, Oudeschouw 6, Akkrum. Phone 0566 65 21 25. Dfl 140 Dbl.
Hotel Goerres, Kanadeeskestraat 45, Akkrum. Phone 0566 65 13 12. Dfl 80 Dbl.
Camping Tusken de Marren, U. Twijnstrawei 33. Phone 0566 65 18 40.

Heerenveen Information
Tourist Information
VVV/ANWB Heerenveen, Van Kleffenslaan 6, Phone 0513 62 55 55.

It is possible to stay in Heerenveen where there are hotels and restaurants, but for a more congenial Dutch town, we suggest Akkrum, located 12 kilometers north of Heerenveen.

Bicycle Shops/Rentals
Heerenveen Railway Station. Phone 0513 62 40 10.

Heerenveen to Dwingeloo: 37 Kilometers
From the VVV head north approximately 100 meters and turn east at the traffic lights in the direction of De Knipe. Just over 1 kilometer up the road,

watch for a small fietspad going off to the right called Jiskelanpaad. Turn right here. Follow the fietspad until you reach the road and turn left. You will come to Oranjewoud and Oranjestein, two mansions set in the forest. You cannot visit the mansions, but it is possible to walk through the gardens on your right as you approach Oranjestein.

When you arrive at Oranjestein, which will be straight ahead, turn left, then take an immediate right. You will be cycling down a road through the forest for approximately 1 kilometer until you reach a fietspad that veers off to the left called Fuotpaden. Ride along that fietspad until you reach Jan Jonkmanweg. Turn right until it hits Kerkelaan. Turn left in the direction of Katlijk and proceed through the village. Stay on same road in the direction of Nieuwehorne; however, the name of the road changes from Kerkelaan to Breedesingel.

After almost exactly 1 kilometer, turn left onto the fietspad along the N380, still in the direction of Nieuwehorne. Go through Nieuwehorne and the adjacent town of Oudehorne where you will turn right onto the N353 and continue on to Noordwolde, passing through the town of Oldeberkoop. Go through Noordwolde and turn left at the bicycle sign to Vledder. Veer right onto Dwarsvaartweg, a small farm road. After approximately 1 kilometer, you turn right onto a small road called Vallaatweg. Vallaatweg is a rural street with lovely, stylishly-built farmhouses on both sides. On your right you will see ANWB mushroom #22592 that indicates 6.3 kilometers to Vledder. Turn right here.

It may appear that you have made an incorrect turn, but for the next several hundred meters, you will be traveling on this tiny fietspad next to a dirt road. The fietspad is covered with crushed shells, unusual for this inland area. After a short time, you will join a small farm road and then continue on into Vledder following the well-marked bicycle signs. The last part of the road is particularly nice with birch trees on either side. At this point you will actually be alongside the road to Vledder on a fietspad.

Leave Vledder in an easterly direction for the 8 kilometers to Diever, a pretty Drenthe village. Stop here and visit the old church and wander around the pretty town center. Then continue 1.5 kilometers to Dieverbrug (translation Diever Bridge) where you will cross the N371 and a canal, the Drentse Hoofdvaart. Continue 3 kilometers farther to Dwingeloo.

Dwingeloo is charming and different than most Dutch towns. Instead of the usual canals, it is centered around a "brink" or village green, ringed by oak trees. The brink is surrounded by quaint houses now converted into shops and cafés. Its church, St. Nicholas, which dates back to the fourteenth century, is also unusual because of the onion-shaped dome on its steeple. Most people come to Dwingeloo to enjoy the outdoors in the nearby Dwingelderveld National Park.

Tourist Information
VVV Dwingeloo, Brink 4a. Phone 0521 59 13 31.

Accommodations
Dwingeloo has two hotels and about six bed and breakfasts in town, approximately Dfl 60–70 Dbl. (Check with VVV.)
Hotel Wesseling, Brink 26. Phone 0521 59 15 44. Dfl 160 Dbl.
Hotel de Brink, Brink 30. Phone 0521 59 13 19. Dfl 110 Dbl.
Camping: There are about 10 campgrounds in the vicinity of Dwingeloo, but

most of the campgrounds are a few kilometers out. When you enter town, a board has a map and location of many of these.

Camping Meisterhof, Lheebroek 33. Phone 0521 59 72 78. Three kilometers north.

Camping De Oude Bargen, Oude Hoogeveensedijk 1. Phone 0521 59 72 61. En route south to National Park.

Bicycle Shops/Rentals

Reiber, Brink 23. Phone 0521 59 13 26. This shop has some good information on bicycle routes in the area.

Dolsma, Brink 13. Phone 0521 59 14 28.

Dwingeloo to Giethoorn: 48 Kilometers

The area around Dwingeloo and this part of the province of Drenthe has many bicycle paths and several signposted ANWB routes, each ranging from 30 to 40 kilometers. Information on bicycling in the area is available from the VVV and the bicycle shops. There is some lovely cycling through the forest of the national park south of Dwingeloo.

The first portion of this stage directs you to the Dwingelderveld National Park. There you can spend some time cycling in the area of the park and rejoin the route in the town of Ruinen, just south of the national park boundary.

From the VVV, cross the brink and head southeast on Moleneinde which turns into Zuidenweg. You'll see bicycle signs for Lhee. Follow these. You will leave on a birch-lined road, characteristic of this area. After 2 kilometers you will arrive in Lhee. Continue through town, leaving to the south. You will see signs for Camping de Oude Bargen. Just past the campground, a fietspad goes off to the left. It is only possible to continue straight on this road if you want to visit the Radiotelescope (as many do who come to this area). The road is restricted, and you must park cars and bicycles in the parking area and continue on foot.

ANWB mushroom #21268 points toward Spier. At the fork, a few hundred meters on, veer right, again in the direction of Spier. This takes you through a lovely forest on a packed dirt fietspad that looks more like a hiking trail than a bicycle path. You are now in Dwingelderveld National Park. Continue exploring or make your way to Ruinen.

Ruinen is a small town. Like Dwingeloo, Ruinen is centered around a brink. You will find the VVV right next to the church, and several shops and restaurants in the vicinity of the brink.

From Ruinen take the bicycle route to Meppel. Do not follow the car sign which will take you to the N371. You will follow the fietspad along the quieter road that goes through Oosteinde and Ruinerwold and eventually into Meppel after approximately 16 kilometers.

Follow the signs to Meppel Centrum. Meppel is a lively town with a pedestrian center area. It is pleasant enough to stay in, but approximately 12 kilometers farther on your extra cycling effort will be rewarded upon entering Giethoorn (see below). The VVV is at Kromme Elboog 2 (phone 0522 25 28 88), and there is a bicycle shop with rentals at the railway station (phone 0522 25 43 69). This is important if you are renting bicycles to explore the gorgeous area of Giethoorn and the lakes. The only youth hostel in the area is located in Meppel at L. Springerlaan 14, phone 0522 25 17 06. There are a couple of hotels in town.

From Meppel Centrum take Eendrachtstraat. Turn left onto Steenwijkerstraatweg, you will see signs for Steenwijk and Giethoorn. Take a left again on Zomerdijk. The fietspad sign to Giethoorn will indicate 12 kilometers. In less than 1 kilometer turn right again. There will be another bicycle sign. This takes you along the Meppelerdiep canal until you meet the N375. Turn left onto the fietspad. Follow the road approximately 2 kilometers to a bicycle sign that points to the right. Cross the N375 and follow the small farm road Lozedijk to the northwest. This is a very scenic stretch with a small canal running alongside the road and fields with cows. In 3 kilometers you will reach the town of Wanneperveen. At the main street there are two bicycle signs. The red one points left to Giethoorn; a green one points straight ahead. Turn left here, following the red sign. You will continue on this road for approximately 4 kilometers until you reach the N334. Turn right onto the fietspad alongside the highway. Continue 2.1 kilometers until you reach the Giethoorn VVV, which will be on your left and across the road.

Giethoorn has three museums, but the village itself is like a living outdoor museum. It is a village along canals like no other you will see in Holland. For approximately 3 kilometers, this incredibly picturesque *dorp* clings to both sides of the canal with quaint thatched roofed houses and well-tended gardens that one only imagines in storybooks.

Using the fietspad, you are forced to cross no less than 40 wooden footbridges as you zig-zag through the town's 3 kilometers. The fietspad is just wide enough for one bicycle in each direction, but apart from the canal, with its Venice-like "gondolas" and row boats, this path is the village's only road. You will find no cars in Giethoorn, another factor that adds to the serenity and beauty.

Giethoorn is a very popular destination and can often be crowded. Even with its "touristy" feel and the canal-side cafés geared to year-round visitors, it is well worth a visit. A tip: The south end of Giethoorn is the most heavily visited. Head north for a short distance to the quieter part of town.

Tourist Information
VVV Giethoorn, Beulakerweg a/b Ark. Phone 0521 36 12 48. On N334 on outskirts of Giethoorn.

Accommodations
There are several hotels in and around Giethoorn, not to mention an abundance of bed and breakfasts. Lists are available from the VVV.

Hotel 't Centrum, Ds Hylkemaweg 39. Phone 0521 36 12 25. Dfl 90 Dbl. Convenient, quiet location.
Hotel De Pergola, Ds Hylkemaweg 7. Phone 0521 36 13 21. Dfl 100 Dbl. Convenient, quiet location.
Hotel De Jonge, Beulakerweg 30. Phone 0521 36 13 60. Dfl 100 Dbl. On main road on edge of town.
Camping: There are no less than 15 campgrounds within the environs of Giethoorn. Stop in at the VVV for listings and directions as some of smaller ones are tucked away and difficult to find.

Where to Eat
Cafés, restaurants, pancake houses, outdoor coffee gardens, and the like dot the canals and area around.

Bicycle Shops/Rentals

Prinsen, Beulakerweg 137. Phone 0521 36 12 61.

Giethoorn to Kampen: 35 Kilometers

Begin across the road from the Giethoorn VVV on the main road, the N334. Head south for 2.1 kilometers until you reach an intersection. Continue straight. The fietspad veers right in the direction of Vollenhove, Zwartsluis, and Zwolle.

Four hundred meters farther is a bridge, De Blauwe Hand, with a large blue hand on it. The plaque tells a rather gruesome story of how the place may have received its name back in the sixteenth century.

As you proceed, you will have lakes on both sides, ideal for yachting and other recreational water sports. Take the road here in the direction of Vollenhove. The sign says 9 kilometers. Go 3.9 kilometers along the dike across the lake (Beulakerwijde). A bicycle sign points left indicating *doorgand verkeer*. Take this left, and it will take you to the town of St. Jansklooster. Take a right at the main road through town. Just before the end of town, there will be a bicycle sign; turn to the left, again in the direction of Vollenhove. This will take you on a small farm road to Vollenhove. Continue straight into town. All the roads lead to the harbor, the most direct way being to take Voorpoort to the Y, then Kerkestraat to the right. However, Bisschopstraat to the left will also get you to the harbor.

Vollenhove has a pretty harbor area. Just before you reach the harbor is Kerkplein (Church Square), where all the town's sights are conveniently located. The fourteenth-century church dominates the square with its mass of towers, spires, and gables. Attached to the church is the beautiful old Stadhuis, now a restaurant. Across Kerkplein is the former Latin school, dating back to 1627, now a bank. The remarkable feature of the old school is the carved entryway. Note: The VVV used to be in the Latin School, and some maps and guidebooks still indicate this, but the new VVV is now directly on the harbor down some stairs on the far side of Kerkplein.

Leave town the same way you came in. Turn right at the N331 and continue south toward Zwartsluis and Genemuiden. It is an agreeable ride along the service road, which then becomes a fietspad, following along the N331. Turn right approximately 10 kilometers after Vollenhove, following the ferry signs to Genemuiden for just a few hundred meters. This is another of the tiny Dutch ferries servicing a river crossing. The cost is Dfl 0.75 per person including bicycle.

On the other side, follow the road along the harbor to the center of town and continue on through.

Bicycles parked outside Kampen Railway Station.

The only thing of particular interest is Achterweg, perhaps the only street in the world where smoking is prohibited. There are signs in this tiny back street indicating that smoking is a risk to the historic wooden warehouse buildings.

For the next stages of the route you will pass through some Hanzestads (Hanseatic towns) and be on part of an LF3 route called the Hanzeroute. In the thirteenth century several cities in northern Europe formed a trading alliance known as the Hanseatic League. These cities were located along major trading routes and included cities such as London, Cologne, Stockholm, plus about 80 more. Several Dutch cities, such as Kampen, Zwolle, and Deventer, were involved, these being along the IJssel River, an important trading route connected to the Rhine River.

Kampen is a Hanseatic town and an IJssel River trading port dating back to the Middle Ages. The center of town is extremely well preserved with numerous buildings with impressive facades, gables, and brickwork. It is a pleasure to just wander or ride through the town's narrow streets admiring the architecture.

Kampen is famed for its beautiful skyline of spires, towers, and turrets, best viewed from the old bridge across the IJssel River. The Stadhuis is one of the most visited buildings, the Oude (Old) Stadhuis built in 1543, and the Nieuwe (New) built in the eighteenth century (open Monday through Friday and some Saturdays). There are some interesting churches and towers in Kampen, but the three Poorts (Gates), remnants from the old city fortifications, are outstanding—Broederpoort, Cellebroederspoort, and Koornmarktspoort.

Tourist Information
VVV Kampen, Botermarkt 5. Phone 038 331 35 00.

Accommodations
There are few hotels in town, and these fill up in high season. The VVV has some bed and breakfast options (approximately Dfl 70 Dbl).

Hotel van Dijk, IJsselkade 30. Phone 038 331 49 25. Dfl 110 Dbl.
Herberg d'Olde Brugge, IJsselkade 48. Phone 038 331 26 45. Dfl 110 Dbl.
Camping Seveningen, Friesweg 7. Phone 038 331 48 91. Two km northeast.

Bicycle Shops/Rentals
Kampen Railway Station. Phone 038 331 50 79.

Kampen to Zwolle: 19 Kilometers

From the center, follow the signs to the railway station, which will take you back across the IJssel River the way you entered. Just across the river, turn right and follow the fietspad in the direction of Zwolle. From this point you will be following the LF3a Hanzeroute. It is well signposted with LF route signs. Once again you will be on top of the dike for part of the route and riding through pastures, so you may have to share the fietspad with sheep, cows, or both. You will pass the small village of Wilsum, which boasts one of the oldest churches in the Netherlands, dating back to the tenth or eleventh century. Although just a village today, it received its city charter in the twelfth century.

Continue to Zwolle, following the LF3a route signs. When you reach the outskirts of Zwolle and pass under the big A28 freeway bridge, you will leave the LF route which continues along the river. Proceed east to Zwolle Centrum.

As soon as you enter the old core of Zwolle, the rich history of this Hanseatic stronghold is evident. The center is ringed by a star-shaped moat, and remnants of ancient fortifications separate the "island center" from the suburbs. The magnificent Sassenpoort with its four octagonal turrets, built in 1406, still guards the southeastern entrance to the city.

Head to the center where the Grote Kerkplein is framed by the fourteenth-century Grote St. Michaelskerk (Great St. Michael's Church) with its seventeenth-century, 4,000-pipe Schnitger organ, the Stadhuis (both the old and new town hall), and the VVV. Turn down Voorstraat, and at #38 is the Provinciaal Overijssels Museum in a sixteenth-century patrician's house and another adjoining house off Melkmarkt 41. The museum has seventeenth-century furnishings, ceramics, and silverware (closed Monday). Just north of here are remnants of the old town walls.

A speciality of Zwolle is *blauwvingers* (blue fingers), a type of shortbread finger with chocolate tips. Excellent ones can be found at Van Orsouw bakery on the corner facing Grote St. Michaelskerk.

While in Zwolle you should make the effort to visit the small town of Hattem across the IJssel River southwest of Zwolle. It can be reached by using the small foot and bicycle ferry, 't Kleine Veer, just south of 't Engelse Werk Park. It operates 10 A.M.–6 P.M., and costs Dfl 1.75 for an adult and bicycle. A plaque on the far side tells you (in Dutch only) that there has been a ferry operating at this location since 1795. Back then it was a 15-minute crossing. Today it takes just 4 minutes.

Once on the other side of the river, you will follow the fietspad about a kilometer until you cross a bridge. A sign will point you toward the center, which you will have already spotted by the church steeple and exceptional fourteenth-century town gate that are visible as you approach.

Hattem, also a Hanzestad, is an appealing town that received its city charter in the fourteenth century. On the main square is the Dutch Reformed Church of Hattem, parts of the church dating back to the twelfth century with the upper tower added in the mid-fourteenth century. The Stadhuis, built in 1619, is also on the main square, as well as the VVV. On the west side of town part of the old castle walls remain, although the castle is no longer there. If you wind your way through the streets, you will come across several attractive, old houses, and on the edge of town there is an elegant windmill. Hattem has three small museums, including the enjoyable Bakkerijmuseum (Bakery Museum) on Kerkhofstraat 13.

Return to Zwolle either by the ferry or via the bridge across the IJssel River approximately 1 kilometer north of Hattem.

Tourist Information
VVV Zwolle, Grote Kerkplein 14. Phone 038 421 39 00.
ANWB Office, Tesselschadestraat 155. Phone 038 453 63 63.

Accommodations
There are no bed and breakfasts in Zwolle, and hotels tend to be on the expensive side. An alternative to staying in Zwolle is the quaint town of Hattem which has a couple of hotels, restaurants, and a bicycle shop.
City Hotel, Rode Torenplein 10-11. Phone 038 421 81 82. Dfl 125 Dbl. Five-minute walk to Grote Kerkplein.
Hotel 't Engelse Werk, 't Engelse Werk 4. Phone 038 421 75 93. Dfl 90 Dbl. South of town in lovely park area.

Camping Schellerberg, Schellerbergweg 18. Phone 038 465 15 02. Set on the Schellerberg family estate. Ten-minute bicycle ride south.

Camping De Agnietenberg, Haerstereerweg 27. Phone 038 453 1530. On River Vecht northeast of town.

Bicycle Shops/Rentals

Zwolle Railway Station. Phone 038 421 45 98.

H. J. Scholten, Luttekestraat 7. Phone 038 421 73 78.

Zwolle to Deventer: 35 Kilometers

From the center of Zwolle, follow signs to the railway station. At Stationsplein, follow the road southeast past the station a couple hundred meters until you see an underpass for foot and bicycle traffic. Take this underpass, as well as a second underpass that follows very shortly. In a few hundred meters, you'll take a right turn onto Schellerallee. Follow this tree-lined road all the way to the river, where you will join a fietspad to the left along the river. You might first want to make a detour in the other direction if you wish to visit 't Engelse Werk, a large city park with English-style gardens. This park starts a few hundred meters north of here. Return to this point and continue south along the IJssel River.

At this point you are following the LF3a, the ANWB Hanzeroute. The ANWB route signs will mark your route from here to Deventer. There are quite a few such signs to keep you on the right route. As you approach a large power plant about 5 kilometers south, there is a point where the sign is hidden by bushes. About 50 meters before you reach the power plant gates, you turn left onto Herculosepad.

Continue on until you reach the tiny village of Windesheim. Just as you leave town, note the impressive gateway on your left. This is the entrance to House Windesheim. The sixteenth-century mansion that belonged to this estate was destroyed by bombs in 1944. All that remains are the smaller outhouses, the grounds, and this gate.

Continue on through the towns of Wijhe and Olst. About 1.5 kilometers south of Olst, notice the fifteenth-century castle, Kasteel Groot Hoenlo, guarded by two ferocious stone lions.

Continue south to the town of Diepenveen, basically a suburb of Deventer, although it retains its village-like character. Continue through Diepenveen. As you enter Deventer, the LF3a turns to the right, rejoining the river road. This would work for you, but we suggest going straight on into town on Zwollestraat. There is a fietspad along the road all the way to the center, and it is a very easy ride.

Deventer is another old Hanzestad. It centers around the Brink (Main Square) where the highlight is De Waag, the old fifteenth-century weigh

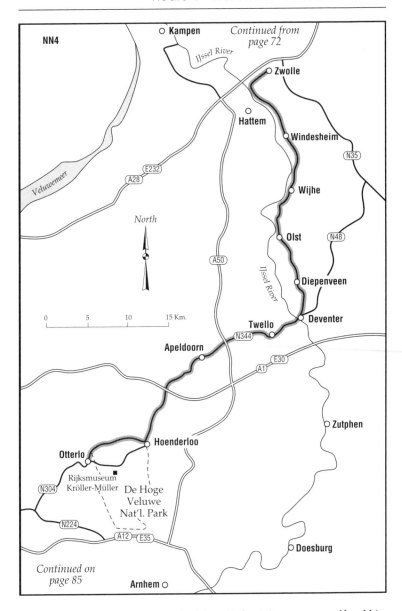

Continued from page 72

NN4

Continued on page 85

house, which is quite an amazing building. Today it is a museum of local history and has an exhibit of bicycles said to include some of the oldest in the Netherlands. Also on the Brink is the Speelgoed en Blikmuseum (Toys and Tins), the largest public collection of vintage toys in the country, as well as displays of antique packaging tins (both closed Monday).

The town is characterized by many wonderful old buildings. Head up Bergstraat, with an actually discernible incline, and visit Bergkwartier, the "hill

Bicycles dominate the traffic in the center of Zwolle.

quarter," with its narrow, winding streets and medieval houses. View the town from the twelfth-century St. Nicholas or Berg Church, where you see the other famous church of Deventer, the huge Romanesque St. Lebuinuskerk, founded in the eleventh century, and alongside it, the Stadhuis.

Tourist Information
Be aware that the VVV (shared with ANWB) is no longer at Brink 55 on the Brink (town square) but in new premises about halfway between the Brink and the railway station at Keizerstraat 2 (corner of Keizerstraat and Brinkpoortstraat). Phone 0570 61 31 00.

Accommodations
There is only one hotel in town, rather surprising for a town the size of Deventer, and any bed and breakfasts are out from the center. Plan carefully, since Deventer is a town worth spending some time in.

Hotel Royal, Brink 94. Phone 0570 61 18 80. Dfl 95 Dbl. Center of town.
Camping De Worp, Worp 12. Phone 0570 61 36 01. Across the IJssel River en route to Apeldoorn.

Where to Eat
What Deventer lacks in lodgings, it more than makes up for in eating establishments. Ethnic offerings include Balkan, Greek, Indian, Japanese, Portuguese, Kurdish, Thai, and more. You will also be able to feast on the ubiquitous Shoarma, pancakes, and Dutch and Indonesian food.

Bicycle Shops/Rentals
Leo Jensen Tweewielers, Stationsplein 3. Phone 0570 61 38 32.

Deventer to Apeldoorn: 16 Kilometers
This will not be the most exciting stage of your trip. From Deventer you basically follow the N344 highway all the way to Apeldoorn. You will leave town over the large bridge spanning the IJssel River. Follow the signs for Apeldoorn from the Brink. You will need to be on the road leading to the bridge a couple blocks before the river as it is quite a high bridge, and there is no access to the bridge from the road along the river.
There is not much to see on this portion of your route, although there are some mansions along the road through the town of Twello. The rest of the route is rural.

As you approach the sizable city of Apeldoorn, continue on the same highway, which turns into Deventerstraat, all the way to the center. The VVV is at Stationsplein 72, phone 06 442 03 30, and the ANWB office is next door at #70.

Apeldoorn itself has little appeal, except for Rijksmuseum Paleis Het Loo (Het Loo Palace) on the northwest edge of the city. The magnificent former palace was built in the late seventeenth century and has been restored to exemplify the lifestyle of the House of Orange with art, furnishings, tapestries, and all the typical palace splendor. The museum is housed in the garage. For a stroll, the formal gardens and grounds are pleasant. Spend a few hours visiting the palace (except on a Monday, as it's closed), then head back to the center of Apeldoorn and south to Otterlo.

Apeldoorn to Otterlo: 21 Kilometers

From Apeldoorn, follow the bicycle signs in the direction of Ede. This will take you out of the center of town, joining Europaweg (the N304), with a fietspad all the way to the town of Otterlo. Once you leave the city, you will ride through a forest, the start of the Hoge Veluwe area. You will actually start using a few more of your low gears as there are some extended inclines en route.

The first town you will reach, in about 13 kilometers, is Hoenderloo, a village on the north end of the Hoge Veluwe National Park. There are lots of campgrounds and restaurants, a few hotels, shops, bicycle rentals, and not much more. The village is there mainly as a tourist base for the park. Continue on to the town of Otterlo 8 kilometers more along the N304. If it sounds like there is a war going on to your right, it's because this is a military shooting range. This is, however, not an everyday occurrence.

Otterlo makes a somewhat better spot than Hoenderloo for exploring this area. It gives you easy access to Apeldoorn, Arnhem to the south, and the Hoge Veluwe National Park. It is less than 4 kilometers from the Kröller-Müller museum. The town itself is small but has a pleasant center with restaurants, banks, some shops, and a supermarket.

Hoge Veluwe National Park

This park, the largest in the Netherlands, covers approximately 13,500 acres. There are 42 kilometers of bicycle paths, and over 400 white bicycles are offered free to visitors at the park entrances. You can buy a map of the park or simply follow the well-marked paths.

Within the park there are natural areas of heath, woodland, sand dunes, and grassy fields where animals such as deer, wild boar, fox, and moufflons (wild sheep) roam. Originally the estate of Willem Kröller and his wife Hélène Müller, in the 1930s it was bequeathed to the nation.

The park truly reflects the harmony of art and nature. Located in the center is the park's highlight, the Kröller-Müller Museum (closed Monday). Its focal point is a fabulous collection of 278 Van Goghs (they don't show all at once) plus works by Mondrian, Picasso, Toroop, and other nineteenth- and twentieth-century artists, some earlier works, as well as ceramics. Surrounding the building is Europe's largest sculpture garden, covering 27 acres and including pieces by Rodin, Moore, and others (open April 1–November 1).

Cycling north from the museum you reach Jachtslot St. Hubertus, the Kröller-Müller's 1920s art deco hunting lodge. It is only open for tours May through November. Also in the park is Museonder, an underground museum featuring displays of subterranean animals. There are lots of picnic possibilities plus refreshment areas. The park is best visited in good weather, and avoid being there on a Monday when the museum is closed.

Tourist Information
VVV Otterlo, Arnhemsweg 14. Phone 0318 59 12 54.

Accommodations
There are three hotels in town plus about half a dozen bed and breakfasts around Dfl 60–70 Dbl (details at VVV). If you are going the youth hostel route, you are midway between two; one is in Apeldoorn and one in Arnhem. Six campgrounds are also in the vicinity of Otterlo.

Hotel 't Witte Hoes, Dorpstraat 35. Phone 0318 59 13 92. Dfl 100 Dbl. Charming old white house.

Hotel Sterrenberg, Houtkampweg 1. Phone 0318 59 12 28. Dfl 150 plus Dbl. Expensive.

Carnegie's Cottage, Onderlangs 35. Phone 0318 59 12 20. Dfl 120 Dbl. Lovely, peaceful setting. Five-minute bicycle ride from the town center.

Camping de Veluwe, Arnhemsweg 63. Phone 0318 59 13 06. Large campground on main road through town.

Camping Beek en Hei, Heideweg 4. Phone 0318 59 14 83. Small, quiet campground on edge of forest.

Bicycle Shops/Rentals
Although there are no bicycle shops in Otterlo, several are close by.

Ede. Railway Station. Phone 0318 61 59 57.

Lunteren. Groot Bammel Tweewielers, Dorpstraat 31. Phone 0318 48 23 08.

Arnhem. Fietsspeciaalzaak Roelofs, G.A. van Nispenstraat 1. Phone 026 442 60 14.

Otterlo to Utrecht: 54 Kilometers

From the Otterlo VVV, go south on Arnhemsweg, take the first right onto Koeweg, and pick up the fietspad to Ede in a few hundred meters. This is a delightful fietspad, taking you through landscape similar to that of the national park. You will be riding alongside a dirt road, but the fietspad itself is paved. The first 5 kilometers or so is forest. Then you have a couple kilometers of open heath, covered with mauve heather during August and September. Just before you reach Ede, you will cycle through more forest.

You will reach the N304 highway 8 kilometers after leaving Otterlo. If you wish to go into Ede, cross the road here. Otherwise, turn right on the fietspad and go along this road for 1.5 kilometers. Turn left, crossing the high-

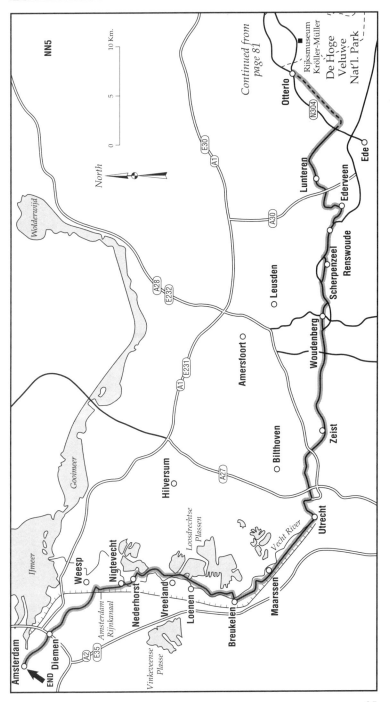

Continued from page 81

way, and take the road to Lunteren. In just under 6 kilometers, you will come to a road with an ANWB mushroom indicating a left turn to Lunteren. Take this road approximately 3 kilometers into town. Both Ede and Lunteren offer numerous hotel, camping, and restaurant possibilities.

In the center of town, take a right, following the car signs in the direction of Utrecht and Veenendaal. Just out of town you go under the big A30 freeway, continuing in the direction of Ederveen. Turn left 3.3 kilometers from town, again following a blue sign to Ederveen. In another 1.5 kilometers, turn right, again toward Ederveen, at the T-intersection. Just as you are entering town, turn right onto Brinklanderweg. The street veers to the left, and in 1.5 kilometers you turn right onto Veenweg. About 0.8 kilometers farther you will come to the N224; turn right.

In just a few hundred meters you will enter the town of Renswoude. As you enter the town, notice the row of nearly identical houses on your right called *kasteel woningen*. The oldest, at the west end, was built in 1773. The newest, at the east end, was built in 1780. You can see the progression in the cast-iron numbers on each house indicating the year it was built. Across the road, notice the house built in 1683, again marked in cast-iron. Take the first left at Kerkstraat and visit the church (originally a castle) with the circular dome. The crest has the year 1639. The church overlooks a beautiful forest area.

In approximately 3 kilometers you will come to the very pleasant town of Scherpenzeel. This is an elongated village, the main street lined with old brick houses. The center of town is dominated by the church.

Leaving town, continue following the red bicycle signs in the direction of Utrecht, basically following the N224 past Woudenberg and on into Zeist. Along the way you can stop and see the sand Pyramid of Austerlitz, built by Napoleon's soldiers in 1804.

Continue on through the town of Zeist in the direction of Utrecht. As you leave Zeist, you will see a number of huge impressive mansions along the road, which is called Utrechtsweg. This road takes you through the town of De Bilt and on into Utrecht. Follow the signs to Centrum.

For sightseeing, accommodations, and other information in Utrecht, see the Southern Netherlands route.

Utrecht to Amsterdam: 49 Kilometers

For this stage, see the Southern Netherlands Route.

Chapter 8

Route 2— Southern Netherlands Route

Including connection to Belgium

Total Distance:	516 kilometers (320 miles)
Terrain:	Flat
Maps:	Michelin Map 211 (1:200,000), ANWB Maps— North Holland, South Holland, North Brabant, Gelderland, and Utrecht (1:100,000)
Connecting Routes:	Route 1—Northern Netherlands
	Route 3—Northern Belgium

The Southern Netherlands takes you inland and lends itself to gentle cycling as the land is mainly flat. The south offers quiet cycling in rustic settings. You will cycle through farmlands and forests, see the highest concentration of windmills in the nation, and cycle through the colorful fields of Dutch flowers. You will also enjoy superb riding along canals and on dikes and visiting historic towns and villages as well as some of the main urban centers in the country.

Art lovers, or those who love museums of any type, might have trouble getting through this route in a timely fashion! The selection of museums, art galleries, and cultural activities offered by the cities along the way is staggering. Haarlem, Leiden, and Utrecht, for example, are filled with world-class exhibitions.

The four major cities of Amsterdam—The Hague, Rotterdam, and Utrecht—are included in the area, known as the *Randstad* or Rim City. It is home to 40 percent of Dutch residents. The Randstad includes the capital, Amsterdam; the seat of government, The Hague; the world's largest port, Rotterdam; plus several other medium-sized cities and villages, not to mention the bulk of tulip fields and other farmlands. Even though this sounds concentrated, riding through this area, which encompasses the western portion of the Southern Route, you will be surprised at the beauty and open space contained in this highly populated area.

Windmills of the Kinderdijk, the largest concentration of windmills in the Netherlands.

Farther east the country is far more rural, and the route takes you through farming areas, small towns, and through or near several nature reserves. Highlights include the entwined Belgian and Dutch towns of Baarle-Nassau and Baarle-Hertog (it is actually one town with two nationalities). Fans of Vincent van Gogh will want to spend some time in the town of Nuenen, where van Gogh started his serious painting. The towns of Heusden and Zaltbommel, both medieval fortified towns, offer the chance to step back a few centuries in time. Bird watchers and nature lovers will want to explore the nature reserves of De Groote Peel south of Asten, the Biesbosch National Park near Dordrecht, and the Schaijkse Heide west of Den Bosch. You will also have the opportunity at several points along the Southern Route to ride south into Belgium to pick up the Northern Belgium Route.

Amsterdam to Schiphol:
18 Kilometers

For information on Amsterdam, see the Northern Netherlands Route.

The large and efficient Schiphol Airport is located 18 kilometers from central Amsterdam.

To begin this stage, make your way to Leidesplein, not too far west of the Rijksmuseum. Signs will direct you to Den Haag (via Park). This takes you to the fietspad through the Vondelpark, with signs for Den Haag and Badhoevedorp. You can also follow the youth hostel signs to get to Vondel-park, as it is at the northeast end of the park where you enter. You will ride a couple of kilometers through the park, a welcome respite from the city traffic. At the far end of the park, you will exit the park and cross the road, back onto a fietspad, always following the signs for Den Haag and Badhoevedorp. You will make a couple of turns following these signs. For much of the way, you will be following a canal on your right.

Just as you enter the town of Badhoevedorp there is a windmill on your right (Molen van Sloten) with an interesting exhibit and a cheese maker next door.

Go through town until you reach a T-intersection at the N232 highway. There are signs for Schiphol Oost and Schiphol Centrum, pointing opposite directions. You will turn right, in the direction of Schiphol Centrum. At this point you can already see the airport terminal across the fields. A few hundred meters farther on you will come to a left turn. If you are headed for the airport, turn left here. You will follow along this farm road for approximately 1 kilometer until the Schiphol signs point you onto a fietspad, turning left. This takes you under a road, through a special *fiets* tunnel built alongside the car tunnel, and on to the terminal. If you don't want to go to the airport, continue straight along the N232, toward Haarlem.

If you are using this part of the route to ride to Schiphol to catch a flight, be sure to allow at least 1-1/2 hours for the ride, an extra hour for bicycle packing plus the 2-hour required pre-departure check-in. In other words, leave really early, or consider taking the train to make sure you don't get lost or have a mechanical problem that would cause you to miss your plane.

For directions from Schiphol to Amsterdam, see the Northern Netherlands Route (Amsterdam).

Schiphol to Haarlem: 17 Kilometers

If you are picking up the route here after arriving at Schiphol airport, you need only head out the door from Terminal 3, where most international flights arrive, take a right, and continue just past the covered walking area to find the start of your first Dutch fietspad. Take this bicycle path until it reaches the N232 highway at Badhoevedorp on the north end of the airport grounds and turn left there in the direction of Haarlem.

This is not a particularly interesting ride as you basically just follow the N232 highway. As you approach Haarlem you will see signs for Centrum, which will take you into the city. It is approximately 17 kilometers from Schiphol Terminal 3 to Haarlem Centrum.

Haarlem, although close to Amsterdam, is a total contrast. It is 15 minutes from Amsterdam by train, so if you'd prefer to stay here and make day trips to Amsterdam, it is an agreeable alternative to the hustle and bustle of the capital

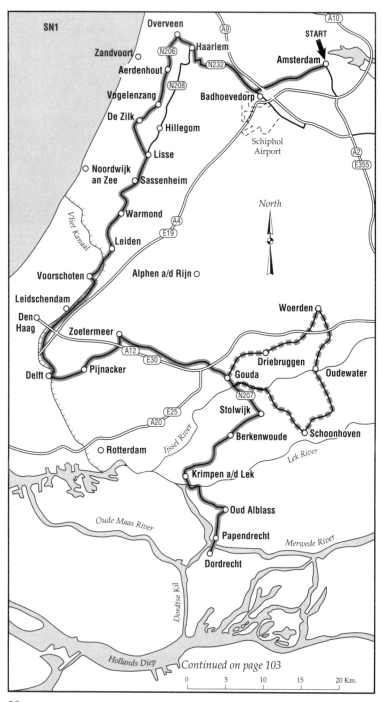

Continued on page 103

city. It is also a suitable base to explore the tulip fields that start just a few kilometers south, as well as the sand dunes along the coast to the west. Both the tulip fields and dunes are covered in the route description below but also make great day trips from Haarlem (on unloaded bicycles) before heading on to Leiden.

Haarlem has a peaceful feel with its canals, hidden courtyards, and seventeenth-and eighteenth-century architecture. The focal point of Haarlem is the Grote Markt (Market Square) dominated by Grote St. Bavokerk with its incredibly beautifully decorated 1738 Müller organ (on which Mozart played). Concerts take place during summer months. Also on the Grote Markt are the medieval Stadhuis (Town Hall), the Vleeshal (Meat Hall), and Vismarkt (Fish Market). The Grote Markt, which comes alive on Saturdays with a colorful flower and fruit market, is surrounded by shopping streets and residential areas, and the museums are close by.

The artist Frans Hals was Haarlem's native son, and the city is very proud to house many of his works in the Frans Hals Museum at Groot Heiligland 62, a former seventeenth-century almshouse (open daily). Other than works by Hals, there are many more sixteenth- and seventeenth-century paintings. The Teylers Museum, the oldest museum in the Netherlands, dating back to 1778, is also close to the Grote Markt at Spaarne 16 (closed Monday). It was originally set up to promote arts and sciences, but today is a mixture of paintings and drawings (including a Michelangelo and Rembrandt), fossils, coins, and scientific instruments.

Also in Haarlem is the Corrie Ten Boomhuis at Barteljorisstraat 19. This is the house where Corrie Ten Boom and her family hid Jews during World War II. The family ended up in a concentration camp, with Corrie the only survivor (tours Tuesday through Saturday). Haarlem is sprinkled with *Hofjes*, originally almshouses for elderly women. These clusters of brick houses around pretty courtyards are now a spot of tranquillity. Ask at the VVV for locations.

Tourist Information
VVV Haarlem, Stationsplein 1. Phone 023 531 90 59.
ANWB Office, Stationsplein 70. Phone 023 531 91 63.

Accommodations
Hotels in Haarlem can be pricey, but the VVV can also book bed and breakfasts.

Hotel Carillon, Grote Markt 27. Phone 023 531 05 91. Dfl 115 Dbl. Excellent location on Grote Markt.
Youth Hostel Jan Gijzen, Jan Gijzenpad 3. Phone 023 537 37 93.
Camping De Leide, Liewegje 17. Phone 023 33 23 60.

Where to Eat
Haarlem is a sizable town with plenty of dining options.

Bicycle Shops/Rentals
Haarlem Railway Station, Rijwiel Shop. Phone 023 531 70 66.

Haarlem to Leiden: 39 Kilometers
Leave Haarlem to the west, following signs in the direction of Overveen and Bloemendaal. Cross over the large A208 and continue to the center of Overveen. Head south toward Vogelenzang. Approximately 1 kilometer out of

town, veer left. The main road continues straight, but you will veer left following the sign to Vogelenzang through a forested area. On your right you will see the entrance to Natuur Reservaat Middenduin. Continue through the town of Aerdenhout. Notice the incredibly large villas in this town. Continue in the direction of Vogelenzang. Just south of Aerdenhout you will start following the N206 south until you reach Vogelenzang, 14 kilometers from Haarlem.

Continue south through Vogelenzang in the direction of De Zilk. Ride through De Zilk. Three and a half kilometers after Vogelenzang, the road veers to the right. Stay on the road until you see signs pointing left to Lisse. Turn here. Continue following signs for Lisse and Keukenhof. In about 4 kilometers you will cross the railway line and pass the Lisse train station, which is actually 3 kilometers from the center of Lisse. One kilometer after the station, you will come to the famous Keukenhof Gardens. The entrance is on your left.

The Keukenhof Gardens is a huge "park" of 70 acres planted with over 6 million bulbs. (Note: The Netherlands itself boasts approximately 41,000 acres of bulb fields.) Prime time is spring when the tulips, daffodils, hyacinths, and other bulb flowers take turns in their full glory. Understandably, the gardens are crowded during this peak time, but due to the nature of the Keukenhof and what it represents, "When in Holland . . . " Note: The gardens are open daily but only from the end of March until late May.

You are currently in the bulb field area, and if it's springtime, you should be treated to beautiful displays as you meander through this area. The fields are a patchwork of color throughout this part of Holland, so take as much time as you can afford to explore.

Continue on to Lisse, another 2 kilometers. There is little of interest in town. The VVV is at Grachtweg 53, phone 02521 142 62. If you are really interested in bulbs, you can visit the Museum Voor de Bloemenbollenstreek at Heereweg 219. The focus is on the history of bulbs and the growing process. There are annual flower parades in April. Lisse has a couple of hotels and a few bed and breakfasts.

From Lisse, continue south along the N208 to Sassenheim, about 4 kilometers. Turn right off of the N208 onto Parklaan following signs to Centrum. Stay on this road as it winds through town. Follow signs to the VVV, located in the Gemeentehuis.

To leave town, head south past the church. Here you will be following the ANWB Bollenstreek Route. At 1.9 kilometers south of the VVV you will turn left, following signposts to Leiden and Warmond. Three kilometers south, four camping areas are off to your left; only Camping De Wasbeek has facilities for tent camping. At 4.5 kilometers you will come to Warmond. Notice Mariehaven on your right and the large houses in town. At 5.5 kilometers do not follow the bicycle sign left to Leiden; follow the Bollenstreek sign straight. At 7.5 kilometers, take a left to Leidendorp and Leiden, leaving the Bollenstreek Route that continues straight. As you approach Leiden, you will notice two windmills. Follow the Centrum/Station signs.

Nearing Leiden, you will begin to wonder why on earth anyone would direct you to come here. The northern approach to the city is, to put it plainly, ugly. You will arrive turning onto a huge road that runs alongside the railway tracks. A wall of huge concrete buildings bars you from the main part of town. Once you reach the center, though, you will discover a lively university city criss-crossed by canals and with plenty of atmosphere. Conveniently located across the road from the railway station is the VVV, which should be your first stop.

Leiden has 11 excellent museums, an amazing number for a town its size. The Rijksmuseum van Oudheden at Rapenburg 28 (closed Monday) has the impressive mini-Egyptian Temple of Taffeh in the foyer plus exhibits of classical Near Eastern, Egyptian, and Dutch archaeology. The mummies on the second floor are well preserved and worth a peek. Another interesting museum is the Molenmuseum de Valk (Windmill Museum), a working windmill for 10 generations from 1747 until 1964. Its seven floors shed light on the miller's lifestyle (closed Monday). Also visit the Stedelijk Museum de Lakenhal at Oude Singel 28, the old cloth hall that now houses decorative arts, paintings, a replica of clothmakers' rooms, and antiques (closed Monday). And there are still more museums to explore.

While in Leiden, walk or ride along Rapenburg Canal and note the arched bridges crossing the canal and the grand houses of the aristocracy that line it. Close to Rapenburg is the fourteenth-century Gothic St. Pieterskerk, and back on Rapenburg at #73 is Hortus Botanicus, one of the world's oldest botanical gardens with the first seeds planted in 1590. Its paths are lined with exotic plants, plus there is a tropical rain forest greenhouse (open daily).

Tourist Information
VVV Leiden, Stationsplein 210. Phone 071 514 68 46.
ANWB Office, Stationsweg 2. Phone 071 514 62 41.

Accommodations
There are several reasonably priced hotels/pensions, plus check the bed and breakfasts through the VVV.

Hotel Witte Singel. Witte Singel 80. Phone 071 512 45 92. Dfl 85 Dbl. Just south of Hortus Botanicus.
Hotel de Doelen, Rapenburg 2. Phone 071 512 05 27. Dfl 120–160 Dbl. Well located in the center.
Youth Hostel Herberg De Duinark, Langevelderlaan 45, Noordwijk. Phone 0252 37 29 20. This is the closest youth hostel to Leiden, 15 kilometers northwest in Noordwijk.
Camping: There is no camping in Leiden itself, but plenty of facilities are in the seaside area of Katwijk. On the route into Leiden, you will pass through Warmond where there are several in the vicinity. Several do not accommodate tent campers; however, Camping De Wasbeek just north of Warmond (and right on the route) takes campers. Wasbeeklaan 7. Phone 071 301 13 80.

Where to Eat
This is a university town, so there are lots of places to eat for reasonable prices, as well as plenty of cafés.

Bicycle Shops/Rentals
Three bicycle shops are in the center of Leiden, two of which are right on the main square. No rentals.

Leiden Railway Station, Terweepark. Phone 071 512 00 68.

Leiden to Delft: 23 Kilometers

Leave Leiden in the direction of Den Haag. About 2.5 kilometers out of town, when entering the town of Voorschoten, watch for the left turn to Vlietland. Approximately 250 meters past a large church on your left, the road veers right, but you want to continue straight, following the yellow sign that says *doorgand fietsverkeer*. Do not veer right as that road takes you to the center of town. In approximately 1 kilometer you will go over a bridge crossing a canal. Across the bridge, turn left, and in less than 100 meters you will turn right onto a fietspad. About 100 meters farther on, a sign tells you to turn right to Leidschendam. Turn here, again onto a fietspad. Follow the Vliet (the canal on your right), which is the main canal through the city of Delft. You will follow this canal all the way to Delft.

Nine kilometers from Leiden you will enter Leidschendam. Note the windmill as you enter town in front of a row of modern housing. This might not be the most scenic view, but it is typical of how Holland often blends the very old with the ultra modern. The old part of Leidschendam, once you've passed the new housing, is a really nice little town. Cross the canal and visit the town if you like, then return to the same side to head farther south.

South of Leidschendam, you will shortly be looking at the town of Voorburg across the canal to your right. At 2.7 kilometers south of Leidschendam you can follow the signs to Den Haag (4 kilometers), Gouda (26 kilometers), or Delft (7 kilometers).

Note: For part of the way, the path along the canal looks like a bicycle path, but note the sign indicating it is for pedestrians only. At this point you'll be on the fietspad on the other side of the road. Shortly after, the fietspad does cross over to be right along the canal again.

Follow the canal all the way to Delft. This is a lovely way to enter the city. When you come to the bridge with the small white and blue sign for the VVV, turn right over the bridge, and follow the road into the center. The main church will be on the right and the VVV on the left in a few hundred meters.

Delft's claim to world fame is the well-known white porcelain painted with blue, which was developed in the sixteenth century to compete with "china" from China. Certainly the ever-present Delftware can be found all over Delft, and for that matter, all over Holland, but the city of Delft has more to offer than just tourist shops filled with souvenirs. You can stroll along the many canals, view architecture, visit a market, and, of course, see Delftware being made.

Delft spreads out from the central Markt. Towering over the Markt is the Gothic Nieuwe Kerk, built in 1381, where the mausoleum of William of Silent is found. Climb the tower to get a view of Delft and to see the 48-bell carillon. Also at the Markt are the Waag, the old weigh house, now a theater; the Vleeshal, the old Meat Hall; the two ox heads on the gable, a reminder of the past; and the Vismarkt, the old Fish Market.

At Sint Agathaplein, Het Prinsenhof Museum (originally a nunnery and then William the Silent's domicile) houses paintings, tapestries, Delftware, and paintings (closed Monday). Should you want to buy some Delftware, the most well-known shop is Koninklijke Porcelyne Fles, founded in 1653, at Rotterdamseweg 196 in the southern part of town. Here you can also see the porcelain being processed and painted (open daily, except Sunday, November–March). Another Delftware factory is De Delftse Pauw at Delftweg 133 in north Delft. They also offer demonstrations.

Delft comes alive on Thursday between 9 A.M. and 5 P.M., when the Markt is transformed into a huge, colorful, and very animated market. It is hard to recognize this as the same tranquil town, but at 5 P.M. when the stalls pack up, Delft reverts back to its quiet self. On Saturday there is a small fruit and vegetable market at the Brabantse Turfmarkt.

Tourist Information
VVV Delft, Markt 85. Phone 015 212 61 00.

Accommodations
There several hotels and pensions in Delft, as well as some bed and breakfasts (check at the VVV).

Pension De Vos, Breestraat 5A. Phone 015 212 32 58. Dfl 70 Dbl. Pleasant bed and breakfast close to center.
Hotel Les Compagnons, Markt 61. Phone 015 214 01 02. Dfl 125 Dbl. Great location on Markt.
Hotel Leeuwenbrug, Koornmarkt 16. Phone 015 214 77 41. Dfl 150–170 Dbl. On canal. Charming.
Camping De Delftse Hout, Korftlaan 5. Phone 015 213 00 40. Located a 5-minute bicycle ride from center in Delftse Hout (Delft Woods).

Bicycle Shops/Rentals
Rijwielshop Delft, van Leeuwenhoeksingel 40A. Phone 015 314 30 33.

Optional Side Trip: Den Haag
(Official Name—'s-Gravenhage)

Amsterdam is the constitutional capital, but Den Haag is the center of Dutch government. Visiting the city offers a glimpse of the royal history and political structure of the Netherlands. It is a city of diplomats and officials. Here you will find the International Court of Justice (World Court), housed within Vredespaleis (Peace Palace), and the royal residence. Other than the central area, the city itself is sprawling suburbs. Also in the vicinity is the beachside town of Scheveningen, with a name so difficult for anyone but a native Dutch person to say, that pronouncing it was used as a test in World War II to detect German infiltrators.

To get your sightseeing bearings, head to the Hofvijver, a lake in the center of town around which most attractions are located. The Binnenhof (inner courtyard), the center of Dutch government for centuries, is there. Guided tours leaving from Binnenhof 8A during the week will show you the Ridderzaal (Hall of Knights), as well as the Chambers, and more. A little farther away is The International Court of Justice (World Court) at Carnegieplein 2, aptly named as the building was donated by Andrew Carnegie.

After your political fill, you can choose to visit several of the museums in Den Haag. Haags Historisch Museum (Korte Vijverburg 7) has a collection of paintings, furniture, and other relics tracing three centuries of Hague history (closed Monday). Mauritshuis (Korte Vijverburg 8) has a collection of seventeenth-century paintings including Rembrandt's *Anatomy Lesson of Professor Tulp* and works by other Dutch masters (closed Monday). Rijksmuseum Gevangenpoort (Buitenhof 33) was a prison for four centuries, and you can now tour the cells and view torture instruments (closed Saturday). Museum Bredius

(Lange Vijverburg 14) was once the home of Abraham Bredius and now houses his collection of lesser-known masters and some more well-known (closed Monday). The Haags Gemeentemuseum, the Municipal Art Museum (Stadtshoudterslaan 41), has Delftware, rare musical instruments, and impressionist and modern art including Mondrians and Eschers (closed Monday).

You can then head to the three royal palaces: Noordeinde Palace (Nooreinde 68), Lange Voorhout Palace (Lange Voorhout 74), and Huis ten Bosch (Haagse Bos). None of these are open to the public, but you can create your own "Royal Bicycle Tour" and cycle from one to the other and take a look from the outside at how the other half have lived over the centuries.

A note about Den Haag: The North Sea Jazz Festival takes place every July and attracts 60,000 people with acts from all over the globe. The city is crowded, so plan around this.

Tourist Information
VVV Den Haag, Koningin Julianaplein 30. Phone 070 354 62 00.

Accommodations
The Hague is quite an expensive city as far as accommodations are concerned due to the international and diplomatic flavor of the city. However, a couple of cheap hotels can be found around the area of the Holland Spoor Station (not to be confused with Centraal Station), or you can ask the VVV to book a bed and breakfast. It is also possible to venture out to Scheveningen, where the accommodations are a little cheaper.

Hotel Aristo, Stationsweg 166. Phone 070 389 08 47. Dfl 110 Dbl. Basic hotel near station.
Hotel Astoria, Stationweg 139. Phone 070 384 04 01. Dfl 110 Dbl. Same as above.
Youth Hostel Ockenburgh, Monsterseweg 4. Phone 070 397 00 11.
Camping Ockenburgh. Located in the Recreatiecentrum Kijuduinpark. Wijndaelerweg 25. Phone 070 325 23 64. Huge.

Both the youth hostel and the campground are located in the same park on the beach near Kijkduin, approximately 10 kilometers southwest of Den Haag. If you are camping, it is closer and easier to stay in Delft.

Where to Eat
Everything from *Shoarma* to *Rijstaffel*. All price ranges. And, of course, some very fine dining at very fine prices to cater to the dignitaries that frequent the city.

Bicycle Rentals
Both railway stations. Holland Spoor, phone 070 389 08 30. Centraal Station, phone 070 385 3235.
Du Nord Rijwielen, Keizerstraat 27-29. Phone 070 355 40 60.

Delft to Gouda: 32 Kilometers
Leave Delft from the VVV the same way you came in and cross the bridge. Follow the camping signs into the Delftse Hout (Delft Woods). Go past the camping area 2.5 kilometers from the VVV. Continue on this road until you come to a T-intersection and turn right toward Pijnacker. Three hundred meters farther, turn left onto the fietspad, also toward Pijnacker. After approximately 1

kilometer you will turn right at another T; go another 2 kilometers until you reach Pijnacker. At the end of the fietspad, turn left and continue following signs to Centrum.

From the center, head northeast to Zoetermeer. Cross the railway line and turn left. Continue 7 kilometers until you reach Zoetermeer. Zoetermeer is incredibly well signposted. You will continue through the town on the fietspad in the direction of Gouda without ever entering the main part of the town.

Information signs such as this one are a usual sight when you enter a Dutch town or village.

Next you will come to the A12 freeway intersection; turn right, continuing on the fietspad alongside the A12 for approximately 15 kilometers. Then cross over the A12 and continue for about 3 kilometers following the signs into Gouda. Continue past the station and take the first right into the Gouda Centrum.

Gouda, identified by most people with its namesake cheese, is a lively town with plenty of interesting attractions. Every Thursday morning in the summer months, you can sample Gouda cheese from the market held in the congenial marketplace in the center of town. Huge wheels of Gouda line the stalls, and farmers weigh in their cheese at the Waag at Markt 36. Gouda (pronounced How-dah, with the first H being a very guttural sound) comes in a variety of ages, the youngest being the most mild. Begin with the *jong,* creamy and mild, and work your way through the aging process to *belegen, extra belegen,* and *oude,* aged for at least two years.

You can't help but be impressed by two exceptional buildings in Gouda, the Stadhuis (open daily), built in 1450, in the center of the Markt and Grote St. Janskerk (open daily) at Achter de Kerk 16. You hardly need the address of St. Janskerk (St. John's Church), which is enormous; in fact, it is the largest church in the Netherlands. There is an admission charge of Dfl 3 to the church, but it is well worth it to see 70 of the most impressive (and largest) stained glass windows you'll ever come across. Some date from the sixteenth century, having survived the years. The windows depict biblical scenes as well as events in Dutch history. Try to find the telescope that is generally available for visitors and view the intricacies of some of the windows through the lens, a totally different perspective.

There are a few notable museums in Gouda. The Stedlijk Museum Het Catharina Gasthuis across from the church at Achter de Kerk 14 was once the hospital and the governor's mansion. The two complexes have been joined into a huge maze of a museum displaying everything from sixteenth- and seventeenth-century paintings to seventeenth-century medical equipment in the old surgeon's room. It also has a period kitchen and antique toys (open daily). Be sure to visit Museum de Moriaan at Westhaven 29, an eighteenth-century tobacconist's shop and pipe museum (open daily). Gouda is also home to the Zuidhollands Verzetsmuseum at Turfmarkt 30, a remembrance and documentation of World War II (closed Monday).

Tourist Information
VVV Gouda, Markt 27. Phone 0182 51 36 66.
ANWB Office, Stationsplein 1b. Phone 0182 52 44 44.

Accommodations

Hotel Utrechtse Dom, Guezenstraat 6. Phone 0182 52 79 84. Dfl 80 Dbl. Worth
    negotiating the winding streets to find this bicycle friendly hotel.
Hotel de Keizerskroon, Keizerstraat 11. Phone 0182 52 80 96. Dfl 110 Dbl. West
    of market.
Camping Elzenhof, Broekweg 6. Phone 0182 52 44 56.
Camping De Breevaart, Bodegraafsestraatweg 52. Phone 0182 58 15 56.

Where to Eat

Gouda has just about anything you'd want. Several restaurants are understandably clustered around the Markt. It is a gorgeous square where you
can sit outside during the summer. Wind your way through the streets and
along the canals, and you'll find some excellent restaurants: Indonesian, Middle Eastern, Greek, and more.

Bicycle Shops/Rentals

Gouda Railway Station. Phone 0182 51 97 51.
    There are also no less than three bicycle shops (no rentals) in the center
of Gouda.

Optional Day Trip:
Gouda/Woerden/Oudewater/Schoonhoven/Gouda
Circle Trip: 54 Kilometers

If you decide not to take this trip, it is worth abbreviating the suggested
route and simply going to Oudewater via the lakes, then returning to Gouda
along the Hollandse IJssel. Note: From Woerden it is only 19 kilometers to
Utrecht, an option for shortening the Southern Netherlands route.

Leave north in the direction of Reeuwijk. Three and a half kilometers out
of town turn right following the ANWB Reeuwijkse Plassen Route sign. This
takes you out over the lake. Take note of the lovely houses. This looks like a
normal road, but it is actually crossing the lake on a thin strip of land. Follow
the ANWB route signs and signs for Driebrugge/Oudewater. You will arrive
at Driebrugge in 11 kilometers. One kilometer out of town your fietspad ends.
Here you will veer right in the direction of Woerden/Oudewater. After a
while the Oudewater route turns right. You will continue straight in the direction of Woerden. You will reach Woerden after 19 kilometers.

Woerden has an extremely well-preserved fifteenth-century moated castle across from the huge 1892 neo-Gothic church, Bonaventurakerk. There is a
municipal museum in the Stadhuis dating from the sixteenth century (open
weekdays only). Woerden is very close to Utrecht, in fact, just 19 kilometers
away. Should you wish to shorten the Southern Netherlands Route, this
would be the place.

Just past the church, turn right over the bridge by the statue of skaters,
in the direction of Linschoten. Go to the station and take the fietspad underpass, continuing south. A white sign with blue writing points the direction to
Linschoten just on the other side of the station. Go in the same direction under several underpasses. When barely beyond the town of Linschoten (which
you do not go into), cross the road to turn right. The bicycle sign reads "Oudewater 6 kilometers." Around the corner, cross the bridge and turn right. There
are 6 kilometers of a wonderful road along a tree-lined canal. You will share
this narrow road with cars, but there is not too much traffic. Approximately 1

kilometer after turning onto this road, look right across the canal, and you will see a castle. It is private and not open to the public. Continue along the canal noting the farmhouses typical of the area. As you enter Oudewater, follow the VVV direction signs to find the center.

Oudewater is one of those Dutch towns that looks like it comes right out of an old Dutch village painting. The town is full of sixteenth-century houses, cobblestone streets, and picturesque canals. As you go through town, it's hard to believe you're in the twentieth century. The Waag in Oudewater is a little different from that of other Dutch towns. Here it is called the Heksenwaag, or Witch's Weigh House. In the sixteenth century, women suspected of being witches were brought here to be weighed. The theory was that in order for a witch to fly, they must weigh considerably less than a normal human being. The Heksenwaag at Leeuweringstraat 1 is now a museum, and today you can be weighed on the huge scales (open April to October, closed Monday). If you are here on a Wednesday, there is a great little local and very traditional farmer's market.

To go to Schoonhoven, leave Oudewater continuing through town until you reach the N228. Turn left in the direction of Utrecht, and in less than 1 kilometer you will see a sign to turn right to Polsbroekerdam. This is 1,200 meters from the VVV. You will go through Polsbroekerdam. Continue straight through the intersection until you reach a T-intersection. Although the car signs for Schoonhoven say turn left, you will turn right in the direction of Cabauw. Go through Cabauw, a lovely village along a canal with many thatched houses. At the church, continue straight, staying on the same side of the road. Again, do not follow the blue car signs in the direction of Schoonhoven. When you reach the N210, turn left. Four hundred meters farther, on your right, you will see signs for Schoonhoven Centrum/VVV. Follow these.

Schoonhoven is located on the confluence of the Vlist and Lek Rivers. The town itself is charming, but the main reason that people come here is for the silver products, which have been produced over the centuries in many of the town's workshops. The Nederlands Goud, Zilver, en Klokkenmuseum (Gold, Silver, and Clock Museum) on Kazernplein 4 is well worth a visit, not only for its fine collection of gold and silver artifacts but for its entire floor of fascinating antique clocks, many still in working order, chiming and cuckooing at regular intervals (closed Monday).

There are many other buildings of note in the town all along the Haven, the main waterway through town. The beautiful fifteenth-century Stadhuis with a 50-bell carillon in its steeple is also the home of the VVV. The Waag, dating back to 1617, is now a restaurant. The Veerpoort, from 1601, the only remaining town gate, is at the far end of town on the river.

Leave Schoonhoven in the direction of Vlist. If you follow the Gouda signs at this point, they will take you to a busy main road, so be sure to look for Vlist signs instead. Just north of town you get on a small farm road. You'll see three windmills right away. One is next to the road, with two in the distance. Follow the road along the canal north to Vlist and through the picturesque village. One kilometer after Vlist, cross the Vrouwebrug bridge to the other side of the canal and continue on in the same direction. If you miss this bridge, there are two more footbridges farther on that you can use to cross (approximately 1 kilometer to each one). As you enter Haastrecht, veer left onto the fietspad. Continue through town following signs to Gouda, heading in a westerly direction. Follow the signs back to Gouda Centrum.

Gouda to Dordrecht via Kinderdijk: 39 Kilometers

From the Gouda VVV, leave town to the south, initially following bicycle signs to Utrecht, getting onto the N207 for a brief time. Just over the IJssel River there is a large roundabout. Continue following the signs to Utrecht, which also point to Stolwijk. There is a fietspad along the N207, separated from the highway by a strip of trees making for pleasant cycling. As you enter Stolwijk, 5 kilometers from Gouda, the street is flanked by canals on either side, each house having a small bridge over the canal as a driveway. It is common in the Netherlands to see this on one side of a road, but it is quite unique to have this on both sides. You get the feeling that you're riding down the middle of a large canal.

At the intersection in Stolwijk (there's really only one), you will turn right in the direction of Berkenwoude, following the bicycle sign. Berkenwoude is another 5 kilometers. About a kilometer before you reach town is a Y-intersection. Again there is a bicycle sign to indicate you should veer right.

Continue straight on through Berkenwoude. You'll see signs now for Lekkerkerk and Oudekerk a/d IJssel. Almost exactly 2 kilometers from the center of Berkenwoude, you will cross a bridge over a canal. Turn left immediately after the bridge onto a fietspad. There is an ANWB mushroom (#22373) here indicating this is the direction for Lekkerkerk. One kilometer farther you come to a T-intersection in the fietspad with another ANWB mushroom (#22363). Take a right here in the direction of Lekkerkerk and Krimpen a/d IJssel. Just 3.3 kilometers farther the trail splits in three directions. You will continue straight here, in the direction of Krimpen a/d IJssel and Rotterdam. In another 1.5 kilometers you will reach a T-intersection with another ANWB mushroom (#21386). Turn left in the direction of Krimpen a/d Lek. In another 2 kilometers you will turn right at another T-intersection, then about 400 meters later you come to a bridge. Turn left over the bridge following directional signs for Centrum and *Veer* (ferry). You then go straight for about 1 kilometer through the town of Krimpen a/d Lek. When you reach the Lek River, you will see the ferry landing for the Krimpen/Kinderdijk ferry. This is a small ferry for both cars and bicycles.

Take the ferry across the Lek (cost Dfl 0.85 per adult and bicycle). Just up from the ferry landing on the Kinderdijk side (less than 200 meters), you will turn left onto the road. Follow the green signs for *Molens* (Mills), which you will already see in the distance. A few hundred meters up the road you will turn right following the green bicycle signs to Alblasserdam and Dordrecht. Go through the parking lot and onto the marked fietspad heading straight for the impressive row of windmills.

This area, known as Kinderdijk, is the place to see the quintessential, picture postcard Dutch windmills. Have extra film ready. There are windmills everywhere! Two kilometers of windmill after windmill, 19 in all. These impressive windmills were built in the early to mid-1700s and worked to keep the polders drained until 1950. One mill is open daily for visits. If you didn't get the chance to visit the windmill museum near Alkmaar, do so here to see an actual working mill.

Once you've had your fill of mills, continue on the fietspad past the mills to the south. Just under 2 kilometers from the last windmill, veer to the right. There is an ANWB mushroom (#20712) pointing in the direction of Alblasserdam and Dordrecht with a small white windmill on your right. In a couple hundred meters you will come to a bridge. Do NOT cross the bridge, but veer left along the canal. This is not signposted. After traveling exactly 1 kilometer, go left in the direction of Oud Alblas, a small village you will reach in about 3 kilometers. When you reach the village, turn right over the bridge, then right again just across the bridge. After about 800 meters, you will turn left onto a fietspad along the road to Papendrecht and Dordrecht. The street is called Veerstraat (Ferry Street), and you are indeed headed for another ferry. In 2.5 kilometers, you turn right over a bridge crossing the A15. There are again bicycle signs to Papendrecht and Dordrecht. You will go straight through Papendrecht on this road all the way to the Dordrecht foot ferry. You'll go through a series of roundabouts, but continue straight through each one. Be careful—one of the roundabouts has two bicycle signs for Dordrecht, one indicating a left turn for Dordrecht via Brug, but this is via the bridge, a much longer route. Continue straight, and take the pedestrian ferry across the Beneden Merweda, an offshoot of the Maas River (cost Dfl 1.30 per adult and bicycle).

From the ferry landing, go straight up the road a few meters until you reach a church. Veer right, and you're in the center of Dordrecht. The VVV is on the other side of town, a block from the railway station. The town is uncharacteristically poorly signposted, so pick up a map when you find the VVV.

Dordrecht, founded in 1220, is one of the oldest towns in the Netherlands. Today the city is a busy river junction. If you like to view ship traffic, head down to the river for a constant parade. There are several buildings in the "old town" that are of historic interest. Just meander through the streets to enjoy the architecture, the market squares, the old city gates, and fine houses.

The Grote Kerk is a Brabant Gothic church dating from the fifteenth century. It has an unfinished 70-meter (230-foot) tower that leans slightly and a 49-bell carillon that usually plays Friday at 11 A.M. and Saturday at 2 P.M. You can climb the tower for a view of the city and surrounding area. The interior of the church has numerous features worth seeing such as the stained glass windows, choir stalls, and organ. There are two museums of note in Dordrecht. One is the Simon Van Gijn Museum, located in an eighteenth-century patrician's house at Nieuwe Haven 29 with period rooms, some fine tapestries, silverware, antique toys, and items of local interest (closed Monday). The other is the Dordrechts Museum at Museumstraat 40. It houses a collection of works by Dordrecht artists, especially from the period around the seventeenth century (closed Monday).

Tourist Information
VVV Dordrecht, Stationsweg 1. Phone 078 613 280 00.
ANWB Office, Spuiboulevard 88. Phone 078 614 07 66.

Accommodations
There are several hotels, plus a few bed and breakfasts (check with VVV).
Hotel Klarenbeek, Johan de Wittestraat 35. Phone 078 614 41 33. Dfl 110 Dbl.
 Near station.
Hotel Dordrecht, Achterbakkers 12. Phone 078 613 60 11. Near harbor area.
Youth Hostel De Hollandse Biesbosch, Baanhoekweg 25. Phone 078 621 21 67.
 Eight kilometers from center on the edge of Biesbosch Recreation Area.
 Also, part of the building is a budget hotel.
Camping De Hollandse Biesbosch, Baanhoekweg 25. Phone 078 621 21 67.
 Next door to youth hostel.
Camping De Kleine Rug, Losalweg 1. Phone 078 616 35 55. Plan ahead and book

here. You will need to take a private ferry, which runs on demand to the sand spit where this tiny campground is located. Seven kilometers from town.
Camping 't Vissertje, Losalweg 3. Phone 078 616 27 51. Alternative to De Kleine Rug. Nearby.

Bicycle Shops/Rentals
Dordrecht Railway Station. Phone 078 614 66 42.

Optional Side Trip: Rotterdam
Although our route does not lead you directly into Rotterdam, the city is easily accessible from this portion of the route. In fact, as you cycle toward the ferry across the River Lek to the Kinderdijk, you can see Rotterdam on your right just a short distance away. Should you decide to veer off the route, it is easy to follow the red and white bicycle signs into Rotterdam. Below is some basic information on the city.

Rotterdam is a large modern port city. Much of the city was destroyed during World War II. The modern buildings serve as a reminder of how cities in Europe suffered from bombing during this tragic war. Another monument to the bombing of 1940 is Ossip Zadkine's 1953 monument *City Destroyed*, the statue of a man screaming with his arms outstretched expressing pain at the bombing.

The statue is behind the Maritiem Museum (closed Monday), which has a collection of memorabilia related to sailing—paintings, models, and masts. While in the area, visit Schielandshuis at 31 Korte Hoogstraat. This museum is dedicated to the history of Rotterdam with paintings, sculptures, and artifacts (closed Monday). Another museum is Museum Bogmans-van Bogningen at Museumpark 18-20 which has artwork, including works by Rubens, Van Gogh, and Magritte.

The VVV is located at Coolingsel 67, phone 06 340 34 065, across from Stadhuis, and they can provide accommodation advice. It is also possible to visit Rotterdam as a day trip from Delft, Gouda, or Dordrecht as it is not much more than 17 kilometers from each of these towns. There is a bicycle shop at the railway station.

Dordrecht to Breda: 33 Kilometers

From the VVV, leave in the direction of the Centraal Station and turn right at the street in front of the station, taking the fietspad along the road for 1 kilometer to a T-intersection. Cross the road and take a left onto the fietspad, going under the big railroad bridge. Continue straight following directional signs for Moerdijk and Breda. You are following the A16 but on a service road set apart from the freeway, so the cycling is still pleasant.

At 11.7 kilometers, you will come to the bridge over the Hollands Diep. The bridge is almost exactly 1 kilometer long. Continue over the bridge, and in approximately 3 kilometers you will turn left, using an underpass under the

A16. Approximately 600 meters farther on you will turn right, following another bicycle sign for Breda. The next couple of kilometers you will follow along next to the main road.

Once you pass through the town of Zevenbergschen-Hoek, you will get away from the freeway onto smaller roads. Continue on, following signs to Breda, going through the town of Terheijden. You'll pass by a windmill that is open to visit but only on Friday 2 P.M.–5 P.M. and Saturday 10 A.M.–4 P.M. and irregularly at other times. You can stop if you like as you literally cycle just a few feet from it on the road. You'll also pass the large church. Notice that as you are heading into southern Holland, there are more Catholic churches than in the north, which is predominantly Protestant.

Proceed on into Breda. You will go through an industrial area north of town. Continue straight, and take a right at the ring road to get to the VVV, which is next to the Centraal Station.

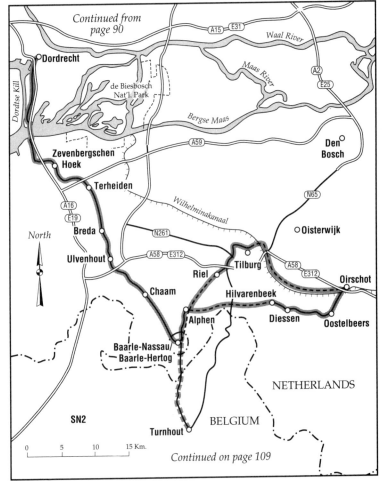

Continued on page 109

Breda at its best is the area from the old city center to the attractive sub-urbs to the south. The city itself is dotted with several parks such as the Burg Sonsbeeck Park to the south and Valkenburg Park, once part of the castle grounds, the northern limit of the old city. Alongside Valkenburg is the serene Begijnhof, dating back to the twelfth century with its houses grouped around its courtyard and medicinal herb garden. Within the park of Valkenburg is the imposing moated Kasteel (Castle) surrounded by fortified walls, part of which is Het Spanjaardsgat (Spanish Gate), consisting of two large impressive towers with onion-shaped domes. The Kasteel unfortunately cannot be visit-ed as today it is the Netherlands Military Academy.

The parks lend a relaxed feel to the city, but come the weekend or Car-nival (Mardi Gras), Breda is the party city of the province of North Brabant. The heart of Breda is the Grote Markt, market days being Tuesday and Friday. Around the Grote Markt and Havermarkt (Hay Market) is an abundance of restaurants, cafés, and bars adding a liveliness to the center. Also on the Grote Markt is the Stadhuis. In Het Lam, a fine seventeenth-century building at Grote Markt 19, is Breda's Museum, with exhibits of the city's history and re-ligious art (closed Monday). The Havermarkt is beside the Grote Kerk, an immense Gothic Brabant style church with a 97-meter (318-foot) onion-domed belfry with a 49-bell carillon. The interior contains the mausoleum of Count Engelbrecht II plus several other tombs of the Oranje-Nassau dynasty.

Tourist Information
VVV Breda, Willemstraat 17-19. Phone 076 522 24 44. Near station.
ANWB Office, Wilhelminapark 25. Phone 076 522 32 32. South part of Breda.

Accommodations
Even the VVV admits there is not much in the lower price range in Bre-da. There is one bed and breakfast.
Bed and Breakfast Graumans, Delpratsingel 14. Phone 076 521 62 71. Dfl 90 Dbl. Not the cheapest bed and breakfast but the cheapest lodging in town. Near the station.
Hotel De Klok, Grote Markt 26-28. Phone 076 521 40 82. Dfl 140 plus Dbl. Ide-al location.
Hotel Van Ham, Van Coothplein 23. Phone 076 521 52 29. Dfl 97.50 Dbl. South of center, 10–15 minutes by bicycle.
Hotel Donkers, Duivelsbruglaan 72. Phone 076 565 43 32. On southern edge of Breda, lovely area near Castle Bouvigne (see next stage of route).
Camping: There is no camping in the close vicinity of Breda. The closest campgrounds are in Ulvenhout and Oosterhout.
Camping Bosweelde, Geersbroekseweg 3, Ulvenhout. Phone 076 561 25 25. Eleven kilometers southwest of Breda (see next stage of route).
Camping Sint Hubertshoeve, Hondstraat 5, Oosterhout. Phone 0162 45 30 35. Seven kilometers northeast of Breda.

Bicycle Shops/Rentals
Breda Railway Station. Phone 076 521 05 01.

Breda to Baarle-Nassau/Baarle-Hertog: 25 Kilometers
Leave south along Ginnekenstraat, then Nieuw Ginnekenstraat. About 3.5 kilometers from the center, you will come to Ginnekenmarkt, a cute little trian-

gular area. Rows of neat brick and sandstone buildings are all along this road. It feels like a separate village, yet it is just the southern outskirts of Breda.

Take the time to make a short detour of less than 2 kilometers to Kasteel Bouvigne. The sight of this appealing castle is well worth a few minutes of riding. Go right and along Duivelsbruglaan for approximately 300 meters. Go left on Bouvigne Road. ANWB mushroom #24538 is located here. It is 0.5 kilometer to the castle, which is on the east side of the road. Built in 1612, it is a small, picturesque castle flanked by octagonal turrets and surrounded by a moat. You can visit the gardens only on weekdays.

Retrace your steps back the 800 meters to the Ginnekenmarkt. Leave to the south via Raadhuisstraat. Veer right as the street name changes to Ulvenhoutslaan, which you will follow to the town of Ulvenhout. After about 3 kilometers you will arrive in Ulvenhout. Continue straight through town. Just before the end of town, a few hundred meters past the windmill on your left, turn left into Chaamsweg, following the bicycle sign direction toward Chaam and Baarle-Nassau.

In approximately 1 kilometer, watch for a bicycle sign indicating a right turn. Cross the road and turn left, following the red and white bicycle sign. After about 4 kilometers there is a camping area, Camping Bosweelde (see Breda camping above).

Ride through the town of Chaam, where there is a youth hostel and lots of camping possibilities. Continue on to Baarle-Nassau/Baarle-Hertog, a very confused town.

Arriving in Baarle-Nassau/Baarle-Hertog, you are excused for not knowing which country you are in. You will begin to see Belgian flags and assume you have arrived in Belgium a little sooner than you anticipated. Dutch flags are still in evidence, and in fact, the VVV has both flags displayed. You will see both Dutch and Belgian banks, churches, post offices, and shops, yet you may notice that each country has its own town hall, police department, schools, and tax system. What confusion!

Baarle-Nassau is actually Dutch, while Baarle-Hertog is Belgian. It's not, however, as easy as being a divided town with a simple border between the two halves. In the twelfth century, the town was divided between the two countries, then over time parts were reabsorbed. Today, due to quirks of history, 21 Belgian enclaves are scattered haphazardly through what is otherwise a Dutch territory. To complicate it even further, several Dutch enclaves are located within the Belgian enclaves. The VVV has a sheet explaining the full history of the two Baarles, a "geographical curiosity." Not surprisingly, the communal symbol of the two towns is two interlocking puzzle pieces.

Wander around and look at the house numbers. On the same street you will notice the houses do not always have consecutive numbers. The numbers with the white center banded by red and blue are Dutch houses. Belgian house numbers are denoted by a small Belgian flag in the corner. As you walk down the same street, you are actually crossing borders several times. One house of particular interest is the house on Loveren Street with the numbers 2 (Belgian) and 19 (Dutch) where the border goes through the house. The family cooks in one country and sleeps in another. This is really borderless Europe!

While in town, you will be able to pay in either Dutch or Belgian currency.

Note: Phone numbers in Baarle-Nassau are local if you are calling from the Netherlands and the same for Baarle-Hertog if you are in Belgium. If you are in the other country, you will need to dial the country code. The country code for the Netherlands is 31, and Belgium is 32.

Tourist Information
VVV Baarle-Nassau/Hertog, Nieuwstraat 16, Baarle-Nassau. Phone 013 507 99 21.

Accommodations
There are three hotels (one in Baarle-Nassau, two in Baarle-Hertog) and one bed and breakfast (in Baarle-Hertog). A lot of campgrounds are in this area, mainly north of town in the Dutch area, as well as in Alphen and Ulicoten.
Hotel Den Engel, Singel 3. Phone 013 507 93 30. Dfl 180 Dbl. Expensive luxury right in the middle of town.
Hotel Het Kasteelje, Past de Katerstraat 3, Baarle-Hertog. Phone 014 69 92 97. Dfl 100 Dbl. A small castle-style hotel.
Hotel Den Bonten Os, Past de Katerstaat 23-25, Baarle-Hertog. Phone 014 69 90 16; Dfl 70 Dbl. Simple and basic.
Camping Rustoord, Bredasweg 12, Baarle-Nassau. Phone 013 507 90 72.
Camping De Heimolen, Heimolen 6, Baarle-Nassau. Phone 013 507 94 25.

Bicycle Shops/Rentals
Jansen-Oomen, Gen. Maczeklaan 13, Baarle-Nassau. Phone 013 507 92 28.

Baarle-Nassau/Baarle-Hertog to Turnhout: 14 Kilometers (Connection to Northern Belgium Route)

To continue south to Belgium, begin on the fietspad just opposite the VVV. There are bicycle signs to Turnhout. Just out of the "Baarles," you will leave Holland and enter Belgium. Then you will leave Belgium and enter Holland. After approximately 5 kilometers you will cross the final border into Belgium. There is no border check. In fact, the only way you will know you've reached the border is by the sign for the Hotel de Grens, meaning Border Hotel. Keep going straight. Several kilometers after the border, you will cross the N119. There is a fietspad along the road, but go straight ahead through the forest as it is more scenic, and it also goes to Turnhout.

The fietspad is the old railway line between Tilburg and Turnhout called the Bels Lijntje. It is a very pleasant fietspad, going through forest most of the time.

Baarle-Nassau/Baarle-Hertog to Oirschot: 44 Kilometers via Tilburg or 35 Kilometers via Hilvarenbeek

About a block west of the VVV, pick up the Bels Lijntje Route heading north (look for the red and white bicycle sign to Alphen right across the street from the Snackbar de Tourist). In 4.6 kilometers, just as you are entering the town of Alphen, take a right turn following the bicycle signs to Tilburg/Riel/Hilvarenbeek. About 300 meters farther on you will come to a small square. Here you will join the LF13a. There are signs for this route in two directions at this point, one in the direction of Tilburg and one in the direction of Hilvarenbeek and Poppel.

The simplest route to follow is to continue via Tilburg. This will continue on the Bels Lijntje all the way to Tilburg, where the LF13a signs will guide you through town. The route joins an experimental bicycle route through Tilburg from west to east where all cross traffic must give way to cyclists. You will pass the train station and the impressive Jezefkerk, a neo-Gothic church built in 1870. On the east end of Tilburg, you will come to the Wilhelminakanaal. Cross the bridge and turn right. You will follow the canal from Tilburg all the way to Oirschot, which is 18 kilometers away. Just outside Tilburg, after you ride under the freeway viaduct, you will come to a smaller bridge called the Trappistenbrug. At this point you can turn off the route to the left if you wish to visit the Trappist monastery Koningshoeve, located about 700 meters down the road. Established in 1893 by monks fleeing France, today it is the only monastery in the Netherlands brewing a traditional Trappist beer. A couple kilometers farther on you will cross a bridge and continue on the south side of the canal through the villages of Biest-Houtakker and Haghorst, both offering only cafés for refreshments. A couple kilometers past Haghorst you will again cross the canal and enter the town of Oirschot.

The alternate route via Hilvarenbeek takes you due east from Alphen through rural areas. It does require a substantial amount of riding on dirt roads and is a little more complicated than the route via Tilburg. If you would like to avoid the city of Tilburg, turn right in Alphen. In 1 kilometer you will take a left after seeing signs for LF35a and Hilvarenbeek. In half a kilometer the road forks. You will veer left. ANWB mushroom #24702 indicates the way to Hilvarenbeek at this point. About 2 kilometers farther you will turn left onto a paved fietspad along a dirt road, again with an ANWB mushroom (#24701) indicating the direction to Hilvarenbeek. About 2.8 kilometers farther, you will turn right onto a dirt road at mushroom #24700. Continue 1.4 kilometers until you come to a paved road. Cross the road and turn left onto the fietspad at ANWB mushroom #21308 in the direction of Goirle, Tilburg, and Hilvarenbeek. Then, in just 30 meters or so, you will take another right turn in the direction of Gorp, Hilvarenbeek, and Rovert at ANWB mushroom #21309. This takes you back onto a well-maintained dirt road through some lovely forested land. At the T-intersection 2 kilometers farther on, you will take a left at ANWB mushroom #21310, then veer right after about 400 meters. Here the road becomes paved again. You will find ANWB mushroom #21311 in the direction of Hilvarenbeek. Just past this point, notice the impressive turreted hunting lodge of De Licenhof.

As you approach the town of Hilvarenbeek, you will see the tall, ornate, double onion-domed steeple of the church long before you reach the town. The LF signs will help direct you to the center built around a brink (village green) dominated by the church, the fifteenth-century St. Petruskerk.

Continue past the church, and one block south, turn left, again following the LF13a route sign. This takes you out of town and in 2 kilometers to the town of Diessen. Ride straight through Diessen using the fietspad alongside the road all the way through Middelbeers and Oostelbeers, following the signs in the direction of Oirschot. About 4 kilometers out of Oostelbeers, the road crosses the A58/E312 freeway. Just beyond this overpass you will turn left into the center of Oirschot.

Oirschot is a small, quiet town with a most attractive square framed by shade trees and congenial cafés. The fifteenth-century St. Pieterskerk is the magnificent striped church dominating the town square. Across from it is the Stadhuis, built in 1463. Just off the main square is the Vrijthof. (Vrijthof is a regional term for a church square.) The small church on Oirschot's Vrijthof dates from the twelfth century. Originally built as a Catholic church, it was used as a Boterwaag (Butter Market) from the mid-1600s until 1800 when it became a Dutch reformed church. It is known today as the Boterkerkje (Little Butter Church). It was restored in 1961.

There are several old cloisters in the vicinity, a couple right in Oirschot. The VVV can direct you to them. Just as you approach the town square, you can hardly miss the giant chair on the corner of Rijkesluisstraat and Gasthuisstraat. This chair (the biggest in Europe) represents the furniture industry of Oirschot. Hoist yourself up into it and take a photo; you'll feel like you are from Lilliput. There are also two small museums in town, De Vier Quartieren at Sint Odulpusstraat 11, which focuses on life in Brabant province, and Hand en Span on Rijkesluisstraat 65, which details the history of farming.

Tourist Information
VVV Oirschot, Torenstraat 2. Phone 0499 57 29 70.

Accommodations
Hotel De Kroon, Rijkesluisstraat 6. Phone 0499 57 10 95. Dfl 125 Dbl. Center of town.
Pension 't Merelnest, Spoordonksweg 11. Phone 0499 57 17 71. Dfl 80 Dbl. Two-minute ride from center. Friendly family, residential setting.
Camping De Bocht, Oude Grintweg 69. Phone 0499 57 19 43.
Camping Latour, Bloemendaal 7. Phone 0499 57 56 25.

Where to Eat
There are several restaurants and cafés in Oirschot. Try the local dessert specialty *oirschotse muts*, a type of apple pie. An especially good slice can be found at Eetcafé De Oude Smidse at Rijkesluisstraat 3, where good meals at reasonable prices are also served.

Bicycle Shops/Rentals
R. van Overdijk Tweewielers, Spoordonkweg 91. Phone 0499 57 29 59.
Smetsers Oirschot, Spoordonkweg 28. Phone 0499 57 12 31.

Oirschot to Asten: 41 Kilometers

Leave to the east on the main street. Continue straight through the roundabout. About 1 kilometer from the center of town, veer right to the canal where you will take a left and follow the lovely fietspad along the canal shaded by lots of trees. The fietspad skirts the town of Best, but you can turn off the fietspad and go into town to visit the Klompen (wooden shoes) Museum at Broekdijk 14 (open daily April through October). The easiest access is when you cross the main road 6.8 kilometers from Oirschot.

A red and white bicycle sign directs you to the center of Best.

Otherwise, continue straight ahead along the canal. In about 3 kilometers the fietspad forks. Cross the road, but do not continue across the bridge. Continue along the road in the direction of the twin towns of Son en Breugel. This takes you away from the canal for about 2 kilometers. There you will veer right at ANWB mushroom #22670 and head back to the canal for about 50 meters on a dirt road. Another mushroom tells you to veer left onto a paved fietspad along the canal. In just under 3 kilometers you will come to a large bridge over the canal. The path along the canal does not go under this bridge.

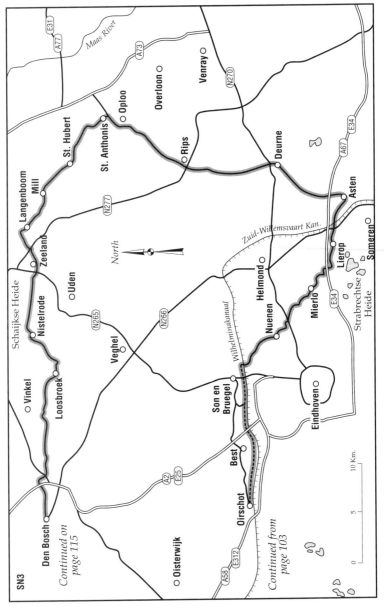

In order to continue, you are forced to make a somewhat complicated maneuver. Follow the path up to bridge level and turn right, crossing the bridge.
Continue straight for a block until you reach the traffic lights. Cross from the
west side of the road to the east side and ride back on this side of the road to
the canal. Cross the same bridge and turn right, rejoining the canal. Continue
another 1.2 kilometers along the canal where you will come to a bridge across
the canal. Cross the bridge, leaving the LF route, and ride south on the tree-
lined road toward Nuenen. In about 4.5 kilometers you will veer right into the
town of Nuenen. On the other side of the road is a lovely old windmill.

Nuenen, like the Van Gogh Museum and Kröller-Müller Museum, is a
mecca for lovers of van Gogh. Van Gogh lived and worked in Nuenen from
1883 to 1885, and here he did his first paintings of peasant life, one of which is
the famous *Potato Eaters*. There are many van Gogh landmarks, tributes and
scenes from his paintings to be visited in the town and environs. A self-guided
brochure is available (easily followed by bicycle or foot) to places in Nuenen associated with van Gogh, many of which have hardly changed over the years. It
is available from the Van Gogh Documentation Center, Papenvoort 15, where
photos, works, and reproductions from the artist's Nuenen period can be
viewed (open weekdays only; if it is closed, try the Gemeentehuis next door).

The first van Gogh landmark you come to is 700 meters from the last turn
you made to enter town. You will come to a small village square with a huge
linden tree, a stone monument to Vincent, and a large pump that used to
serve as the town's water pump. A little farther on you will come to a larger
park-like square with a pond, gazebo, and a statue of van Gogh. Next to this
park is a large church, and next to that is the house where van Gogh had his
studio. Other points of interest are van Gogh's parental house, the tiny old
church where his father was the vicar (recognizable from a well-known van
Gogh painting), the location of the *Potato Eaters* house, and lots more.

From the main square follow bicycle signs in the direction of Helmond
and Mierlo. This takes you through the new part of Nuenen. The route splits
about a kilometer out of town. Follow the signs to Mierlo, which involve a
right turn then an immediate left and another right in a couple of hundred
meters, bringing you back to the LF13a. You will cross the A270 freeway
shortly after the fork, then cross railway tracks after about 1 kilometer. Continue on to Mierlo (which is 6 kilometers from Nuenen) following LF13a route
signs that take you along small farm roads.

Go through Mierlo still following LF13a route signs. You will go past the
church and out of town in the direction of Lierop. Five hundred meters out of
town, veer left at ANWB mushroom #20683. In 1.5 kilometers, veer left at
ANWB mushroom #20768. In another 400 meters, you will veer left again at
ANWB mushroom #20809 in the direction of Lierop and Asten, staying on the
main road. At this point there is also a Kempen route sign. In approximately
100 meters, you reach an overpass and cross the big A67/E34 freeway. In
about 3 kilometers you come to Lierop, a small town with a mammoth
church. The church has a unique domed roof and beautiful brickwork. Take a
few minutes to admire it from all sides. The LF13a signs again lead you
through town, past the church, to the left one block farther, and out of town
in the direction of Asten.

One and a half kilometers past the church you will come to the N266 highway and the Zuid-Willemsvaart Kanaal. You will cross both. Note the locks in
the canal. Continue east. A fietspad starts along the road just after the bridge. In

2 kilometers the LF13a turns left. Ignore this turn and go straight into Asten.

Asten is a pleasant but ordinary town. Other than as an overnight point (in Asten, Someren, or Deurne), the main reason to stop in Asten is to visit the Nationaal Beiaardmuseum and Natuurhistorisch Museum de Peel. The first of these two museums is a Carillon Museum, devoted to the history of chimes and bells, plus it has a clock collection. The second museum focuses on the natural area of the Groote Peel just 8 kilometers southeast of Asten. It focuses on the history of the area and on the flora and fauna. The Groote Peel Nature Reserve is an area of woodland, heath, lakes, and swamps that are ideal for several species of birds. The area has both hiking and cycling possibilities.

Optional Side Trip: Groote Peel
Minimum of 13 Kilometers

If you're interested in birds, marshes, or natural areas or in taking a hike, consider this small side trip to De Groote Peel, a designated natural area. Turning off the main road and riding a loop around the area will be anywhere from 13 to 20 kilometers. Or you can just turn off at the sign to De Groote Peel, ride in a few kilometers, and turn around at anytime.

Follow signs to Heusden along Heesakkerstraat, then take a right on Meijerstraat. Don't take the N279 all the way from Asten, but instead take the quieter backroad through a rural farming area on which the small farm town of Heusden lies. Keep going along this road, and soon you will be on the northern edge of De Groote Peel. Eight and two-tenths kilometers south of Asten, you will join the larger N279, heading south toward Meijel (Meyel on Michelin map), where you will ride alongside the road on a fietspad. You can head to De Groote Peel shortly after Heusden, but soon after arriving at the N279, you are actually riding through the north tip of the reserve. Meijel is 14 kilometers south of Asten and is the town on the eastern edge of De Groote Peel. There are hotels and several campgrounds in the vicinity of Meijel.

Practical information for this area is given for Asten/Someren/ Deurne, which are within a few kilometers of each other.

Tourist Information
VVV Asten, in bookshop Henk Berkers, Burg Wijnenstraat 15, Asten. Phone 0493 69 29 99.
VVV Deurne, in bookshop Hub Berkers, Stationstraat 42, Deurne. Phone 0493 31 58 13.

Accommodations
Asten has a large motel on the main road and one pension where the owner is not too friendly. Someren has a couple of hotels, and Deurne has five hotels and a pension.
Guesthouse Zeuve Meeren, Wilhelminaplein 14, Someren. Phone 0493 49 27 28. Dfl 120 Dbl.
Hotel Centraal, Wilhelminaplein 3, Someren. Phone 0493 49 48 15. Dfl 115 Dbl.
Hotel Stationszicht, Spoorlaan 21, Deurne. Phone 0493 31 29 55. Dfl 90 Dbl.
Pension Rodts, Stationsstraat 45, Deurne. Phone 0493 31 47 70. Dfl 70 Dbl.
There are several campgrounds in the area of Asten.
Camping De Peel, Belhap 13, Asten-Heusden. Phone 0493 69 32 22. Small campground near Heusden.
Camping Kranenven, Kranenvenweg 10, Asten-Ommel. Phone 0493 69 24 88.

Camping Oostappen, Kranenvenweg 23, Asten-Ommel. Phone 0493 69 14 33.
Many more campgrounds can be found around the area of De Groote Peel.
Listings available from VVV Meijel, Dorpstraat 7. Phone 077 466 32 73.

Bicycle Shops/Rentals
Tweewielers Wim van Veghel, Burg Wijnenstraat 21, Asten. Phone 0493 69
    13 55.
Theo Verstappen, Emmastraat 57-59, Asten. Phone 0493 69 14 83.
Manders Rijwielhandel, Deurne Railway Station, Stationsstraat 108. Phone
    0493 31 23 54.

Asten to Den Bosch: 75 Kilometers

Note: This is a long stretch, but the riding is easy, taking you through rural farmlands and some pretty forest areas. Plenty of camping en route, but the
towns are small, and there is not much lodging except for a bed and breakfast
in the town of Zeeland.

Leave Asten heading north in the direction of Deurne. Just after the outskirts of Asten you will cross the A67/E34 freeway. Continue along the fietspad the 7 kilometers into Deurne. Go through town continuing north in the
direction of Rips and Oploo. There is a fietspad the entire way to Oploo. After leaving Deurne you will ride through a pleasant "green" area, the Neder-
heide. Soon you cross the N277. Blink and you'll miss the tiny village of Rips.
Continue on for 8 kilometers until you reach Oploo, staying on the same fietspad until you reach the N272. At the N272, turn right and cycle a couple of
kilometers into St. Anthonis.

St. Anthonis is a pleasant little town with a large forest, Boswachterij St.
Anthonis, fringing the west side of town. It offers lots of hiking and recreational activities. There are several campgrounds around St. Anthonis.

St. Anthonis Camping Information
Camping de Ullingse Bergen, Bosweg 36. Phone 0485 38 17 00. At 1.5 kilome-
    ters from St. Anthonis. Large campground.
Camping Vlagberg, Bosweg 42. Phone 0485 38 27 63. Two kilometers from St.
    Anthonis. Small, basic campground in wooded area. Part of Natuur-
    camping system.
Recreatiecentrum De Breyenburg, Beckerstraat 56A, Ledeacker. Phone 0485
    38 15 75. Approximately 1.5 kilometers northwest of St. Anthonis in an
    adjoining village. Camping plus lots of recreational activities.

Continue straight on through town on the road to Wanroij. You will pass
through the adjoining village of Ledaeker after just 1 kilometer and reach
Wanroij in 6 kilometers with a fietspad all the way. You'll pass a windmill just
before town. There is another campground here.

Continue on to the town of Mill, 3.7 kilometers farther. Turn left on
Hoogstraat (look for the sign to the VVV). Go straight through the roundabout, following signs to Langenboom and Zeeland. Just past the roundabout
is a lovely town park. Just past that on your right is a World War II tank and
plaque honoring the First Canadian armored regiment who fought here in
1944. In 4.5 kilometers you will reach Langenboom. Just past the town at the
T-intersection, turn left on the fietspad toward Zeeland.

In about 5 kilometers you will reach a roundabout as you enter the town of Zeeland. Turn right onto the continuation of Lanenboomsweg. In about 600 meters, turn left onto Kerkstraat; go past the church, then turn right onto Oude Molenstraat, where you'll see the old windmill. While in town you might want to stock up on picnic supplies as you will be entering a natural area in a few kilometers, an ideal place for picnics. Go to the end of Oude Molenstraat, turn right and immediately left again onto Tweehekkenweg, where you will cross the main road. As the road veers left, the name changes to Zevenhuis. You'll notice a horse farm on the left. About 100 meters past the horse farm, turn left onto Weversweg. A small sign at the intersection points left for the town of Nistelrode. This route will take you through the Schaijkse Heide, a park area of forest and grazing land. About 1.5 kilometers from this turnoff, the road ends for cars but continues through the park as a fietspad. Two and a half kilometers along the fietspad you will come to a picnic area with a map of the park. Take the time to explore some of the paths through the park if you like, or continue on. At 3.3 kilometers from the picnic area you will come to an intersection. Follow the paved road to the right, then in about 100 meters, left again. Both turns have signs to Nistelrode. Continue on and under the main road into town. At the T-intersection, follow the VVV sign to the left and on into town. The Nistelrode VVV is 8.4 kilometers from Zeeland.

Just past the VVV is a Y-intersection. Veer left toward Loosbroek. About 1 kilometer out of town turn right. Ride through a tunnel of shade trees and on to a roundabout. Veer right into Loosbroek which is 4 kilometers from Nistelrode. Continue through town. When you are 4.1 kilometers out of town, you will reach a Y. Veer right in the direction of Vinkel and Berlicum. At the next Y, veer left (do not go in the direction of Vinkel). At the next intersection, go straight through. The sign will point toward Rosmalen. Seven and seven-tenths kilometers out of Loosbroek a fietspad starts alongside the road. After 3 kilometers you will come to a main highway. Turn right for about a kilometer, and you will come to a big intersection. Cross with the bicycle traffic lights, then go left onto the fietspad along the highway. When you come to the information map, check your bearings. Then turn left by crossing the street and follow Graafseweg into the center of town. It is 1.5 kilometers from the information sign to the center of Den Bosch. Continue straight into town.

Den Bosch is officially known as 's-Hertogenbosch, which translates as "the Count's Forest." Centuries ago it was shortened to Den Bosch, the second word pronounced like the English "boss." The center of the town is designated almost entirely for foot traffic. Bicycles are allowed but must be wheeled occasionally. Life in Den Bosch centers around the triangular-shaped Markt where you find the VVV in "de Morian," the town's oldest building with its thirteenth-century crow-stepped gable, and the Stadhuis, a fifteenth-century building with a classic facade and a 35-bell carillon that chimes on the half hour. The cellar is now a restaurant. Market days (at the Markt) are Wednesday and Saturday mornings.

Head down Kerkstraat to St. Janskathedral (St. John's Cathedral) one of the most ornate Brabant gothic-style churches in the country. Building began in the fourteenth century, and it took nearly 200 years to complete. The church has a most impressive interior, including works by Den Bosch native Hieronymus Bosch, and the belfry has a 50-bell carillon. The exterior is elaborately decorated with statues. Next to the church is the Parade, a square that is the site of a general food market on Fridays. If you want to leave your bicycle to wander around the town, there is an attended fietsenstalling on the north side of St. Janskathedraal at approximately Dfl 0.75 per bicycle.

Behind the cathedral at Choorstraat 16 is the Slager Museum containing the works of three generations of the Slager family of Den Bosch. The Noordbrabants Museum is housed in the eighteenth-century former governor's mansion on Verwerstraat 41. The museum showcases the region's history, archaeological finds, paintings (including ones by van Gogh), sculptures, and more works by Hieronymous Bosch (closed Monday).

Look around for signs for *Bosshe Bollen*. These scrumptious chocolate-coated choux pastry balls filled with whipped cream are a specialty of the town. Treat yourself to one; you'll soon ride off the calories. They are available in many of the town's bakeries and cafés.

Tourist Information
VVV Den Bosch, Markt 77. Phone 073 12 30 71.
ANWB Office, Burg Loeffplein 11-13. Phone 073 614 53 54.

Accommodations
Hotel Terminus, Stationsplein 19. Phone 073 613 06 66. Dfl 80 Dbl. Near railway station.
Eurohotel, Hinthamerstraat 63-65. Phone 073 613 77 77. Dfl 120 Dbl. In center.
Camping: There is camping southwest of the city in Cromvoirt. This is approximately 8 kilometers from Den Bosch, and there are three campgrounds. Take Vughterstraat from the Markt, crossing the bridge into the suburb of Vught. Follow the signs toward Tilburg, then take the turnoff to Cromvoirt.
Camping De Vondst, Pepereind 13, Cromvoirt. Phone 0411 68 14 31. Large, overcrowded campground.
The other two campgrounds are on Louvensestraat at #7 and #11.

Bicycle Shops/Rentals
Den Bosch Railway Station, Stationsplein 22. Phone 073 613 47 37.
Cyclepoint, Hoek Zuid Willemsvaart, Hinterhamereinde. Phone 073 613 90 20. Bicycle shop.

Den Bosch to Zaltbommel: 37 Kilometers

To leave town, take Visstraat to the new station. Follow around to the right of the station and through the tunnel. Continue a couple blocks to Copernicusstraat and turn left past the college. At the end of the street, turn right. The fietspad to Vlijmen starts just after the BP service station. Watch for a small sign on the right side of the road pointing left. This is 2.4 kilometers from the VVV. In another 5 kilometers you will reach Vlijmen. Go across the bridge toward town (you'll see the church

steeples). Turn left on Grotekerkstraat. At the roundabout, veer right toward Haarsteeg on Akkerstraat. Follow the main street through Haarsteeg, arriving

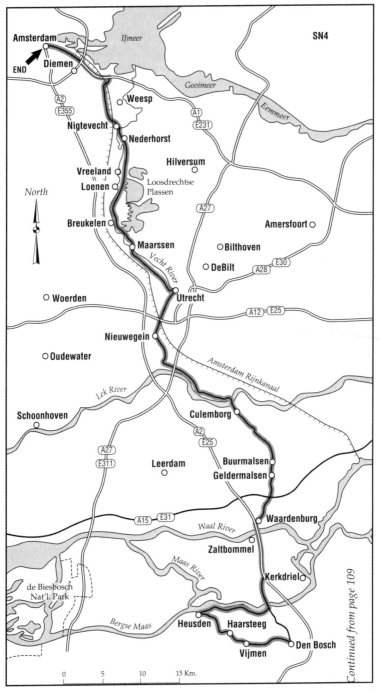

Continued from page 109

there just 2.5 kilometers past Vlijmen. One kilometer past the church turn right toward Heusden. In the tiny town of Herpt, go straight through the roundabout.

Heusden is a gorgeous, old, restored fortified town where it's possible to walk around the town's sixteenth-century star-shaped ramparts. There are no museums in Heusden, but the tiny town is like an outdoor museum. The architecture is mainly from the sixteenth and seventeenth century, houses complete with gables and attractive facades. The center is the Vismarkt (old fish market) framed by lovingly restored buildings, several of which are now restaurants, many specializing in fish. To complete the picture are the ubiquitous Stadhuis, a Gothic church, a pretty harbor, and, of course, canals and windmills.

The VVV is at Engstraat 4, adjacent to Vismarkt. There is one rather expensive hotel in town, a bed and breakfast in the adjoining village of Herpt, and camping in the nearby towns of Aalst and Wijk en Aalburg.

Leave town the way you came in, but turn left onto the dike in the direction of the large shipyard. You'll follow the small road past the shipyard, then turn onto a fietspad along the dike. It's a glorious ride as you are on top of the dike above the fields, the Maas River to your left. About 8 kilometers along, the fietspad takes you down off the dike into the village of Bokhoven.

Ride into Bokhoven, and when you reach the church, turn left, noting the old town wall and moat as you do. Follow along through the village, another one of those picture postcard towns where time has stood still. You will notice many thatched roof houses and detailed brick work.

Two kilometers past Bokhoven, turn left over a bridge just past the lock. Follow the road until you come to a highway, which you will cross, following signs that say *(Brom)fietsers richting Hedel*. This will take you across a large bridge over the Maas. Go north through town, following signs to Zaltbommel. You will follow along the A2/E25 freeway 7 kilometers to the town of Zaltbommel. At the big roundabout just out of town, go straight, continuing north, then through a smaller roundabout, again continuing straight ahead.

The small town of Zaltbommel is one of those surprising towns that seemingly no one has heard of. It is overlooked by guidebooks but has lots to offer the visitor. It is certainly a town full of ambiance, steeped in history with some remarkable buildings, but more than that, has had its share of illustrious figures tread upon its cobblestones.

In 1842, Franz Liszt, passing through Zaltbommel, heard the musical tones of the town's 35-bell carillon (east of the Markt and still chiming today). He then took the carillonneur's daughter to Paris where she met impressionist painter Edouard Manet. They returned to Zaltbommel and married in the fourteenth-century St. Martinuskerk with its gorgeous frescoed ceiling and imposing 63-meter- (207-foot-) high belfry. Also, Karl Marx visited his cousins, the Philips family, and spent the winter of 1863–1864 working on *Das Kapital* here. The Philips worked on the design for the first electric light bulb and went on to begin the now multinational Philips company.

Apart from the notables in the town's past, there is much to see. On the Markt is the Stadhuis dating from 1763, and across the Markt in the former eighteenth-century Waag is the VVV. The Markt is the scene for a lively market on Saturday morning. Also of note is the fourteenth-century Waterpoort (Water Tower) guarding the town along the River Waal. Walk along the banks of the river and around the town along the remaining ramparts. The beautifully facaded house, Huis van Maarten van Rossum, at Nonnenstraat 5 is home to the local museum (closed Monday).

Tourist Information
VVV Zaltbommel, Markt 10. Phone 0418 51 81 77.

Accommodations
Hotel Tivoli, Steenweg 2. Phone 0418 51 25 17. Dfl 90 Dbl. Only place to stay
  in town.
Hotel de Gouden Molen. Waaldijk 5, Rossum. Phone 0418 66 13 06. Dfl 100
  Dbl. Next town approximately 5 kilometers southeast.
Camping den Bol, Maasbandijk 1a, Kerkdriel. Phone 0418 63 19 63. The clos-
  est camping is approximately 10 kilometers southeast of Zaltbommel.
  Camping den Bol is on the peaceful harbor right in Kerkdriel and is a
  combination campground/marina.

Bicycle Shops/Rentals
Zaltbommel Railway Station. Phone 0418 51 42 54.

Zaltbommel to Utrecht: 44 Kilometers

Leave town on Waalbrandijk. Follow the ANWB signs for Grot Rivieren
Route. About 1 kilometer out of town you will see a huge bridge over the Waal
River. Take the path to the right up to the bridge level. Turn left across the
bridge. Follow the Utrecht signs through the small town of Waardenburg,
which you will hardly notice. On the highway out of town, notice the thatched
roof cottages and farmhouses on the canal that you will follow for several kilometers. Continue over the A15 motorway, using the overpass, and on into and
straight through the town of Geldermalsen. Following 1 kilometer later is the
village of Buurmalsen. You then have about 7 kilometers of straight, flat road
with fietspad before you come to the charming town of Culemborg.

To enter Culemborg, follow the road you are on straight into town. Do
not take the left turn at the roundabout with the sign to Utrecht; that is for
cars. Like Alice through the looking glass, you enter another world, this one
of centuries past, as you pass through the one remaining, and very impressive, town gate, Binnenpoort, and enter the medieval town center. The gorgeous town square is ringed with well-preserved old houses, crowned at the
far end by a stunning Gothic Stadhuis built in 1534.

Culemborg is 22 kilometers from Zaltbommel and can be considered as an
overnight stop if convenient. The VVV is at 't Jach 32 right by the post office,
phone 0345 53 12 52. There are two hotels, two campgrounds, and several
restaurants. There are two bicycle shops with rentals, one at the railway station,
phone 0345 51 37 08, the other Dokman, Zandstraat 70, phone 0345 51 35 07.

From the main square, continue a few blocks north where you will take
a small ferry across the Lek River (cost: Dfl 1 for adult with bicycle). On the
other side, turn left (Utrecht sign to the right is for cars). This is a great road
along the top of the dike for 12 kilometers. Go under the freeway viaduct and
then across the bridge at the locks. You will soon descend from the dike and
enter Nieuwegein, an industrial suburb of Utrecht. Stop at the information
map to get your bearings. Take the first right and go almost 2 kilometers. You
will see a bicycle route sign for Utrecht Centrum. Take a left there. Follow the
fietspad 4.5 kilometers until it ends. Continue on through residential suburbs
in the same direction to the center of Utrecht.

Utrecht is a bustling city, and its claim to fame is the atmosphere. Stroll
along canals with the unusual warehouses dating back to the thirteenth cen-

tury lining Oudegracht (Old Canal). Wind your way through streets with lovely old gabled houses. Much of the activity and the attractions of Utrecht are centered around Domplein. Utrecht is home to a large university.

The Domtoren (Dom Tower), located at Domplein, is the tallest tower (112 meters/367 feet) in the Netherlands. Climb the 465 steps for a magnificent view. If it's a clear day, they say you can see as far as Amsterdam. Adjacent to Domtoren is the Domkerk (Dom Church), begun in 1254 and completed approximately 250 years later. In the same vicinity is Pieterskerk, the oldest Romanesque church in the Netherlands, built in 1048.

Across the canal to the west is the Nationaal Museum van Speelkok tot Pierement (Mechanical Musical Museum), located in the Buurkerk at Buurkerkhof 10, displaying all sorts of musical instruments from the eighteenth to twentieth century, with everything from music boxes to street organs, musical clocks, and even musical chairs (closed Monday). A few blocks south on Nieuwe Gracht (New Canal) at #63 is the Rijksmuseum Het Catherijneconvent. The former convent is now a museum that documents the story of Christianity in the Netherlands; it contains the largest collection of medieval art in the country (closed Monday).

Utrecht has several other museums of note such as the Centraal Museum (paintings and exhibits), the Nederlands Spoorwegmuseum (Railway Museum), the Univeriteitsmuseum (interesting old instruments formerly used by members of the university), and the Museum voor het Kruideniersbedrijf (Grocery Museum, an old-fashioned grocery store). Some more buildings to seek out are the Stadhuis, some of the Cloisters, and the buildings along both Oude and Nieuwe Gracht.

Tourist Information
VVV Utrecht, Vredenburg 90 (at Hoog Catherijne Mall). Phone 06 340 340 85.
ANWB Office, Gildenkwartier 177. Phone 030 232 14 21.

Accommodations
It is not easy to find lower priced lodgings in Utrecht, and most of the reasonably priced hotels are on the outskirts. As an alternative DeBilt, 5 kilometers east, has a couple of bed and breakfasts as well as a campground.
Park Hotel, Tolsteegsingel 34. Phone 030 251 67 12. Dfl 90 Dbl.
Hotel Kay, Wittevrouvensingel 44. Phone 030 271 21 14. Dfl 110 Dbl.
Youth Hostel Bunnik, Rhijnauwenselaan 14. Phone 030 656 12 77. In Bunnik area. Seven kilometers southeast of center.
Camping de Berekuil, Arienslaan 5. Phone 030 271 38 70. Large complex situated in a lovely park 3 kilometers east.

Where to Eat
Utrecht is a cosmopolitan city with a variety of cuisine. There are many restaurants along the picturesque canal, Oudegracht. If you're craving Cajun food, stop for a bowl of gumbo at Mad Mick and Big Mamou (Oudekerkhof 29, phone 030 231 8004), probably the only Cajun restaurant in the Netherlands.

Bicycle Shops/Rentals
Utrecht Railway Station. Phone 030 31 11 59.

Utrecht to Amsterdam: 49 Kilometers

From the main station, follow bicycle signs to Maarssen. You will follow the large Amsterdam Rijnkanaal as far as Maarssen, about 6.5 kilometers. Continue straight in the direction of Breukelen. About 1 kilometer before Breukelen, notice the impressive castle on your left. It is not open to tourists, unfortunately. Go straight through Breukelen until you come to the bridge over the Vecht River. Cross the bridge and turn left.

The Vecht River will be on your left. Note the old stately homes lining the river on both sides as you head toward Nieuwersluis. Continue along the Vecht River to Loenen, then go on to Vreeland, always staying on the same side of the Vecht River. If you want to visit the towns of Nieuwersluis or Loenen, cross the bridges into town but return to the other side to continue. It is possible to continue on the other side, but you would then follow the main road rather than the river, and it is not as scenic or pleasant.

Continue on through Vreeland. When you come to Nederhorst den Burg, turn left into Brilhoek. There is a sign for the Nigtevecht ferry. If you come to the information map for Nederhorst, you've come one block too far. This road goes through fields back to the Vecht River. In about 2 kilometers you will see the town of Nigtevecht across the water. Take the tiny little ferry across to Nigtevecht. From the small ferry landing, you will take a path a few meters up to the road. Turn right in the direction of Weesp. Several red bicycle signs will guide you through the small town to the fietspad along the Amsterdam Rijnkanaal. Follow this north approximately 4 kilometers until you join the N236. You will recognize this by the large bridge that crosses the canal. Turn right just before the bridge, riding up the incline, then left onto and across the bridge, following the signs to Amsterdam and Diemen.

If you don't want to take the tiny, somewhat rickety looking Nigtevecht ferry, or if you arrive after 5:30 P.M. when it stops, you can continue along the same side of the river until you reach the N236. This adds about 3 kilometers to your trip. Either way, take the N236 in the direction of Diemen.

Here you'll start seeing signs for Amsterdam. Follow signs that say just Amsterdam (sometimes abbreviated as A'dam) or Amsterdam Centrum. Don't follow signs to Amsterdam Zuid (South) or any other direction. You will have designated bicycle lanes and great signage. Amsterdam will be the easiest big city you have ever negotiated on a bicycle. Once in the central area (Centrum) there will be signs to Centraal Station. There is an always crowded VVV at the station with maps, information, accommodation service, etc.

If this is the end of your trip and you want to head straight for the airport, there are signs to turn off for Schiphol at Diemen.

For practical information on Amsterdam, see Northern Netherlands Route.

Chapter 9

Route 3— Northern Belgium (Flanders) Route

Total Distance: 550 kilometers (341 miles)
Terrain: Flat, hills in the Flemish Ardennes and Limburg
Maps: Michelin Maps 212 and 213 (1:200,000), ANWB Maps—North Brabant, Zeeland, and Limburg (1:100,000); Geocart Maps—Brabant, Limburg, Antwerpen, Oost-Vlaanderen, and West-Vlaanderen (1:100,000)
Connecting Routes: Route 2—Southern Netherlands, Route 4—Southern Belgium

Northern Belgium is known as Flanders. This region is generally flat and crisscrossed with tree-lined canals. The area has its fair share of diversity, stretching from Belgium's 65 kilometers of coastline in the west to the gentle hills of Limburg in the east. While the south of Belgium claims the country's most beautiful scenery, the north maintains the cultural edge with Belgium's major cities: the capital Brussels (actually an autonomous area within Flanders), Antwerp, Gent, and Brugge. Add to this the inclines of the Flemish Ardennes to the southwest of Brussels and several other towns steeped in history, such as Oudenaarde and Tongeren, plus interesting museums and architecture in the major cities, and there is something for everyone in Flanders.

The people speak Flemish, a Dutch dialect, and in the larger cities English is widely spoken as a second language. Although this is the most populated part of Belgium, the bulk of the population is concentrated in the cities. It is not difficult to find pleasant cycling through farmlands and along the major water routes such as the Albert Canal and the River Schelde, where barge traffic still plays an important role in transport.

The Northern Route takes an elliptical shape as it circles Flanders. Much of the route follows the Vlaanderen Fietsroute. This is an earnest attempt by the Belgians to offer cyclists a scenic and less trafficked route around Flanders avoiding major roads. In order to do this the Vlaanderen Fietsroute uses a lot of backroads and skirts major cities. For the purposes of the route in this book, we have used the Vlaanderen Fietsroute in part but have tailored the route to take in the cities as well as other highlights not found on the very rural Vlaanderen Fietsroute.

An important thing to note about Flanders is that the quaint image of delightful old-world cobblestone roads becomes a tiresome reality to the cyclist. Rough cobblestones can make for tough cycling. But when weighing the options, putting up with cobblestones on quiet backroads is a small price to pay when the other option is busy roads with trucks and cars whizzing past. Road surfaces are also often not paved on the backroads and on some fietspads. Where the route is not paved, it is usually hard packed dirt or gravel and not difficult to deal with. It can, however, become quite muddy after heavy rains. If you are using a hybrid, mountain, or rented Belgian bicycle, you should not encounter any problems with the surface except the occasional bumpy ride. However, if you are using a road bicycle with narrow tires, study the route carefully and try to avoid those potential problem parts, mainly on the portion of the route between Geraardsbergen and Leuven (specific routes contain more details).

Brussels

Brussels (Brussel in Flemish/Bruxelles in French) is an autonomous region. It is the place where the Flemish and the Walloon cultures meet. Brussels falls into two linguistic categories. Officially, both Flemish and French are spoken here, a compromise by the government to keep everybody happy. All street names are in both Flemish and French, as are public signs.

Brussels is the capital of Belgium, and it also holds the honor of being the headquarters of the European Union and NATO. The city is an interesting

The market square in the center of Brugge.

mix of culture and history. It is a city of politics and bureaucrats, as well as home to some of the finest food in the world. It is a city of old and new, from the cobblestone streets and old world feel around the Grand'Place to newer areas with modern skyscrapers.

The centerpiece in this large sprawling city is the Grand'Place, fringed with ornate seventeenth-century buildings and the Gothic Hôtel de Ville (town hall). Both look like they are out of a storybook with their perfect gables and gilt edges. Make sure you visit the Grand'Place to see it lit up at night. In the summer months, take in the early morning flower market and the Sunday morning bird market. Every second even-numbered year in mid-August, the spectacular event Tapis de Fleurs occurs when the whole square is covered in a carpet of flowers. Also on the Grand'Place is Musée de la Ville de Bruxelles (City Museum), exhibiting the history of the city, maps and models of old Brussels, silverware, ceramics, artwork, and costumes worn by the Manneken Pis (open daily). Hint: It is inviting to sit at a café on the Grand'Place, but you'll pay more. Explore a little and go down a side street or two, and you will find ambiance and cheaper prices.

Everyone who visits Brussels feels the necessity to view the Manneken Pis, a fountain with a statue of a small (very small) boy urinating. (Note: *manneken* means little man in Flemish.) It is located a few blocks from the Grand'-Place at the corner of Rue Chêne and Rue de L'Etuve. Don't be surprised to see him dressed up, as Brussels' "oldest citizen" has a wardrobe.

Every European city has its selection of churches, and Brussels is no exception. Cathédrale de St. Michel, famous for its Gothic towers, stands high on the Truerenberg (Mount of Tears). Eglise Notre Dame de la Chapelle, in the interesting Marolles District, houses the tomb of artist Pieter Brueghel. And Eglise Notre Dame du Sablon is a flamboyant fourteenth-century Gothic Church on Place du Grand Sablon.

Brussels has an excellent array of museums, far too many to list. A selection includes the Musée d'Art Ancien (Museum of Ancient Art) on Place Royale with a fine collection of fifteenth- to nineteenth-century works by early Flemish masters such as Breughel the Elder, Van Eyck, and Rubens (closed Monday). The Musée d'Art Moderne (Museum of Modern Art) at Place Royale 1 houses nineteenth- and twentieth-century contemporary Belgian art, including works by Magritte and Ensor (closed Monday). The Musée Royaux d'Art et Histoire (Museum of Art and History) is located at the entrance of Parc du Cinquantenaire and displays ancient Roman, Greek, and Egyptian art (closed Monday).

Brussels has a few museums with unusual collections such as Musée de la Bande Dessinée (Belgian Comic Strip Museum) in Art Nouveau Waucquez Warehouse at 20 Rue des Sables. Here one finds originals of many famous Belgian comic strips, including *Tintin* comics (closed Monday). For fans of Art Nouveau, Musée Horta (Horta Museum) can be found in the Art Nouveau house of architect Victor Horta. There is a splendid display of his famous Art Nouveau style with its graceful curves enhanced by glass and iron. It is on Rue Américaine 25 in the St. Gilles area (closed Monday). Musée Instrumental (Museum of Musical Instruments) has over 6,000 instruments from the Bronze Age to the present in its collection (only a part is ever on display). It is located on Place du Petit Sablon at Rue de la Régence (closed Monday).

Brussels offers the visitor numerous other sights such as the elaborate Bourse, the Stock Exchange built in 1871; the Palais Royale (Royal Palace) at one end of the Parc de Bruxelles (open from end of July until end of September); and the Palais de la Nation at the other end of the park where the Belgian Parliament meets (closed Sunday). There are several other squares and quaint streets especially around the Ilot Sacré. If you are interested in flea markets, visit Place du Jeu de Balle (open daily from 7 A.M.). When hunger sets in, stroll down the Rue de Bouchers, the most famous "restaurant row" in Brussels.

Tourist Information
Tourist office specifically for Brussels. Hotel de Ville, Grand'Place. Phone 02 513 89 40.
Tourist information on the rest of Belgium. Regional Tourist Office, 63 Rue du Marché aux Herbes. Phone 02 504 03 90.

Brussels Airport
The airport is located in the suburb of Zaventem, 14 kilometers northeast of the city center. The best way to get you and your bicycle into Brussels is by train. Trains leave directly from the airport, going to Gare Centrale or Gare du Nord approximately every 20 minutes. One train per hour continues to Gare du Midi. You should purchase your tickets in advance at the booth in the terminal. The trip takes about 20 minutes.
As for cycling, we did not find a suitable and safe route to recommend.

Arriving and Departing by Train
This may be an odd section to include in a book on biking, but this is the one city of all those in this book that we would recommend not riding. If you choose to take the train in from a point close to Brussels, we suggest Leuven, but you may look at the map and find a location better suited to your needs.
The most important thing to know about arriving by train in Brussels is that there are three main stations, all with both Dutch and French names. Brussels Noord/Gare du Nord (north) has trains to Antwerp, Amsterdam, and the airport; Brussels Zuid/Gare du Midi (south) handles trains to the south and west such as Oostende and Paris. The other station is Centraal Station/Gare Centrale and is the closest to the Grand'Place. Most trains stop at all three stations.

Accommodations
As you would expect, Brussels has several hotels to choose from in all price ranges. Try to stay close to the city center between Gare du Nord and Gare Centrale.

Welcome Hotel, Rue du Peuplier 5. Phone 02 219 9546. BEF 3,200 Dbl. Tiny (six rooms) but charming.
Hotel Sabina, Rue du Nord 78. Phone 02 218 2637. BEF 2,400 Dbl. Near Metro Station Madou. Comfortable.
Hotel Pacific, Rue Antoine Dansaert 57. Phone 02 511 84 59. BEF 1,800–2,200 Dbl. Basic hotel in great location. Five minutes from Grand'Place.
Youth Hostel Brueghel, Rue de St. Espirit 2. Phone 02 511 0436. Closest hostel to Grand'Place.
Youth Hostel Jacques Brel, Rue de la Sablonnière 30. Phone 02 218 0187. About a 15-minute walk to Grand'Place.

Youth Hostel Jean Nihon, Rue de l'Eléphant 4. Phone 02 410 3905. About a 20-minute walk to Grand'Place.

Camping Paul Rosmant, 52 Warandeberg. Phone 02 782 10 09. In northeast Brussels suburb of Wezembeek. Not a convenient location as it is quite difficult to negotiate by bicycle through hectic Brussels traffic.

Where to Eat
Brussels is a feast. There is no lack of places to eat, just walk in any direction from the Grand'Place. Close to the Grand'Place it tends to be more touristy and expensive. Walk around and check menus. You will find a mix of both traditional and ethnic food throughout the city. Rue des Bouchers near Grand'Place provides an entire street of restaurants specializing in seafood, and there are plenty, seafood being a specialty of this landlocked city.

Markets
There are many markets throughout the city including Place Ste. Catherine (food/general, Mon.–Sat.), Place du Jeu de Balle (flea market, daily), and Grand Sablon (antiques, weekends).

Bookshop
WH Smith, 71-75 Blvd Adolphe Max. Phone 02 -219 -27 08.
FNAC, City 2 Shopping complex.

Bicycle Shops
Cycles Devos, 500 Kroonin. Phone 02 648 62 72. No rentals.

Getting to Leuven from Brussels
There are two ways to get from Brussels to Leuven. The easiest, and the way we recommend, is to put your bicycle on the train. There are two to three trains per hour from Brussels to Leuven, although only one train per hour allows bicycles. Check at the station to find out. You can depart from any of the three stations. The trip will take between 20 and 30 minutes. A bicycle needs its own ticket and registration prior to boarding.

If you choose to ride, we suggest leaving to the south through Zoniënwoud (Forêt de Soignées). See the Huizingen to Leuven stage of this chapter for details.

Leuven
Leuven (Louvain in French), home to Belgium's oldest and largest university dating from 1425, is very much a university town. This is reflected in the atmosphere with the "student" cafés and events around town, such as concerts, theater, and the like. Around the Oude Markt, a large and very lively square, many of the stately buildings, such as the Lakkenhalle (old Cloth Hall), are part of the university. Leuven is a city of cyclists, most being students using their bicycles for transport.

The Grote Markt centers around the flamboyant fifteenth-century Gothic Stadhuis, the facades having some of the most intricate sculpture you will ever see on a building (daily tours of interior). In front of the Stadhuis is the Font Sapienza, a humorous fountain of a student being literally brainwashed by the book he is reading. Across from the Stadhuis is St. Pieterskerk (St. Peter's Church), a fifteenth-century church with a collection of paintings by Dirk

Bouts including his famous Last Supper.

For a change of pace, go south down Naamsestraat and step into the tranquil surrounds of the Groot Begijnhof (Large Beguine Convent), a collection of brick and sandstone houses built in the seventeenth and eighteenth centuries for the Beguines (see appendix for more details). It is a peaceful setting, a "city within a city," with narrow cobbled streets, quaint houses, and lovely gardens. The whole area is extremely intact due to the restoration and constant maintenance by the university, which acquired the area and now uses it for student residences.

Leuven makes an excellent base for visiting Brussels. For information on the train, see above.

Tourist Information

Recently moved from Grote Markt to L. Vanderkelenstraat 30. Phone 016 21 15 39.

Accommodations

There is a cluster of reasonably priced hotels across from the station on Martelarenplein.

Hotel Industrie, Martelarenplein 7. Phone 016 22 13 49. BEF 1,400 Dbl. Pleasant hotel. Good value on daily menu at restaurant.
The two closest campgrounds are on the outskirts of Leuven, Kessel-Lo to the east and Heverlee to the south.
Camping Ter Munck, Campingweg, Heverlee. Phone 016 23 86 68.
Camping Schoolbergen, Sneppenstraat 58, Kessel-Lo. Phone 016 25 59 69.

Where to Eat

There are many trendy and well priced restaurants due to the student and faculty population. Tiensestraat, near the Grote Markt, is restaurant row with a good selection of cuisine. Several cafés are around the Grote Markt and Oude Markt.

Bicycle Shops/Rentals

Leuven Railway Station. Phone 016 21 23 27. This is the only place to rent bicycles in Leuven.
Huis Boydens, Diestestraat 205. Phone 016 22 12 20.

Leuven to Sint Truiden: 45 Kilometers

To leave Leuven, join the N2 just north of the railway station in the direction of Diest. This is a busy road, but you do have a fietspad alongside. Continue along the N2 for 10 kilometers, then turn right onto a smaller road and ride into the town of Lubeek about 2 kilometers off the highway. At the main intersection just before the church, turn left and head in an easterly di-

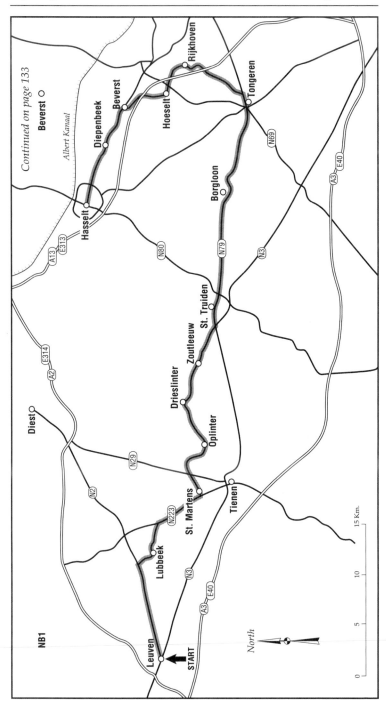

Continued on page 133

rection. About a kilometer out of town at the tiny village of Brakum, veer right at the fork, and in another 2 kilometers you will reach the N223. Turn right on the N223 in the direction of Tienen, using the two-way fietspad for about 5.5 kilometers.

Turn left on the small road to Sint Marten, just off the highway. Continue straight through Sint Marten, and proceed east for 2.5 kilometers to Bunsbeek, where you will veer left and cross the N29 highway. Just past the highway you will reach Boeslinter, where you will turn right in the direction of Oplinter, another 3.5 kilometers. In Oplinter, veer left in the direction of Budingen. Continue straight through the village of Neerlinter and on to the next village of Drieslinter, where you will turn right in the direction of Zoutleeuw. One and a half kilometers past Drieslinter the road forks. Veer left, again in the direction of Zoutleeuw.

As you approach Zoutleeuw, notice the spires and massive church tower in the distance, giving you the impression you are approaching a town much larger than it in fact is. Follow the road over the canal into town.

Zoutleeuw's prosperity during the Middle Ages was due to the cloth industry, which declined in the fifteenth century. Today, this tiny town is graced by buildings reflecting this glorious past. Not to be missed is the massive Gothic St. Leonarduskerk (St. Leonard's Church), built in the thirteenth century. The church contains a wealth of treasures—sculptures, paintings, statues, gold and silverware, and a huge 18-meter- (59-foot-) high stone tabernacle (open daily Easter through September 2–5 P.M., except Monday). Across from the Church on the Grote Markt is the sixteenth-century Renaissance Stadhuis where the tourist office is located. Next door is the striped brick and sandstone Lakenhalle (Cloth Hall) dating from the fourteenth century. Note some of the interesting facades, especially the "Mirror House" with its ornate gable also found on the Grote Markt.

Leave from the Grote Markt in the direction of Tienen. The road veers right. Follow the road for about 600 meters, and then take a left turn onto a fietspad marked with the green and white LF35a Kempenroute sign as well as a sign for the Yzerenweg. (This paved path is part of an unused railway track.) Follow this path for 3 kilometers until you come to a road on the outskirts of Wilderen. Take a left onto this road and follow it through town past the church and turn right in the direction of Sint Truiden. A fietspad on the side of the road leads 4 kilometers to Sint Truiden, where you follow the Centrum signs to the Grote Markt.

Sint Truiden is located in the center of the Haspengouw fruit-growing district. In spring, the approaches to the town are a mass of blossoming apple and cherry trees. The tourist office offers a couple of signposted "Fruit Blossom" cycling routes. Although these are especially appealing to ride in the spring, they are pleasant rides any time of the year. The tourist office is on the Grote Markt in the eighteenth-century Stadhuis, recognizable by its striped brick facade and elegant belfry.

Sint Truiden itself is based on a religious community begun by St. Trudo in 655, thus there is a predominance of religious architecture. The huge Benedictine Abbey is not far from the Grote Markt, and the Begijnhof's thirteenth-century church features murals dating from the thirteenth to seventeenth centuries. The Onze Lieve Vrouwekerk (Church of Our Lady) is on the Grote Markt, and St. Pieterskerk (St. Peter's Church) and St. Gangulfus Church are nearby.

Tourist Information
Stadhuis, Grote Markt. Phone 011 68 62 55.

Accommodations
There are four hotels in the area of Sint Truiden plus one bed and breakfast. The two lower priced hotels are just out of town in Brustem:

Hotel Cicindria, Abdijstraat 6. Phone 011 68 13 44. BEF 3,600 Dbl. Right in the center of Sint Truiden.
Hotel Hera, Vliegveldlaan 129, Brustem. Phone 011 67 35 29. BEF 1,900 Dbl.
Inter Hotel, Vliegveldlaan 3, Brustem. Phone 011 68 73 22. BEF 1,500 Dbl.
Camping De Egel, Bautershoven 95. Phone 011 68 76 37.

Where to Eat
There are several restaurants around the Grote Markt and throughout the town.

Bicycle Shops/Rentals
Bicycle rentals, April–October from the VVV.
Bers, Diesterstraat 19. Phone 011 68 20 16.

Sint Truiden to Tongeren: 24 Kilometers

Leave the Grote Markt on Luikerstraat, which turns into the N76 highway. You will have a good fietspad along the side of the road. This takes you in a fairly straight line to Borgloon, and on to Tongeren. There is a fairly long but relatively gentle incline approaching Borgloon 14.4 kilometers out of Sint Truiden. As you are climbing up toward the town, notice Kasteel Hulsberg on your right, an impressive old château, now a private residence. It is not open to the public, but you do get a good view as you ride past. As you approach Borgloon, you can either veer left and ride through the town itself or stay on the N76 and skirt it to the south. The total distance is roughly the same. About 5 kilometers past Borgloon the fietspad ends for about 3 kilometers. Continue along the highway using the shoulder, and you will pick up the fietspad again as you enter Tongeren. Continue straight on into the center.

This is the easiest and most direct route from Sint Truiden to Tongeren but not the most scenic. We suggest this route because it requires quite a detour into the surrounding countryside to avoid the main highway. If you have the time, though, it is rewarding to simply wander the smaller side roads in an easterly direction, passing through towns like Hoepertingen, Wellen, Kerniel, and Jesseren.

Tongeren's claim to fame is that it is the oldest town in Belgium. Its origins date back to the first century B.C. when it was set up as a camp by Caesar's lieutenants. Today it is a charming town with a lively center, and residents are proud of its rich past.

Heading for the Grote Markt, you will be struck by the massive Onze Lieve Vrouwebasiliek (Basilica of Our Lady). This magnificent Gothic basilica from the thirteenth century, with its subsequent additions, is like a museum. The Treasury houses an incredible selection of "treasures," and there are several pieces worth noting in the church itself. The statue in the Grote Markt is of Ambiorix, said to be the victor over Caesar's army. Also on the Grote Markt is the Stadhuis in which the tourist office and the Stedilijk Museum (Municipal Museum) are found (open daily).

Other points of interest are the Begijnhof, a peaceful area in the southeast of town, and the Moerenpoort, the fourteenth-century town gate, now a military museum. Another museum of note is the Provinciaal Gallo-Romeins Museum at Kielenstraat 15, displaying objects found in the excavations of the Limburg region dating to prehistoric and Roman times (open daily). Not to be missed is the Sunday morning antique and flea market, one of the most well-known in Belgium (between Leopoldwal and Veemarkt).

Tourist Information
Stadhuisplein 9. Phone 012 39 02 55.

Accommodations
Hotel Chemin de Fer, Stationslaan 44. Phone 012 23 31 05. BEF 1,100 Dbl. Cheapest in town.
Hotel Lido, Grote Markt 19. Phone 012 23 19 48. BEF 2,300 Dbl. In the center on the market square.
Youth Hostel Begijnhof, Sint Ursulastraat 1. Phone 012 39 13 70. In the area of the Begijnhof. Renovated historic building.
Camping Pliniusbron, Fonteindreef 3. Phone 012 23 16 07.

Where to Eat
Plenty of restaurants and cafés throughout the city.

Bicycle Shops/Rentals
Claessens Jos, Hasseltsesteenweg 94. Phone 012 23 05 70. Bicycle shop, no rentals.
Baillien, Hasseltsestraat 28. Phone 012 23 17 11. Bicycle shop, no rentals.
Bicycle rentals available from the youth hostel.

Optional Side Trip: Exploring Two Limburgs

This trip utilizes the superb network of bicycle paths recently introduced in the eastern region of Belgian Limburg. It also takes you to the edges of Dutch Limburg. This unique Belgian cycling program has several hundred kilometers of immaculate, brand-new fietspads, crisscrossing the province. Pick up the brochure "Fietsen in Limburg" at the VVV in Tongeren or Hasselt and use the map in the center pages to supplement our suggested route. The route system is set up using a series of numbered points (*knooppunts*) marking every route junction in the network. Signposts indicate not only the points themselves but the directions to all nearby points. It is a great system once you have it figured out. The only drawback is that it is difficult to use without a map. Although map boards are strategically placed along the way, it is important to pick up the

Clearly marked bicycle signs direct you through the network of bicycle paths in Belgian Limburg. This is Knooppunt #44 (Junction 44).

brochure and map and have it with you at all times. The paths wind their way through beautiful forests, along canals, and through the gently undulating hills and towns of Limburg.

Using the network you can follow the numbers to make your way to Lanaken, then directly across the Maas (Meuse) River to the cosmopolitan Dutch city of Maastricht with its Vrijthof, (elegant central square), impressive churches, and winding tunnels of casemates. Head back to Belgium and go north to Maaseik with its beautiful market square and historic buildings. Approximately 12 kilometers from Maaseik, cross the border and visit the pretty Dutch village of Thorn, known as the "white town" due to the predominant color of its houses and buildings.

Suggested Limburg Route

Begin by following the Tongeren to Hasselt route (below) as far as Alden Biesen, which is #68 on the network. From here go to #67, then #65, and on to Lanaken. If you wish to go to Maastricht, continue to #59, cross the bridge, and follow the signs approximately 5 kilometers into Maastricht. If you want to continue to Maaseik from #59, go to #58, #57, #56, #55, #48, #44, and #45 and on into Maaseik. For most of this you will be riding alongside the picturesque Zuid Willemsvaart Canal. To go to Thorn, leave Maaseik; go to #25, on to Kessenich, over the Dutch border, and into Thorn.

You can return using the same route in reverse or wind your way southwest to Hasselt, deciding on your own route. Some superb sections of fietspad through lovely forest lie between #45, #44, #43, #42, and #41. Also consider riding part of the way back to Hasselt along the Albert Kanaal rather than through the sprawling suburbs of Genk.

The route from Alden Biesen to Thorn is approximately 68 kilometers. Hotels are available in Maastricht, where there is also a youth hostel and camping. Maaseik and Thorn both have several hotels, with camping nearby.

Tongeren to Hasselt: 29 Kilometers

Start on the N79 in the direction of Maastricht. After the railroad underpass, take a left onto the N758 in the direction of Alden Biesen. Go under the A13/E313, then turn left onto a small road, again in the direction of Alden Biesen. Follow the main road as it winds through the town of Rijkhoven, and just after the town you will come to majestic Alden Biesen Castle. Stop in and wander around the moated fortification, built in the sixteenth and eighteenth centuries; visit the small museum and stroll through the grounds (open daily, museum closed Monday).

When you leave Alden Biesen, take the road just opposite the castle in the direction of Hoeselt. Cross over the freeway after about 1 kilometer, then the railway tracks after another kilometer. Take a left after the tracks. The road curves around to the right. At the traffic lights go straight across the intersection, direction Centrum. Take the first right after the lights, going past the church. In one block, just past the fire station (Brandweer Hoeselt), turn left onto Bruiloftstraat. At the T-intersection a block farther, take a left and then immediately right again onto Oude Nederbaan. Follow this 2 kilometers to the suburb of O. L. Vrouw. Continue straight past the church, where you will see a directional sign for Beverst. Cross over the A13 again shortly and continue 2.5 kilometers to the town of Beverst. Turn left there along the N2 in the direction of Hasselt. There is a fietspad along the side of the highway. Stay on the N2 through the center of Diepenbeek. One block past the church and Stadhuis turn right. There is a sign here for the railway station as well as a blue and white Kempen en Maasland fietsroute Netwerk sign at this turn. In about 200 meters you will cross the railway tracks, and in another 400 meters you will turn left onto a well-marked fietspad with bicycle signs for Hasselt.

This fietspad takes you away from the road and through lovely farmland and forest for 4 kilometers before you come to a Y in the path. Veer left, and about 500 meters farther on the path joins the N2 highway, although it remains separate from the road. Follow it another 2.5 kilometers into the center of Hasselt. On this stretch you will feel like you are riding on a mini bicycle freeway as the much-used path widens, with signs indicating turn-offs to various streets. You even have a bicycle roundabout. As you continue into town, always follow the directional signs for *andere richtingen* (other directions) until you go under the freeway just past the roundabout and see a sign for Centrum. Take this to the left. Shortly after this turn you will pass the entrance to the Japanese Gardens (sign reads *Ingang Japanse Tuin*). This is one of the largest Japanese gardens outside of Japan, created for Hasselt by its sister city of Itami, Japan, and worth a visit. Continue on, following *andere richtingen* and Centrum signs until you reach the Centrum.

Hasselt is the capital of Belgian Limburg and has a bustling town center. Its streets are lined with fashionable shops and boutiques radiating out from the Grote Markt. On the market square, notice the half timbered house on the corner called Het Zweert, "the sword," dating from 1639. Across the way is the thirteenth-century St. Quintiniuskathedraal (St. Quentin's Cathedral). Onze Lieve Vrouwekerk (Church of Our Lady) is the other prominent church in town. Visit the quiet Begijnhof a few hundred meters northeast of the Grote Markt.

Hasselt's selection of museums is varied. The most famous museum is the Nationaal Jenever (Gin) Museum at Witte Nonnenstraat 19; it is housed in the distillery which dates back to 1803. You can view the step-by-step process, collections of bottles, and advertising materials and taste the various gins (closed Monday). The Modemuseum (Fashion Museum) at Gasthuisstraat 11 illustrates the development of fashion and trends over the last two centuries (closed Monday). Some other museums include Stellingwerf-Waerdenhof Museum with a collection of decorative arts and Hasselt history and the Carillon museum at the top of St. Quintiniuskathedraal with a 42-bell carillon.

Out of town are two outdoor attractions, the Japanese Garden (see above), and 7 kilometers toward Genk, Bokrijk, a large open air museum with restored buildings and villages from all over Flanders, as well as a nature reserve plus theme gardens (open daily April–October).

Tourist Information
Lombaardstraat 3. Phone 011 23 95 40.

Accommodations
Hotel Pax, Grote Markt 16. Phone 011 22 38 75. BEF 2,000 Dbl. In center of town.
Hotel De Nieuwe Schoops, Stationsplein 7. Phone 011 22 31 88. BEF 1,600 Dbl. Cheapest in town. Near station.
Youth Hostel (closest located near Bokrijk; see above). De Roerdomp, Boekraklaan 30, Genk. Phone 089 35 62 20. Nine kilometers northeast of Hasselt.
Camping (closest camping in Zonhoven). Zwanenstraat 105. Phone 011 81 34 37. Eight kilometers north of Hasselt at Heideastrand.

Bicycle Shops/Rentals
Hasselt Railway Station. Phone 011 22 11 01.
Royal Nord, Guffenslaan 96. Phone 011 22 24 50.

Hasselt to Turnhout: 80 Kilometers

This is a long day, but the riding is easy; most of the route is alongside two canals on a *jaagpad* (tow path), and the entire route is flat. If this distance is too much, there are possibilities en route for accommodation or camping at Mol, Balen, Postel Abbey, or Beringen.

From the center of Hasselt, head north to Kolenkaai, a small boat harbor formed by an extension of the Albertkanaal. Note the large globe called "Global Watership" next to the canal. Join the bicycle path on the west side of the canal. It takes you through an underpass, and you will immediately turn right and head north as the fietspad follows alongside Slachthuiskaai until it joins up with the main Albertkanaal and veers left. Less than a kilometer after you join the main canal, just before you reach the next bridge, the fietspad forks, and you will veer right, crossing the road, and continue on the path along the canal itself.

Just past the town of Stokrooie, 6 kilometers from Hasselt, as you approach the bridge, veer left onto the fietspad along the side of the road up to the bridge. Cross the bridge and return to the canal down the cobblestone and concrete steps. There is a rough cobblestone groove on the right side of the stairs for bicycles to make it easier as the descent is rather steep. Once back alongside the canal, continue west again but now on the opposite side.

In about 4 kilometers you will lose the jaagpad for 2 kilometers but just continue on the road alongside until it veers away from the canal and the jaagpad starts up again. Rejoin it.

At 16.5 kilometers you will come to the town of Beringen off to your right. You can leave the canal and head into town for shops, restaurants, or hotels. Return the same way to the canal and continue.

After Beringen, the area gets very industrial for a while. The cycling along the jaagpad is good and very popular with local sport cyclists. About 8 kilometers after Beringen, the path veers right, leaving the Albertkanaal and heading north along the Dessel-Kwaadmechelenkanaal. You will pass several villages off to your right, but none of consequence until you reach Balen about 8 kilometers farther on. You will see the road leading from the canal straight into Balen if you wish to stop there.

About 5.5 kilometers past Balen the fietspad on this side of the canal ends. Veer right at this point onto the road. In 2 kilometers you will reach the N136. Head north on the N136 in the direction of Postel. One kilometer farther, turn left over a one lane bridge (with the traffic lights). One and two-tenths kilometers after the bridge a fietspad heads off to the right. Look for the Grenspark Route sign and a small white sign that says Abdij Postel fietspad. This takes you through farmland and fields away from the traffic until you rejoin the N136 in about 8 kilometers. If you're in a hurry, you can just

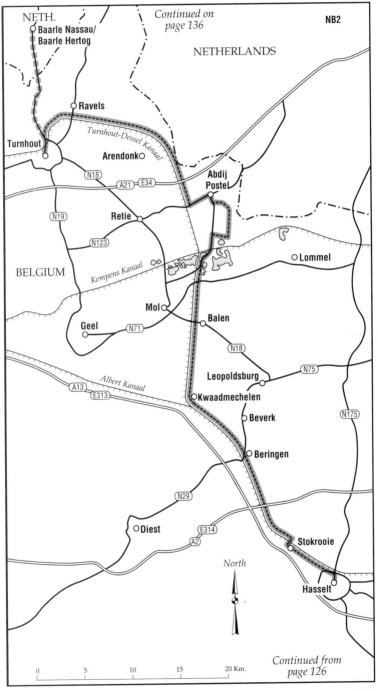

Continued on
page 136

Continued from
page 126

133

continue straight up the N136. It will cut a few kilometers off your route but is less pleasant.

Once you rejoin the N136, turn right, and in 1 kilometer you will come to Postel Abbey. You can wander around the grounds and visit the church built in 1190 as well as some of the other buildings. Stop for a meal or pick up some of the beer, cheese, bread, or smoked ham produced at the abbey.

After visiting the abbey, backtrack on the N136 for just a few meters and turn west on the road to Retie. In 3 kilometers you will come back to the canal. Turn right onto the path along the canal, which is beautiful at this point, lined with tall trees on both sides. Follow the canal as it veers left over the next several kilometers. You will cross the N12 just south of the town of Ravels, and then the canal veers left again, taking you under the big R13 freeway. Shortly after this you will come to a bridge that you will cross, heading into the town of Turnhout.

From the descriptions in the guidebooks (if they bother to include it, most do not), you wonder why anyone would consider visiting Turnhout. It is usually described as "typical of the industrial towns of the area." In fact, it is a surprise. It is a lively town centered around the Grote Markt with the giant St. Pieterskerk (St. Peter's Church) towering over the square. The church dates from the fifteenth and eighteenth centuries.

Just a few blocks north of the Grote Markt is the stately Kasteel (Castle). Originally built in the twelfth century as a hunting lodge for the Dukes of Brabant, it underwent some renovations in the seventeenth century. The best ambiance around the Kasteel can be found on Sunday mornings when a spirited flea market lines the area beside its moat.

A little farther north on Begijnstraat is the impressive Begijnhof (Beguine Convent), one of the finest and most intact in Belgium. You will enter through the huge gates (which, incidentally, are still closed each night at 10 P.M.). This Begijnhof is a large rectangle, 400 meters deep, with a church in the center and neat rows of houses along each side. There is even a small apple orchard with sheep and chickens within the walls. Notice the little alcoves above many doors adorned with religious objects and art. It is now used as an old people's home, and at the time of this writing one very old Begijn nun was still living there.

Visit the Nationaal Museum van de Speelkaart (Playing Card Museum) at Druivenstrat 18 in an old playing card factory. There is a collection of playing cards through the ages and card games from all around the world.

The forested area around Turnhout offers pleasant cycling, and the Antwerp-Turnhout Canal on which you cycle both into and out of Turnhout has some superb tree-lined stretches.

Tourist Information
Grote Markt 1. Phone 014 41 89 96.

Accommodations
Prices for the four hotels in Turnhout are surprisingly high for a small town. There is one bed and breakfast in town, but it is only available in the summer months. Ask at the tourist office.

Hotel Terminus, Grote Markt 72. Phone 014 41 87 57. BEF 2,500 Dbl. Right on Grote Markt. This is the cheapest in town. Also check out Astoria Hotel.
Camping Baalse Hei, Roodhuisstraat 10. Phone 014 42 19 31. A few kilometers

north of town. Follow the signs east off the Bels Lijntje (Old Railway Line Fietspad) between Turnhout and Baarle Nassau/Hertog.

Where to Eat
There are several restaurants to choose from, many on or near the Grote Markt. The Hotel Terminus has some good value meals.

Bicycle Shops/Rentals
Turnhout Railway Station. Phone 014 41 38 01. Bicycle rentals.
Vriens, Korte Gasthuisstaat 45. Phone 014 41 20 20. Bicycle shop, no rentals.

Connection to Southern Netherlands Route (see Chapter 8)

Turnhout to Antwerp: 50 Kilometers

From the main square, head north to the canal. Cross over the bridge and head west on the fietspad along the canal. This canal will take you all the way to Antwerp. Keep the canal on your left, and you can't get lost. The route is partially along *jaagpads*, the old tow paths along the canals, and partially on small roads along the canal. Some are nice quiet tree-lined paths and roads, although you do go through some industrial areas as well.

For the first part you will be following the LF5b Vlaanderen Route. Approximately 8 kilometers out of town you will pass along the edge of the tiny town of Rijkevorsel. At 21 kilometers you will pass along the edge of St. Lenaarts. If you go into town, there is a church, St. Leonarduskerk, with an impressive brick and sandstone steeple. The center of town is only about 500 meters from the canal.

After St. Lenaarts, notice the series of locks in the canal, one every few kilometers, which allow the boat traffic to change water levels along the canal. The jaagpad along the canal for this portion is excellent.

At 40 kilometers the canal you've been following enters a larger canal. The jaagpad continues, though veering right along the new, larger canal. At this point you are on the outskirts of Antwerp, one of the largest port cities in the world and the second largest city in Belgium. As you continue, you will enter a heavy industrial and shipping area. Follow the Steden Route signs. You will still follow along the canal, keeping it on your left. At some points you will have a jaagpad to follow; at other points you will be on the road alongside the canal. You will pass under a number of bridges across the canal. After you have passed under the second railway bridge, watch carefully for the next bridge. It is 6.6 kilometers after joining the large canal and is the bridge that will take you across the canal and into Antwerp. Once again, the Steden Route signs will be your guide. Just after passing under the bridge, you will see a route sign indicating a right turn. You will leave the canal. About 200 meters from the canal, you will make a U-turn onto the

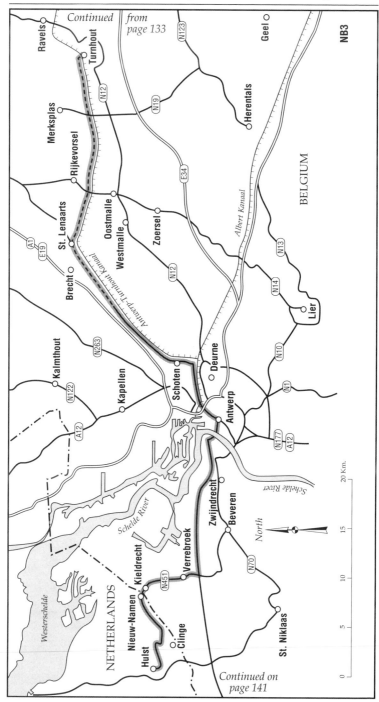

Continued from page 133

NB3

BELGIUM

NETHERLANDS

Continued on page 141

bridge and go over the bridge on the fietspad, still following the signs for the Steden Route.

The fietspad will take you all the way into the center of Antwerp. You will enter along Italienlei. The old center of town will be to your right, and the main train station to your left.

As is evident from your entry into Antwerp (Antwerpen in Flemish, Anvers in French), this city, on the Schelde River, is a huge port city. It is, in fact, the fifth largest port in the world. Once you leave the environs of the port, Antwerp takes on a different feel. It is a sophisticated, artistic, and very lively city. You may choose to cycle, but if you can discard your bicycle for a day or two, the center is better for walking than pedaling.

The hub of the city is the Grote Markt, surrounded by some of the most beautiful guild houses you'll ever see, each complete with a gold statue crowning the building indicating the trade of that particular guild. Here you will also find the ornately decorated Renaissance Stadhuis built between 1561 and 1565. The feature that truly dominates the Grote Markt is the fourteenth-century Gothic Kathedraal van Onze Lieve Vrouwe (Cathedral of Our Lady), the largest Gothic church in Belgium. This imposing building contains two paintings by Peter Paul Rubens, *The Raising of the Cross*, painted in 1610, and *The Descent from the Cross* from 1612 plus works by other artists from the fourteenth century to present (open daily, except during services).

The Meir is a wide pedestrian shopping street, lined with chic boutiques and department stores. This is essentially the main thoroughfare between the Grote Markt/Groenplats area and the Centraal Station.

Peter Paul Rubens made Antwerp his home, and the house where he spent a good portion of his life can be found just off the Meir at Wapper 9. Although his greatest works are in the Cathedral, in Rubenshuis you will find a self portrait, some of his private collection, along with works by some of his contemporaries (closed Monday).

Even if you are not interested in diamonds, any visitor to Antwerp should pay a visit to the Diamond District (near the railway station, which is an incredible piece of architecture itself) bearing in mind that more than half the world's diamonds are cut in Antwerp. Walk along Pelikaanstraat and the streets running off it to get a feel for the Diamond District. The Provinciaal Diamantmuseum (Diamond Museum) is at Lange Herentalestraat 31-33 (open daily with cutting and polishing demonstrations on Saturday afternoons).

One of our favorite streets in Europe is Cogels Osylei in the southeastern part of the city. This street of eclectic mansions is worth the detour. As you stroll down the street you will see an amazing assemblage of Art Nouveau, Art Deco, and neo-Renaissance houses that will leave you with your mouth wide open.

Antwerp has some fine museums. In the late 1500s the Plantin-Moretus Museum was originally a printing workshop. Today the Renaissance building at Vrijdagmarkt 22 houses many first editions, engravings, and manuscripts and is superbly decorated (closed Monday). A little farther out in the south of the city center is the Koninklijk Museum voor Schone Kunsten (Royal Museum for Fine Art) at Leopold de Waelplaats 1-9. Its 1,500 paintings display Rubens, Van Eycks, Hals, Brueghels, plus more Flemish masters (closed Monday). There are many more museums to explore in the city, but avoid Mondays when many attractions are closed.

Markets include the Vrijdagmarkt on Friday mornings for secondhand goods and the Vogelmarkt on Sunday mornings in the square a block south of Wapper.

Tourist Information
15 Grote Markt. Phone 03 232 01 03.

Accommodations
Hotels in Antwerp tend to be on the expensive side. Hotels are found either south of Grote Markt or near the train station, but some hotels too near the station are a bit seedy. The tourist office has a free brochure listing lodgings, not only in Antwerp City, but in the entire province. Some of the cheaper hotels are as follows:

Hotel Terminus. Franklin Rooseveltplaats 9. Phone 03 231 47 95. BEF 2,000–2,400 Dbl. Not far from the station.

Tourist Hotel, Pelikaanstaat 20. Phone 03 232 58 70. BEF 2,000–2,800. Large hotel close to station. Basic.

Pension Cammerpoorte, Steenhouwerstraat 55. Phone 03 231 28 36. BEF 2,700 Dbl. Small hotel in center.

Hotel Cammerpoorte, Nationalestraat 38-40. Phone 03 231 9736. BEF 2,400–3,200 Dbl. Economical hotel in heart of town. Same owners as Pension Cammerpoorte.

New International Youth Hotel. Provincestraat 256. Phone 03 230 05 22. BEF 1,500 Dbl.

Youth Hostel Op Sinjoorke. Eric Sasselaan 2. Phone 03 248 19 32.

Camping Vogelzang. Jan van Rijswijklaan on Vogelzanglaan. Phone 03 238 57 17.

Camping De Molen. Antwerpen-Strand, Thonetlaan, St. Annastrand. Phone 03 219 60 90.

Where to Eat
Antwerp has a great variety of restaurants, ranging in price from cheap to very high-priced. One of the best areas to look for restaurants is around the Grote Markt in almost every direction. You will find everything from traditional Belgian fare around the market square to an abundance of ethnic cuisine (at very reasonable prices) along a street called Oude Koornmarkt which runs off the Grote Markt.

Bicycle Shop
At the time of this writing there was nowhere to rent a bicycle in Antwerp.

Cycle Eddy. Dambruggestraat 351. Phone 03 231 1309. Bicycle shop only, no rentals.

Antwerp to Hulst: 35 Kilometers
Leave town using the St. Annatunnel, a pedestrian/bicycle tunnel under the river Schelde. The entrance to the tunnel is a couple blocks south of the Grote Markt, near the Plantin Moretus Museum. Pedestrians use escalators to get down to the level of the tunnel. Bicycles use the huge elevator in the middle of the entrance building. Press the button to call for the elevator, but once in the elevator it is controlled via closed circuit TV, so just get in the elevator and wait for the doors to close. The elevator will take you down to the start

of the long tunnel. It's fun to ride, even if it gives you a somewhat eerie feeling knowing the River Schelde is flowing along above your head.

At the far end of the tunnel, take the elevator up. As you exit, turn right. You'll notice a large sign for hikers, indicating part of the Grande Randonnée route system. Just beyond this, take a left onto Lode Zielenslaan. In about 600 meters turn right onto the fietspad running along the center nature strip of the boulevard. At the first intersection with traffic lights, Charles de Costerlaan, turn left and join the two-way fietspad along the right side of the road.

Pass the Antwerp city limits sign. It's a big, busy highway. You will notice lots of turnoffs to the *Haven* (Harbor). About 10 kilometers along the highway, you will need to cross over the road. Car signs indicate a turn here for Knokke-Heist and Zeebrugge. There is no bicycle sign to tell you to turn here, although you will notice a sign for cyclists coming the other direction, pointing them to Antwerp. The turn comes 1 kilometer before the R2 crosses the highway. This is a strange intersection. You will follow the two-way fietspad on the left side of the road as it takes you up an incline to an overpass. Turn right down an incline from the overpass. At the bottom of the ramp, turn right, doing a U-turn onto a service road, and you will finally see a bicycle sign to Zelzate. In approximately 2 kilometers you will come to another overpass. Turn left just before you go under this highway. If you continue straight, the road ends in approximately 200 meters. The left turn takes you around the big highway interchange, and you continue on in the same direction. An additional 3.5 kilometers and you will come to another highway crossing. You will want to turn here. The road veers left, taking you to the crossroad. Turn right. There is a Polderland Route sign indicating this turn. This takes you over the overpass, joining the N451. You will have a marked fietspad along the road.

In 2 kilometers you will reach the small town of Verrebroek. Continue on through, following the fietspad in the direction of Kieldrecht, which you will come to in another 4 kilometers. Continue through town until you see a sign telling you to turn left for Hulst. You will then see a series of signs to Nederland (Netherlands). Follow these until you unceremoniously cross the border into the Netherlands and the town of Nieuw-Namen. There you will see a sign for Hulst. Follow this, and in about 6 kilometers you will pass the town of Clinge. Turn right just as you enter Clinge, again following the signs to Hulst, which you will reach in 4 kilometers.

Hulst is an old fortified town with many of its seventeenth-century ramparts and bastions still intact. Head through the colorful streets to the center. The attractive Grote Markt is flanked by the sixteenth-century Stadhuis and the elegant Gothic church St. Willibrordusbasiliek. The church is unusual as it was shared by both Catholics and Protestants for over a century (1807–1931).

From the Grote Markt, follow Steenstraat past the church, following the blue signs for Axel. Steenstraat has some well-preserved step and gabled houses, as well as the Streeksmuseum at #28, a local museum. You can recognize this building by its beautiful tower (open daily May through mid-September). Continue on Steenstraat to the edge of town, where you can stop and climb up on the embankment that follows the moat surrounding the town. Take a walk and visit some of the ancient town gates, such as Gentsepoort and Dubbelepoort.

Tourist Information
VVV Hulst, Stadhuis, Grote Markt 21. Phone 0114 38 92 99.

Accommodations
Hotel de Korenbeurs, Grote Markt 10. Phone 0114 31 22 13. Dfl 130 Dbl. Center of town.
Hotel Hulst, v.d. Maelstedeweg 2. Phone 0114 31 05 31. Dfl 100 Dbl. Edge of town.
Hotel L'Aubergerie, v.d. Maelstedeweg 4. Phone 0114 31 98 301. Dfl 100 Dbl. Next door to Hotel Hulst.
Camping Den Hamer, 1e Verkorting 10, Axel. Phone 0115 56 14 22. Right off N258 a few kilometers before Axel.

Bicycle Shops/Rentals
JCS Bogaert, Dubbele Poort 1, Hulst. Phone 0114 31 21 85.
Klassen, Kerkdreef 18, Axel. Phone 0115 56 17 81.

Hulst to Brugge:
78 Kilometers

From Hulst, follow the blue directional signs for Axel. This will take you back out the way you came in, but you will veer right and head west as you reach the edge of town. You will have a fietspad along the N258. In about 12 kilometers you will come to the town of Axel. If you want to visit the town, turn right and cycle the 1 kilometer into the pleasant town. Otherwise, continue on.

Just under 4 kilometers from the Axel turnoff, you will cross the N253, and the fietspad ends. About 350 meters along the road, turn left into the town of Westdorpe, which claims to be the "longest village in the Netherlands." You'll see why as you follow the road into town for about 2.5 kilometers before you reach the center. This is a good example of what is called a "ribbon village" in the Netherlands, a small town that stretches out along a single main road.

Westdorpe has existed as a town since 1276, although the original site, north of the present location, was abandoned due to flooding. The houses of the present town are recent, at least by Dutch standards.

Continue straight all the way through town. Although you are heading for Sas van Gent, do not turn left in the center of town following the sign to Sas van Gent. That is for cars. You will continue all the way through on the same road. About 1.5 kilometers past the church, as you reach Kanaalweg, take the fietspad which veers off to the left. This takes you onto the bridge over the canal and immediately into the town of Sas van Gent. Turn left on Canadalaan, so named in honor of the Canadian 9th Infantry Division that liberated the town in September of 1944 (yes, that's all on the street sign). There is a small sign indicating the direction to the VVV. Follow Canadalaan to Stationstraat. Turn left and continue until you come to the main street along the canal.

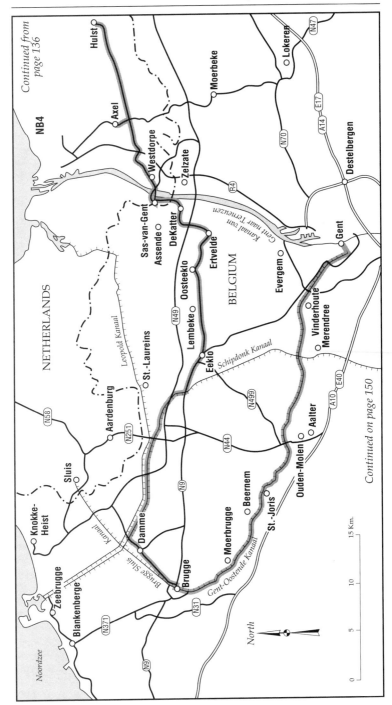

Continued from page 136

Continued on page 150

141

To explore the town, turn left, or turn right to continue the route. Follow the fietspad along the N253. Just out of town you will cross back into Belgium. With the border crossing you will lose your separated fietspad, but you will at least have a marked path along the highway. About 2.5 kilometers out of Sas van Gent you will veer right off of this highway, following signs to Centrum and Andere Richtingen. One and one-tenth kilometers farther on, turn right, following the car signs to Asseneda and Bassevelde and the bicycle sign in the direction of Brugge. This road, the N448, takes you through the village of De Katte and veers left, crossing the larger N49. Continue straight across to the town of Ertvelde, where the N448 meets the N458. You will turn right onto the continuation of the N448 in the direction of Eeklo.

In approximately 7 kilometers, the N448 joins the N456. Be sure to veer left, staying on the N448. Look for the signs to Eeklo.

In another 5 kilometers, you will reach the town of Eeklo. Note the beautiful building on your right just as you enter town. This is the psychiatric hospital Sint-Jan. Just past here you will veer right, joining the N9, following the sign to Brugge. A couple hundred meters farther you will come to the center of Eeklo, and on your right you will see the ornate Stadhuis, with the large St. Vincent Church behind it. The Stadhuis, the former sheriff's house, was built in the early 1700s and restored in 1932.

The VVV is a couple of streets back behind the Stadhuis hidden away on a small square next to the Jenever Museum. Should you wish to stay in Eeklo, there are a couple of hotels in the BEF 1,500–2,000 range per double.

The Jeneverhuis van Hoorebeke, or Jenever Museum, is in an old distillery next to the information office. *Jenever* is a distant relative of gin, and the museum takes you through the distilling process as well as the history of the van Hoorebeke family, brewers and distillers since the fifteenth century. Naturally, you receive a sample of the finished product at the end of the tour (closed Monday).

Just past Eeklo, veer right onto the N455 in the direction of Balgerhoeke and Knokke-Heist. There are bicycle route signs for the Kreker Route at this point. You will reach the town of Balgerhoeke quickly. Continue on through. Two kilometers from the turnoff you will come to the larger N49. Turn left along the N49 and take the bridge over the canal. At the first traffic light after the bridge, in about 2 kilometers, turn right in the direction of Sint-Laureins. In about 600 meters you will reach a canal. Cross the bridge over the canal and turn left onto the small road along the canal. You will notice the Café de Roos here as you turn.

There is a beautiful stretch of road for about 1 kilometer along the canal, then the road veers away from the canal, and you come to a Y. Veer left. When you come to the pub, the Populierenhof, turn right. In a couple hundred meters, turn left again. The road becomes a dirt road, which shortly joins a second canal. Follow this for about 1 kilometer until you come to a bridge. Turn right over the bridge, then immediately left onto the small road along this canal. You'll follow the canal for about 11 kilometers. This portion of the ride is the epitome of the picture perfect canal. It is lined with trees, and cows and sheep graze peacefully on the banks. At the third bridge after passing under the big N49, turn left. Soon you'll see the town of Damme across the fields to your right. The road will take you right into town, past the church and then the Stadhuis.

It is hard to believe today, but Damme was once the port for Brugge. Before the River Zwin silted up in the fifteenth century, Damme thrived as a port between the twelfth and fifteenth centuries with a population of 60,000. Today the quiet core of this medieval town of 10,000 remains centered around its market square with its elegant fifteenth-century Stadhuis and pretty gabled buildings. The statue in the center of the Markt is Damme native Jacob van Maerlant, a thirteenth-century poet. The Tourist office is in the Stadhuis, at Markt 1, phone 050 35 33 19.

The main street of Damme is Kerkstraat, and along this you will find Museum Sint Jans Hospitaal, a hospital dating back to 1249. It now houses a museum with furnished period rooms, liturgical objects, and ceramics (open daily, except Monday and Friday, fewer hours in winter months). Just a little farther along Kerkstraat is the Onze Lieve Vrouwekerk (Church of Our Lady), built in Gothic style in the thirteenth century. In the summer months it is sometimes possible to climb the tower for a fine view of the area, and on a clear day you can see all the way to the coast.

Many lodgings are available in Damme. As far as meals are concerned, Damme, known as a gastronomic center, is well-endowed with eating establishments. Many people make the trip to Damme along the canal from Brugge on one of the "tourist" boats that make the journey up and down the canal in the warmer months.

As you leave Damme, just past the Stadhuis you come to another canal, the Brugge Sluis Kanaal, lined with stately poplar trees almost all the way to Brugge. Turn left, joining the fietspad along this canal. As soon as you leave Damme, you can already see the tall spires of Brugge. A short time after turning onto the fietspad you will notice a white windmill on the western bank. This is the Schellemolen, a windmill rebuilt in 1867. In about 6 kilometers you will reach Brugge.

Brugge (Bruges in French) is a beautiful city, Belgium at its best. This gorgeous, medieval city, with cobblestone streets, serene canals, historic buildings, and pretty squares, is everything that the visitor expects to see. For this reason it has become a major tourist destination and tends to be quite crowded in the summer months. If you must visit then, be prepared to reserve accommodations in advance and at least try to avoid the weekends.

Despite the crowds, Brugge does have much to offer. For the cyclist, the area around Brugge is one of the best areas for cycling in Belgium. There are several picturesque bicycle paths, scenic backroads, and inviting tree-lined canals, as is obvious from the last 10 to 15 kilometers when entering Brugge from the north and through Damme. Cycling within the city is also fairly easy. The respect the people of Brugge have for the bicycle is evidenced by the impressive "bicyclists" statue at 't Zand Square. Be sure to go and see the statue and fountain and do as all cyclists do—take your photo in front of it.

Brugge is centered around the impressive Markt, encircled by picture postcard architecture. Most of Brugge's attractions are within easy reach of the Markt, the first one being the thirteenth-century Belfort tower (Belfry). Climb the 366 steps to the top for a spectacular view (open daily). On your way up, take a close look at the workings of the carillon. There are carillon concerts throughout the year.

Follow Breidelstraat to Burg, the "square next door." Here you can visit the fourteenth-century Gothic Stadhuis. Be sure to check out the "Gothic Room" (open daily). The Hellig-Bloed Basiliek (Basilica of Holy Blood) was built to enshrine a vial supposedly containing Christ's blood. Inside the Basiliek are various chapels and the Museum of the Holy Blood containing some interesting relics (open daily).

Brugge boasts several excellent museums. The Memling Museum at Mariastraat 38, formerly St. Jans Hospital, houses the work of fifteenth-century Brugge native Hans Memling. Groeninge Museum at Dijver 12 has a collection of fifteenth- to twentieth-century Flemish art including works by Van Eyck, Gerard David, Memling, and Hieronymous Bosch, as well as some contemporary works by Delvaux and Magritte. Gruuthuse Museum (Museum of Decorative Flemish Arts) at Gruuthuse 17 is the former residence of a fifteenth-century beer magnate and aristocrat and contains furniture, sculptures, tapestries, and many historic Flemish objects from Brugge. Although not a museum, Onze-Lieve Vrouwekerk (Church of Our Lady) at the corner of Mariastraat and Gruuthustraat has a sculpture by Michelangelo, *Madonna and Child,* plus some other interesting religious artifacts. The church was built between the thirteenth and fifteenth centuries and the tower, at 122 meters (400 feet), is the tallest in Belgium. The Lace Centre at Balstraat 14 presents Brugge's living tradition. Here you can watch the intricate process of lacemaking in progress. Note: All the attractions above are open daily; however, the Lace Centre is closed on Sunday.

If you've had your fill of buildings and museums, relax in the serene part of Brugge. Stroll through the Begijnhof, the thirteenth-century enclave of simple houses and pleasant gardens. From the Begijnhof walk toward the train station to Minnewater, a lake and park, and then around the edge to where three windmills can be found between this point, Kruispoort, and Dampoort. (You can also cycle this portion and will enter Brugge through Dampoort on the route.) Boat tours of the canals are also offered and give you a different perspective of the city.

There are a couple of events worth noting. Festival van Vlaanderen (Flanders Festival) from approximately July 25 to August 8 is an international fortnight of music. Ascension Day, a quiet public holiday in most of Belgium, is a day when Brugge comes alive for the Festival of the Holy Blood.

Tourist Information

The tourist office is located in the center at Burg Square adjacent to the main square (Markt) Burg 11. Phone 050 44 86 86. Also a smaller tourist office is located at the train station. The tourist office has a pamphlet for sale called *5 x op de fiets rond Brugge* with five suggested bicycle day trips in the area ranging from 18 to 29 kilometers.

Accommodations

You will find there is no lack of lodging in various price ranges all over Brugge. For bed and breakfasts, check with the tourist office.

Hotel 'T Bruegelhof, Ostmeers 128. Phone 050 34 34 28. BEF 1,500–2,000 Dbl. Between the station and center near Beguinage. Basic rooms, but quiet and cozy.

Hotel 'T Keizershof, Oostmeers 126. Phone 050 33 87 28. BEF 1,300 Dbl. Similar to hotel above and is next door.

Hotel Het Geestelijk Hof, Heilige Geeststraat 2. Phone 050 34 25 94. BEF 1,500–2,000 Dbl. Simple hotel with friendly patron.

Hotel St. Christophe, Nieuwe Gentweg 76. Phone 050 33 11 76. BEF 1,800–2,800 Dbl. Pleasant. Close to center.

Hotel Fevery, Collaert Mansionstraat 3. Phone 050 33 12 69. BEF 2,000 Dbl. Small family hotel not far from center.

Youth Hostel Europa, Baron Ruzettelaan 143. Phone 050 35 26 79. Modern hostel 2 kilometers from the center of Brugge.

Youth Hostel Herdersbrug, Louis Coiseaukaai 26. Phone 050 59 93 21. Located 6 kilometers due north of Brugge in Dudzele on the canal running from Brugge to Zeebrugge.

Note: There are also a couple of unofficial hostels in Brugge.

Camping Memling, Veltemweg 109. Phone 050 35 58 45. Three kilometers northeast of town center in suburb of St. Kruis.

Camping St. Michiel, Tillegemstraat 55. Phone 050 38 08 19. Three kilometers southwest of town center in suburb of St. Michiel.

Where to Eat

There are lots of places to eat, especially around the Markt. Many of these cater to the tourist crowd, but because of the concentration of restaurants, this lends itself to competition, which results in better prices. Choose carefully. Menus are usually posted outside, so you will know exactly what you're getting. Also, wander around side streets and note any good menus you come across during the day that may interest you for the evening meal. Make a note of the address or mark them on your map as after a while all the cute streets in Brugge start to look the same. Be sure to try the local specialty, *waterzooi*, a thick, creamy soup, the main ingredient either chicken or fish.

Markets

't Zand Square on Saturday morning, Burg every Wednesday morning, and also a Fish Market appropriately held at Vismarkt, daily except Sunday and Monday.

Bicycle Shops/Rentals

Brugge Railway Station. Phone 050 38 58 71.

't Koffieboontje, Hallestraat 4. Phone 050 33 80 27 (near Grote Markt/Belfry).

Eric Popelier, Hallestraat 14. Phone 050 34 32 62 (near Grote Markt/Belfry).

De Ketting, Gentpoortstraat 23. Phone 050 34 41 96 (near Gent Gate).

Beyond Brugge—The Beach Areas

To the west and north of Brugge lies Belgium's 65 kilometers of coastline, lined with its beach resort towns. This is Belgium's beach playground. If you base yourself in Brugge, it's an easy day trip by bicycle through scenic areas to reach Oostende, Blankenberge, Zeebrugge, and Knokke-Heist. Both Oostende and Zeebrugge offer ferry connections with England, and because of this, most of the bodies you see sunbathing other than Belgians are British.

Oostende, in medieval times, was a quaint fishing town. Look carefully, and you will find the core of the village, but anything that's left today is flanked by seaside hotels. The St. Petrus en Sint Pauluskerk, across from the train station, was built in 1905. Museum voor Schone Kunsten (Museum of Fine Arts) on Wapenplein, the main square, has works by local artist James Ensor and other local artists. James Ensorhuis (James Ensor's House) at Vlaanderenstraat 27 was the artist's home, and you can see his studio on the second floor. The tourist office is located at Wapenplein, phone 059 70 11 99, and there are plenty of hotels, a youth hostel, camping, and many eateries.

Heading northeast along the coast, you will come to Blankenberge, another beach resort town. The next town of note is Zeebrugge, smaller and quieter than Oostende. Its claim to fame is its huge harbor area, and it is a deep water coastal port and large fishing port. It is linked to Brugge by the Baudouin Canal, and it is possible to cycle the 14 kilometers along the canal back to Brugge.

Continue on to Knokke-Heist, a stretch of several kilometers along the Belgian coastline, with Zeedijk and its boardwalk following the entire length. Knokke-Heist is the name given collectively to the five small towns in the area, Heist, Duinbergen, Albertstrand, Knokke, and Het Zoute, each with its own character. This is a favorite beach area for Belgians. The Knokke-Heist "resort" is a mass of hotels, casinos, restaurants, boutiques, and shops, and prices can be high. The beach is crowded in the high tourist time. The tourist office is located at Zeedijk Knokke 660, phone 050 62 08 13. There is also camping in the area and all along the coast from Oostende to Knokke-Heist.

Brugge to Gent: 44 Kilometers

Leave Brugge via the Katelijnepoort and go along Baron Ruzettelaan, following the marked fietspad along the road. In just over 2 kilometers, cross a bridge over a canal, crossing the road to veer left onto the small road along the canal. Cross carefully.

You are now following the LF5a Vlaanderen Route, and these route signs will guide you all the way to Gent. This small road along the Gent-Oostende Canal is lovely. Notice several well-preserved brick and concrete World War II bunkers along the way. Pass by the town of Moerbrugge on the other side of the canal. You will cross the road, staying on the same side of the canal. There is an interesting piece of art here dedicated to peace and referring to the "Slag on Moerbrugge, September 1944." (Slag is battle in Dutch.) Continue on, hugging the canal.

In another 6 kilometers, you will come to a large bridge over the canal with the name Beernembrug on the side. Ride under the bridge, and the LF5a signs will direct you right, then over the bridge. Across the canal, take the first right, then go left the same canal. This is a long and complicated way to cross from one side of the canal to the other, but it is the only way. You can go into the village of Beernem by taking the first left along the canal, but there's not much except some shops and houses.

Three and a half kilometers farther on you will come to a bridge leading to the town of St. Joris. Again ride under the bridge and follow the LF5a signs around and over the bridge, back onto the original side of the canal. Continue along the canal until the road veers away from it in about 3 kilometers. Stay on the paved road until it turns into a gravel road in another 6 kilometers. You will have about 2 kilometers of gravel. Some of the route is industrial, but it does follow the canal, and there is virtually no traffic.

Five kilometers past the gravel stretch, the road veers right away from the canal. Again there is an LF5a route sign. This takes you up onto a bridge over the Schipdonk Canal, where you will get a good view of the two canals joining up. Across the bridge, the route signs indicate to continue straight across a highway, heading onto a small farm road. You will see the sign for the town of Lovendegem. About 800 meters farther, you will turn right. You will make another quick left, right, and left again, all signposted LF5a, then you will come to a pretty windmill. About 1 kilometer past the mill you will reach the town of Vinderhoute. Continue on through, and in another 1.5 kilometers you will go over the Speybrug. To this point you've had the luxury of great signage with LF5a signs.

After you cross the Speybrug, you will leave this route. It will head off to the right, and you will continue straight along the canal in the direction of Mariakerk. The road at this point is called Trekweg. Stay on that, hugging the canal, until the name changes to Gerard Willemot and a two-way fietspad starts on the left side of the road next to the canal. Follow this until you see bicycle signs for Gent Centrum, about 4 kilometers from the Speybrug. Take the bridge over the canal and on into the center of town.

Gent (Gand in French), overlooked by many travelers, is a feast of twelfth- to seventeenth-century architecture, the core of the city containing some of the most beautiful buildings and public squares in Belgium. Gent's Oude Stade (Old City) has more protected monuments than any other Belgian city and beckons you to put aside your bicycle and walk, strolling along beautiful canals lined with spectacular architecture. Don't miss the superb houses lining Graslei, especially at night. Gent, overall, is stunning at night when these magnificent buildings are floodlit and take on a romantic air. In the fourteenth century Gent was the second largest city in Europe, playing second fiddle only to Paris. It owed its prosperity to its successful textile industry, and remnants of this grandeur live on in many of the splendid buildings.

The traffic in Gent seems almost as bad as Brussels and feels worse because of narrow streets, many cobblestones, and traffic congestion, all day! Stay in the center, leave your bicycle at your lodging, and walk, using your bicycle just to enter and leave. If you are camping, use public transport to come into town as the campground is approximately 3 kilometers out with quite a crowded route into the center.

You will have no problem getting an aerial view of Gent as the center of the city is dominated by three impressive towers. First, the fourteenth-century Belfort (Belfry) attached to the Lakkenhalle (Cloth Hall) affords spectacular views from the top of the 91-meter (298-foot) tower (open daily). The two other prominent church towers in the center (which you cannot ascend) are

The medieval castle of 's Gravensteen in Gent.

St. Niklaaskerk and the tower of St. Baafskathedraal. St. Baafs is a cathedral but could almost be classified as a museum. It houses the famous painting by Van Eyck *The Adoration of the Mystic Lamb*, which alone is worth the visit. Wander around the church, and you will see an incredibly ornate and beautifully sculpted oak and marble pulpit, church art, and furnishings. Make sure you spend some time in the crypt, which has silverware, old books and scrolls, and more paintings.

If you'd like a view of the city from another angle, head to 's Gravensteen (open daily). This castle, begun in 1180, has had its periods of neglect, which you can learn about as you wander around the maze of rooms. Go up to the top for another great view of Gent. The castle, partially restored and sparsely furnished, gives you an excellent sense of a medieval castle. View torture objects in a room that could be categorized as a small museum. Across the road is an attractive square, Veerleplein.

Some other buildings of note are the Stadhuis on the Botermarkt, a mixture of Gothic and Renaissance architecture. Surprisingly, the post office on Korenmarkt 6 is a massive building that looks like it should be a site to visit, not the functional post office that it is. Other than Botermarkt and Korenmarkt, be sure to wander some of the other squares, such as Vrijdagmarkt, Groentemarkt, and Oude Beestenmarkt.

The Museum voor Schone Kunst (Museum of Fine Arts), located in Citadel Park, is a little south of the Oude Stade and a brisk 20-minute walk. The museum has a collection of Flemish art, some Brueghels, works by Hieronymous Bosch, and a contemporary section. The Begijnhof (Beguine Convent) in the southeast of Gent was founded in 1234 but abandoned in the nineteenth century when it became too small for the community. Some attractive gabled houses and the narrow "main" street remain.

Gent is a university city with a large student population, lending itself to some very reasonably priced eateries. The city has several markets—fruit and vegetables available daily at the Groentemarkt, a flower market held every day at Kouter since 1772, animals at the Oude Beestenmarkt on Sunday, a busy Friday (and Saturday) street market at the Vrijdagmarkt, which then becomes the scene of a bird market on Sunday.

Tourist Information
Basement (actually the crypt) of the town hall. On Botermarkt. Phone 09 224 15 55.

Accommodations
Hotels in Gent tend to be expensive. Check at the tourist office for one of the dozen bed and breakfasts in town.

Hotel Flandria, 3-7 Barrestaat. Phone 09 223 06 26. Dbl from BEF 1,400, including a substantial breakfast. Good economical lodging in three old houses connected by a series of hallways.
Hotel Cour St. Georges/Sint Jorishof, Botermarkt 2. Phone 09 224 24 24. Dbl from BEF 3,500. Oldest guest house in Europe dating from 1228. Across from town hall. A splurge, quite gorgeous, best location in town. Even if you don't stay here take a peek when you're at the tourist office.
Youth Hostel De Draecke, St. Widostraat 11. Phone 09 233 70 50. More like a hotel than a hostel. Well located. One street away from 's Gravensteen

Castle. Some private rooms available with shower and toilet in the room. Book this hostel in advance as it is one of the best values in Gent and often full.

Camping Sport and Rekreatiecentrum Blaarmeersen, Zuiderlaan 12. Phone 09 221 53 99. For directions, see beginning of stage to Oudenaarde. Quite far out for sightseeing. This is one city where staying in the center is highly recommended. If you are on a budget and strictly on the camping route, try the youth hostel, but do reserve in advance.

Where to Eat
Because of the student population, there are several reasonably priced ethnic restaurants along the stretch from Kraanlei to Oudeburg. Lots of cheap student cafés are located in the vicinity of the university along Overpoortstraat near the Museum voor Schone Kunst. Many fine restaurants are scattered throughout the city.

Bicycle Shops/Rentals
Gent-Sint Pieters Railway Station. Phone 09 241 22 23. Only place for rentals.
Plum, Nederkouter 141. Phone 09 225 44 62. Bicycle shop closest to center.
Fietsen Godefroot, Sint Denijslaan 127. Phone 09 221 76 76. Bicycle shop.
Bike City, Sint Lievenspoortstraat 250. Phone 09 233 02 71. Bicycle shop.

Gent to Oudenaarde: 40 Kilometers

Leave to the southwest. Find the Rozemarijnbrug over the Coupure Canal. Go down Rozemarijnstraat for a couple hundred meters. At the next big intersection you will start seeing signs for camping at the Sport and Rekreatiecentrum Blaarmeersen. Follow these signs onto Europalaan then Zuiderlaan along the Watersportbaan Canal.

Just over 3 kilometers from the Rozemarijnbrug, you will see the sign indicating you are leaving Gent, and you will come back to the canal you followed from Brugge to Gent. Turn left onto the two-way fietspad along the busy road along the canal and note that at this point you are back on the LF5a Vlaanderen Fietsroute with the familiar green and white route signs to help you.

In 6 kilometers you will come to the Zwijnaardebrug. You will need to turn left onto the street approximately 150 meters before the bridge into Gestichtstraat. Go across the bridge and into the town of Zwijnaarde, now following the LF30a Scheldedelta Route signs. Watch for the signs indicating a left turn into Dorpstraat, where you will ride past two churches, then take another left into Hondelee past the soccer field, go left again into the small Zwartekoben Straat. These turns are all signposted with LF route signs.

Soon after this turn you will reach the River Schelde. You will follow the river going south, staying on the right side for approximately 7 kilometers until the LF signs indicate a right turn, veering you away from the river. This takes you

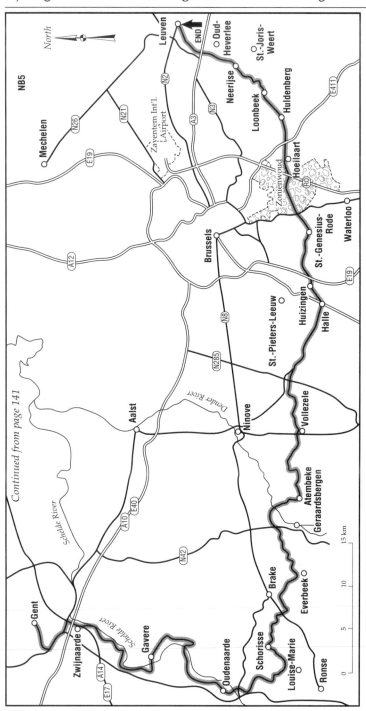

Continued from page 141

150

through a small farm community, then onto a bridge over the Schelde, skirting the town of Gavere, then heading south into farm country. At this point you will have two route signs to help you. You still have the green and white LF30a Scheldedelta Route signs and also the red and white Scheldevallei Route signs. There are actually a few hills in this area, a novelty for those who have been in Holland. The route does take you on a couple kilometers of dirt road just south of Gavere. Note: If the weather has been extremely wet, this could be muddy.

The next town you come to is the tiny farm village of Meilegem. Shortly after Meilegem, you will take a right turn over a bridge. You're still on the LF30a, but you will lose the Scheldevallei Route signs here. Once across the bridge, take the first left along a small farm road. This takes you through the town of Zingem and back to the road along the Schelde. Again you are following the road along the right-hand side of the river. In a few kilometers you will come to the Ohiobrug (Ohio Bridge). Here the LF turns right, but you will continue straight along the river to Oudenaarde. In about 4 kilometers, you will see the center of town. Turn right on Tussen Bruggen which will veer left onto Broodstraat, which brings you right into the Markt, where you will immediately see Oudenaarde's famous town hall.

Oudenaarde's most visited attraction is the Flamboyant Gothic Stadhuis built in 1525 and currently undergoing a 15-year restoration project (parts are already completed). Try to take one of the tours of the Stadhuis that are offered daily April through October. Inside you will see vaulted ceilings, a carved door, in itself a work of art, a silver collection, a huge Gothic fireplace, and the pièce de résistance, some Verdure Tapestries, the signature tapestry form of the town. Should you wish to see more of the tapestries, there is a Tapestry Museum and Restoration Workshop in Huis de Lalaing at Bourgondiestraat 9 (open weekdays only).

Also of interest in the town are some lovely old buildings, especially around the Markt and on Hoogstraat. St. Walburgkerk and Onze Lieve Vrouwekerk van Pamele are two churches of note, dating from the twelfth and thirteenth centuries respectively. The small begijnhof dates from the thirteenth century, its special feature being the tiny, and very cute, chapel.

Tourist Information

Located in the town hall. Phone 055 31 72 51. Around Oudenaarde is excellent for cycling, and if you are interested in exploring more of this area, the tourist office has a number of cycling routes.

Accommodations

Oudenaarde is a small town with a half dozen hotels and no bed and breakfasts.
Hotel Elnik, Dienzestraat 55. Phone 055 33 50 31. BEF 1,500 Dbl. Simple hotel.
Hotel De Zalm, Hoogstraat 4. Phone 055 31 13 14. BEF 2,500 Dbl. Pleasant hotel across from the Stadhuis.
Camping Vlaamse Ardennen, Kortrijkstraat 342. Phone 055 31 54 73. Huge camping complex. Two kilometers from the center.

Where to Eat

There are several restaurants in town, some in hotels, many around Markt.

Bicycle Shops/Rentals

Oudenaarde Railway Station. Phone 055 31 17 52.
Fietsen Peter, Beverestraat 119. Phone 055 68 02 31. Bicycle shop, no rentals.

Oudenaarde to Geraardsbergen: 38 Kilometers

From the Stadhuis, go past the church. At the roundabout, take a left onto the bridge over the Schelde. Across the bridge, take the first right into the town of Leupegem. At the first traffic light take a left, then the first right into Vlaamse Ardennesdreef. This immediately takes you up a hill, a big hill, which comes as quite a shock after the flatlands of the north. You are entering the Vlaamse Ardennes (Flemish Ardennes), so named because they resemble the hilly Ardennes region of southern Belgium and Luxembourg. Some guidebooks indicate that this is a bit of an exaggeration. These guidebook writers were obviously not on bicycles. With this first hill you know without a doubt you have left the flat Flemish north behind. To make you feel better, though, this is the worst hill you will encounter all day.

In 3 kilometers, you will join a fietspad along the N8 in the direction Brakel for half a kilometer. Then turn right onto a small road in the direction of Maarke-Kerkem. Go down the hill. The road is cobblestone, and it is rather difficult to ride on, so keep to the dirt on the side where possible. At the bottom of the hill is a stop sign. Continue straight through the intersection onto Ellestraat. This takes you up a hill. At the top the name changes to Aatse Heerweg. You will come to a small windmill on your right. Turn around for great views of the valley. You can detour a couple hundred meters over to the mill to take a look, then return and continue on the same road.

Just past the mill is an intersection with a sign for Louise-Marie. Continue straight. In about 2 kilometers, before you reach the town of Louise-Marie, you will join the LF6a Vlaanderen Fietsroute by turning left into Boskant. You will see the green and white LF route sign. Soon you will not have to pedal for 2 kilometers as you go down a lengthy hill. The route continues through rolling hills and beautiful pasture land, taking you through the south end of the town of Schorisse, then on through Zegelsem and Opbakel, always following the LF6a route signs.

You will cross the N48 highway, and in about 2 kilometers you will come to a large brick windmill. Continue on through the towns of Nederbrakel and Everbeek. Five kilometers past the windmill you will join a larger road with a marked fietspad for a short distance before turning left and riding through Zarlardinge, Deftinge, and into Schendelbeke. Once through Schendelbeke, you will cross the Dender River. On the far side of this bridge, the route takes you down to the river itself. There is a youth hostel here on an old farm. The LF route turns right at the river, but you will turn left and ride the fietspad alongside the river for about 4 kilometers into the town of Geraardsbergen.

Geraardsbergen (Grammont in French) is a lovely town cut down the middle by the Dender River and is unusual because it rises steeply on both banks of the river. High on the east side you will find the Stadhuis. With fourteenth-century origins, it is an impressive gabled and turreted building on the Grote Markt. At its base is the oldest Manneken Pis (see explanation under Brussels heading in this chapter) in the country, believed to date back to 1455. At the "high" end of the Grote Markt is the fifteenth-century Sint Bartholomeuskerk (St. Bartholomew's Church). Sint Adriaansabdij (St. Adrian's Abbey), a few blocks from the Markt, was originally a Benedictine monastery begun in 1081. The eighteenth-century abbey buildings are now a museum containing artifacts from the area, and the grounds have been converted into a pleasant park (open daily from Easter to October).

If you are a fan of the Tour de France, you might be familiar with the "Geraardsbergen Wall" (Mur de Grammont), the name given to the steep cobblestone street climbing out of town on the slope of the Oudenberg. It is often included as part of the Tour de France and other bicycle races. It is marked with signs "Muur," so if you are feeling energetic after your day's ride, you can try it yourself. This road leads up to the Oudenberg Chapel, where there are fine views of the town and the surrounding area. A word of advice, take your panniers off before attempting this feat.

Tourist Information
Stadhuis, Markt. Phone 054 41 41 21.

Accommodations
Hotel Geeraard, Lessensestraat 36. Phone 054 41 20 73. BEF 2,500 Dbl. Small
   hotel (converted nineteenth-century mansion) in center of town.
Youth Hostel 'T Schipke, Kampstraat 59. Phone 054 41 61 89. Old farmhouse
   (plus new wing) in a quiet setting on Dender River 4 kilometers from
   Geraardsbergen.
Camping De Gavers, Onkerzelestraat 280. Phone 054 41 63 24. Five kilometers
   from Geraardsbergen, not far from the youth hostel.

Where to Eat
There is a good selection of cozy restaurants scattered throughout the town. Several are located around the Grote Markt and the main street, Brugst, which leads off the Grote Markt down to the Dender River and continues up again.

Geraardsbergen is famous for *mattetaarten*, a sort of cheesecake tart. You can buy them at most bakeries, and cafés offer *mattetaart en koffie*. One bakery with excellent tarts is the Van Belle Bakery at Brugst 36 on the main street between the Dender River and the Grote Markt. Also try the excellent Trappist beer produced at the St. Adriaansabdij and served at local restaurants.

Bicycle Shops/Rentals
Fietsen Magazijn Patrick, Vredestraat 31. Phone 054 41 14 01. Bicycle shop
   only, no rentals.

Geraardsbergen to Huizingen: 41 Kilometers
From Geraardsbergen, backtrack along the Dender River the way you entered town for 4 kilometers. At the bridge you crossed coming in back at the youth hostel, turn right in the direction of Onkerzele. At this point you are following the LF6a Vlaanderen Route. This route is well signposted and will take you through several small farm villages.

A word of warning for your stomach: unless you leave the route, you will not go through any towns of note (except Halle toward the end of the stage), so bring food and drink for the day. The small towns you pass through are farm towns, or clusters of houses, often without shops. Very close to this portion of the route are the larger towns of Galmaarden and Oetingen where you can detour, and provisions can be found.

Following the LF route signs, you will ride past the church in Onkerzele and continue to the village of Atembeke. Just past Atembeke you will come to one of the steepest climbs you will have to endure today with grades up to 10 percent as you climb the Bosberg (literally translated as "Forest Mountain"). Once you reach the top, the route evens out a bit, and you will ride through some gorgeous farmland. At 13 kilometers you will come to Vollezele. You have a great view of the town of Oetingen, although the route bypasses the town itself and winds on to Leerbeek.

Here the route crosses the N285 and very shortly brings you to the N28, which heads southeast in the direction of Halle. In a couple of kilometers the LF route veers left, but you will stay on the N28 through Pepingen and straight on to Halle, with a fietspad along the road for most of the way. (If you are interested in seeing Gaasbeek Castle you can follow the LF route, but it adds 10 kilometers or so to the route, partially on unpaved roads.) Gaasbeek Castle is a sixteenth-century castle, restored in the nineteenth century. It is indeed a castle/museum. Apart from beautiful castle furnishings, there are magnificent tapestries from the sixteenth and seventeenth centuries, and Ruben's will is housed in the Archives Room.

If you stay on the N28, you will rejoin the LF route a few kilometers before Halle, as it loops back to the same highway. The LF route signs will then take you right through the Grote Markt in Halle.

For the cyclist who is not camping or taking the youth hostel route, Halle is a suitable stopping point for this stage of the trip. Otherwise, continue on to Huizingen.

Whether you are staying or not, a worthwhile stop in Halle is the area around the Grote Markt. The square is dominated by the huge Gothic Onze Lieve Vrouwebasiliek (Basilica of Our Lady), built between 1341 and 1409. Inside the basilica is the "black" virgin, the objective of pilgrims here since the thirteenth century. Still today, the town comes alive with religious processions several times a year, including Whitsunday, the first Sunday in September and October. Both the exterior and the interior of the basilica hold interest with sculptures and works of art (open daily). Also on the Grote Markt is the Renaissance Stadhuis dating from 1616 which houses the tourist office, phone 02 356 42 59. The one hotel in town is Hotel les Eleveurs, Basiliekstraat 136, phone 02 361 13 40. There are two bicycle shops in Halle, Cycles Union, 132 Sint Rochusstraat, phone 02 356 55 33; and J. Hendrickx, 4-6 Minderbroedstraat, phone 02 356 59 82.

You leave Halle along the Brussel-Charleroi Canal, passing through an industrial area that includes a Côte d'Or chocolate factory. At the first bridge the route takes you over the canal, as well as over the railway line, and on into the town of Huizingen. Huizingen is 4 kilometers northeast of Halle.

The town of Huizingen is tiny, but its surroundings are an oasis of gardens, forest, and green space, surprising for an industrial area so close to Brussels. The Provinciaal Domein van Huizingen (Provincial Domain of Huizingen) is an estate covering 225 acres where you can stroll through the grounds of the château, which has been converted into a restaurant, and partake in many recreational activities. From here it is not far to the medieval Château de Beersel.

Both the youth hostel and camping are found in the Provincial Domain of Huizingen, phone 02 383 00 26.

Huizingen to Leuven: 46 Kilometers

For this stage, follow the LF6a Vlaanderen Route which keeps you off main roads and goes through some lovely, scenic areas. It is in part on dirt paths and cobblestones, so it may be difficult if you are on a bicycle with very narrow tires. These are not difficult trails and are of hard-packed dirt, but if it has been raining, it can be a bit muddy. We rode this section on hybrid bicycles with 35-millimeter tires with no problems.

From Huizingen rejoin the LF route, which takes you out of town and almost immediately onto a dirt path through the Begijnbos, a small forest area. Following the LF signs, the route continues partially on rural dirt and cobblestone roads past the town of Alsemberg and descends to Sint-Genesius-Rode. Past Sint-Genesius-Rode you will have a hefty climb, 4 kilometers of steady incline, although it is not too steep, along a main street, Zoniënwoudstraat, which will bring you to the large N5 highway.

Waterloo Detour

It is here that you will see signs for Waterloo, which is approximately 5 kilometers south of this point. If you are interested, turn right here and simply follow the road south. There is no fietspad for the first part which is quite busy, but there is a fietspad for the last part as you enter Waterloo. This is the site of Napoleon's final battle on June 18, 1815, when Wellington and von Blücher led their English and Prussian troops to victory against the French. You can climb the Butte de Lion (Lion's Mound) to view the surrounding battlefields where Napoleon was defeated and visit Musée Wellington (Wellington Museum) at Chaussée de Bruxelles 147 for more on the history of the battles and the times.

If you are not taking the detour to Waterloo, cross the N5 highway. Here you will enter the Zoniënwoud (Dutch), or Forêt de Soignés (French), the large forest that stretches all the way to the edge of Brussels. This forest was at one time the hunting domaine of the dukes of Burgundy. Here you will leave the cars behind, as the road that gently undulates through the forest is for bicycles and pedestrians only. You will ride through about 6 kilometers of forest, crossing just one road about halfway through. The first few kilometers are paved until you cross the road where the path becomes hard-packed dirt. The route passes by a race track and comes out of the forest just before the town of Hoeilaart, descending into the area known as Groenendaal.

Cycling to Brussels? Try It from Here

If you intend to cycle into Brussels, your best bet for approaching the city by bicycle is from here. Cycling into Brussels is, to say the least, difficult. Of the three major capitals of the Benelux, Brussels is definitely the most difficult to enter on two wheels. We experimented with various options, and the general consensus, by us and others, is take the train. (See Brussels/Leuven information for more details.) The urban sprawl of Brussels, intense traffic, and the lack of cycle paths into and within the city make a bicycle trip through the traffic jungle of Brussels somewhat of an adventure. This may sound very negative, but trust us. After approaching Brussels from various angles, this southern access is by far the least stressful.

One reason we prefer this approach to Brussels is that it is part of the LF2 cycling route, or Stedenroute. This gives you the advantage of the LF signposting. (Note: When heading north to Brussels, the route is the LF2b. When leaving Brussels in a southerly direction and retracing your tracks, you will be looking for LF2a signs.)

Also, this section of the approach takes you through the pleasant surrounds of the Zoniënwoud, or Forêt de Soignes, continuing through the forest to as close as you can possibly get to the center of Brussels from any direction. This offers the least amount of heavy traffic in Brussels for you to tackle on the final part of the entry.

Route to Brussels

From the race track just north of Groenendaal in the park at the east end, go north on LF2b past another race track and hippodrome approximately 2 kilometers farther. Go past the lake at the north end of park. For the last part of the LF2b you will be basically following alongside the N24 (which will be to your right). Exit the park at the N24 which becomes Avenue Louise. At the end of Avenue Louise is Place Louise; here you will cross the R20 and be in the center. (To exit Brussels, reverse this, starting at Place Louise.)

Note: If you have difficulty finding the start of the route, go to the Hoeilaart Tourist Office (just a couple of kilometers east of the forest at the Gemeentehuis, Jan van Ruusbroeckpark, phone 02 657 90 50). Here you can ask for directions or look at a detailed map of the area or one of the books describing the LF route.

To Continue on the Huizingen to Leuven Stage

Leaving the forest, you will cross the N275 as you ascend a couple of kilometers toward Hoeilaart. An LF6a route sign will direct you to turn left, then right, so you are skirting the main part of the town. You will, however, cycle past the castle of Hoeilaart. The town is known as "glass town" because of the abundance of greenhouses.

Do not be surprised to see a second set of LF signs between here and Leuven. It is here that the LF6, Vlaanderen Fietsroute, and the LF2, the Stedenroute ("city" route), share the same path. You will continue to follow the LF6a route signs, continuing another 5 kilometers to the town of Overijse, so named for its position on the banks of the IJse River. Overijse is in the heart of the Belgian wine region. There are several campgrounds in the area around the town.

Leaving Overijse, the LF6a follows the N253 for 4 kilometers to Huldenberg. At Huldenberg, the LF6a signs take you away from the main road to ride on a dirt track alongside the small IJse River. This track is hard-packed dirt and narrow, but it does prove to be more pleasant than riding on the busy N253. For most of this ride along the river, the N253 is within sight to your left as you are riding almost parallel to it. On our hybrids this part of the route was no trouble, but be aware that it may be muddy after rain, and if you have thin tires, you may want to take the road and rejoin the route at Neerijse. You will continue on the river path until Neerijse, where you will climb up into town from the river.

At Neerijse the LF route goes northwest, climbing away from the N253 for a few kilometers. Then it rejoins the N253, crossing it as it goes over the A3 freeway, and there is a fietspad for a while. Then you will leave LF6a and go through the forest on the outskirts of Leuven, coming out near the newer part of the university on the edge of Leuven. Continue into Leuven Centrum. For information on Leuven, see the start of this route.

Chapter 10

Route 4—
Southern
Belgium
(Wallonia)
Route

Including
connections to
and from
Luxembourg

Total Distance: 357 kilometers (221 miles)
Terrain: Gently undulating hills in the north, inclines in the south in Ardennes
Maps: Michelin Map 213 and 214 (1:200,000), Geocart Maps—Brabant, Namur, and Luxembourg (1:100,000)
Connecting Routes: Route 3—Northern Belgium
Route 5—Luxembourg

The southern area of Belgium is known as Wallonia. The people are French speakers and are closer to France historically and culturally. Not as much English is spoken as in Flanders, but the Walloons are warm people and will have patience if you try to communicate as best you can. The part of Wallonia known as Hainaut is an industrial area and Belgium's main steel-producing area. The terrain is the least interesting in Wallonia, and the route avoids this province, instead concentrating on the picturesque areas of the provinces of Namur and Luxembourg, heading into the Belgian Ardennes. This part of Belgium is much less populated than Flanders, and the rural roads are not nearly as crowded.

Much of this route takes you through the hilly forests of the Ardennes, through southern Belgium, and into the Grand Duchy of Luxembourg (see Route 5). This peaceful and beautiful area has some prolonged hills and is a far cry from flat northern Belgium. Some pretty towns are nestled in the valleys of the Ardennes, and you will be rewarded with expansive views not found in the north. Due to the lay of the land some of the stages are longer distances than in the more populated areas in the north of the country. Expect to see little habitation for several kilometers, and be prepared to carry food and water for the day. Also, be aware that unless you are camping, there are often no other lodgings between the beginning and end points of some of the stages.

As you cycle through the valleys, forests, and farmlands of this serene part of Belgium, bear in mind that some of the most severe battles of World War II took place in this part of Belgium and Luxembourg, including the Battle of the Bulge. From time to time you will notice battle sites and monuments in memory of lives lost. Today this tranquil landscape offers pleasant biking, hiking, caving, kayaking, and numerous other outdoor activities, as well as some interesting museums and pretty towns.

Leuven to Namur: 68 Kilometers

For sightseeing and practical information on Leuven, see Route 3—Northern Belgium Route.

Leave Leuven from the Namsepoort, named for the old city gate that was located here on the south end of the city walls. If you are leaving from the center, take the Namsestraat, which begins at the main square. When you reach Namsepoort, cross over the ring road and immediately veer right onto the first road you come to, which is not signposted. Soon you will see signs for Oud-Heverlee, which you will follow to the town of Oud-Heverlee, 6 kilometers from the center of Leuven. Continue straight through town, riding the bicycle path along the road in the direction of St. Joris-Weer. In about 2 kilometers you will pass through the lakeside resort town of Zoet Water (meaning Sweet Water).

Continue on to St. Joris. The bicycle path along the road ends here. Go through the town of St. Joris, crossing the railway tracks. In approximately 400 meters, just before the AGIP service station, turn left onto a smaller road with a bicycle path alongside in the direction of St. Agatha-Rode and Grez-Doiceau. Continue through the town of Nethen and on to Hamme-Mille. Here you will find a large intersection where you will take a sharp right onto the N25 in the direction of Wavre. Exactly 4 kilometers from this turn, when you reach the town of Archennes, turn left in the direction of Grez-Doiceau. Another 1.4 kilometers brings you to an intersection in the center of Grez-Doiceau. Turn left in the direction of Jodoigne. You will ascend and in 500 meters, just as you leave town, turn right, in the direction of Bonlez.

For the next 4 kilometers or so you will be winding your way through the valley of the Train River. This is a pretty pastoral area with lovely vistas of the surrounding countryside. In 4.5 kilometers you will reach the center of Bonlez. Just as you leave town, veer left in the direction of Chaumont-Gistoux until you meet the N243 at Gistoux. Turn left onto the two-way bicycle path along the N243. Continue through Chaumont-Gistoux. Climb approximately 1 kilometer past the town, then turn right toward Walhain and Tourinnes. Go under the A4 freeway, arriving shortly in Tourinnes-St. Lambert. Continue through town and on to Walhain. From Walhain, take the bicycle path along the straight, tree-lined road to the west for 2 kilometers until you reach the N4 highway. Turn left and follow the bicycle path along the N4.

The N4 is a busy road; however, to compensate for the traffic on this main road, there is a bicycle path for almost the entire way into Namur. (You do lose the bicycle path for a short time as you ride through the town of Gembloux, then you pick it up again on the other side of town.) Namur is a sizable city, and unfortunately there are no quiet approaches, so bearing with the N4 for 16 kilometers is the best alternative. Cycling the N4, you will have a few

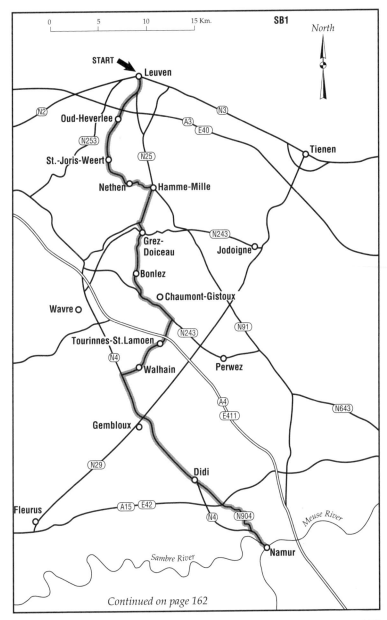

Continued on page 162

hills to tackle until the final descent into Namur.

Continue along the N4 for 6 kilometers through Gembloux. Ten kilometers past Gembloux, you will reach Carrefour de Didi (Intersection at Didi). Just beyond this intersection, the N4 forks. You will be taking the road to the left, the N904, which has less traffic, and is a more pleasant route. In order to do this, you must cross the N4 at the fork. (This is a hazardous crossing, so be cautious.) Continue along the bicycle path through Rhisnes, and soon you will descend through a few kilometers of very welcome forest as you reach the outskirts of Namur.

At the bottom of the descent you will rejoin the N4 for a few hundred meters. Just across the railway tracks you will veer left onto the Rue Melot, which will take you to the train station, and just past the station is the tourist information.

Namur (Namen in French) is a busy city nestled at the confluence of the Meuse and Sambre rivers. As far as the tourist is concerned, the focal point of Namur is perched high on the cliffs that overlook the Meuse River, this being the Citadelle. It is believed that the site has been in use since Roman times; however, most of the current structures were built between the seventeenth and nineteenth centuries. It is worth spending several hours there, enjoying the view, touring the fortifications and underground caverns, and wandering around the grounds (open daily April to October). It's a narrow, steep, and winding road up to the Citadelle, so treat yourself to the *téléférique* (cable car) for the ride up. If you want to cycle up the road, you need to take Route Merveilleuse or the "back way" on Route des Panoramas.

Namur is home to some interesting museums. On the waterfront is Musée Archéologique (Archaeological Museum) in the handsome sixteenth-century Butchers' Hall on Rue du Pont. Collections include artifacts from excavations in the region dating from Roman and Merovingian eras (open daily except Tuesday). Musée Félicien Rops at Rue Fumal 12 houses hundreds of the satirical paintings and drawings as well as engravings by Rops, a native of Namur (open daily). In town there are a couple of other small museums and some churches, including Cathédrale St. Aubain, built in 1751, with works from the Rubens school inside, and the baroque Eglise St. Loup, dating from the 1600s. Near Place d'Armes, the Tour St. Jacques (St. James' Tower) has been used as a belfry since the eighteenth century.

The city itself has a good shopping area centered around Rue de L'Ange and Rue de Fer. Other than the Citadelle and a few museums and churches, consider Namur the "Gateway to the Ardennes."

Tourist Information
Place de L'Europe Unis, just east of train station. Phone 081 22 28 59.

Accommodations
A couple of reasonably priced hotels are near the station, a few minutes walk to the center. Also ask at the tourist office about bed and breakfasts as there are a couple in Namur, but they are only open in the summer months.
Queen Victoria, Avenue de la Gare 12. Phone 081 22 29 71. From BEF 2,000 Dbl. Near the station.
Hotel Excelsior, Avenue de la Gare 4. Phone 081 23 18 13. From BEF 1,600 Dbl. Near the station.
Hotel Opera Parisien, Rue E. Cuvelier 16. Phone 081 22 63 79. From BEF 1,600 Dbl. In the center.

Youth Hostel Auberge de Jeunesse de Namur "Félicien Rops," 8 Avenue Félicien Rops. Phone 081 22 36 88. A 10-minute bicycle ride from the center
of town but worth it for its great location on the Meuse River, the incredibly wonderful staff, and excellent amenities, bar, kitchen, evening
meal, and ambiance in the house of artist Félicien Rops.
There is no camping in Namur, but the youth hostel is a great alternative. The
closest campground is approximately 8 kilometers out of town to the east
off N17, and it is Camping des Quatre Fils Aymon, Chaussée de Liège
389, Lives-sur-Meuse. Phone 081 58 83 13. Also 8 kilometers to the west
is Camping Trieux, Rue des Trîs 99, Malonne. Phone 081 44 55 83.

Where to Eat
Namur has a variety of restaurants. For an area with ambiance and several good restaurants, head to Place Marché aux Légumes in the heart of the
old town. Otherwise restaurants are scattered all over town.

Bicycle Shops/Rentals
Namur Railway Station. Phone 081 35 21 11.
Seitta, 3D Ave. de la Plante. Phone 081 22 03 14. Bicycle shop with rentals.
Also the youth hostel has five bicycles available for rental.

Namur to Dinant: 47 Kilometers via Maredsous or 28 Kilometers Direct

From the Pont de Jambes, the
bridge crossing the Meuse to the
suburb of Jambes, head south along
the road to Dinant without crossing
the bridge, staying on the west side
of the river. In a few hundred meters
you will veer left and join the path
along the river. On your right across
the road you will notice the youth
hostel. The path you are following
along the river, at times shared with

pedestrians, has a decent surface with just very short stretches of cobblestones
or gravel. Notice the locks at 7.3 kilometers for ship traffic on the river. At 9.2
kilometers, the path narrows as it continues along the side of the main road.
Stay on the path, and at the end of this short stretch, a smaller road veers left as
the main road veers away from the river again. Take the small road that hugs
the Meuse. You will share this portion with cars, but only local traffic.

At 14 kilometers the surface deteriorates, and you will have cobblestone,
then dirt and gravel, and back to cobblestone again. Endure this for 2 kilometers until you come to the town of Annevoie. Ride under the bridge crossing the Meuse and take an immediate right turn through a parking lot up to
the main road.

Note: The route includes a detour up the hill to Abbey Maredsous. If you
are in a hurry to get to Dinant or would prefer to include the abbey as a separate day trip, simply turn left here and follow the main road for 12 flat kilometers. The suggested route will add about 20 kilometers but is a beautiful detour.
As there is a major hill to climb, it is more pleasant on an unloaded bicycle.

Take the road going up the hill. You will see directional signs for the town of Fraire, as well as signs indicating that this is the direction for the Jardins-Annevoie and Bioul Abbey. You will have an ascent of about 3 kilometers, although only the first 500 meters is steep. About 600 meters up the hill you will come to Jardins d'Annevoie (Gardens of Annevoie), the grounds of the eighteenth-century château. This gorgeous 30-acre area is a blend of formal French- and Italian-designed gardens. The peaceful gardens filled with

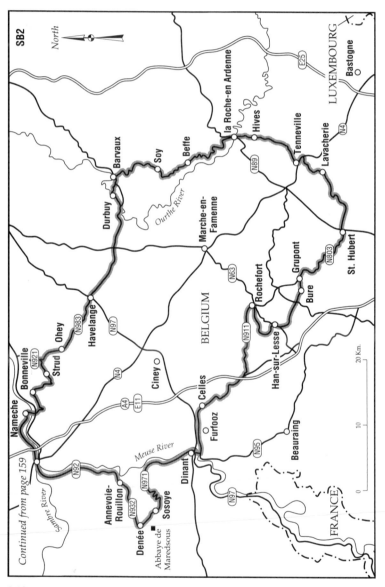

beautiful flower beds and statues are interspersed with ponds, waterfalls, and fountains. You can visit the gardens and the château on weekends April through June and in September and daily in July and August.

Continue on the N932 past the old château just beyond the gardens until you reach the cute town of Bioul. Ride past the stone church and the neighboring château (private) and veer left, continuing on the N932. In about 4 kilometers, watch for the sign to Denée and turn left onto the tiny farm road. In less than a kilometer you will reach the town of Denée where you will veer left following the sign to Maredsous. Descend 2 kilometers and take the second road to the right in the direction of Maredsous. Climb 1 kilometer up the hill to the Abbey of Maredsous. A Benedictine abbey established in 1872, it is still very much a working abbey. You can visit the church and wander through part of the grounds. Stop at the visitor's center for lunch or a snack. You can purchase cheese, bread, and beer, all made at the abbey. They also have desserts, coffee, and other refreshments. There is a huge outdoor dining area with tables and chairs.

Ride back down the hill and turn right, going through the village of Sosoye onto the N971. Stay on this road in the direction of Dinant/Anhée. About 6 kilometers after leaving the abbey, take a short detour onto the small farm road to the right, signposted ruins of Château Montaigle. In about 200 meters you will have a great view of the ruins. Return to the N971 and continue down, following the babbling brook. You will again pass the ruins, but the view is not as spectacular from this road.

In approximately 7 kilometers you will reach the town of Anhée. Turn right through town. At the end of town, you will rejoin the highway, the N96, in the direction of Dinant. Follow the highway for 6 kilometers into the town of Dinant.

Due to the spectacular setting of the town on the banks of the Meuse River, Dinant is one of the most visited cities of the Ardennes. The town stretches along the river, and as you ride across the bridge into Dinant, the town's two most prominent sights vie for attention. The Citadelle, high atop the cliff, looks down on the church with its onion-shaped bulbous spire.

The Citadelle has had many lives. Originally built in 1051 as a castle, it was re-built in 1523 and destroyed in 1703, with the present structure dating from 1821. Today it is a museum, but the main reason to go there is for the spectacular view of the town and the Meuse Valley (open daily April to October, closed Friday November to March). It is accessible by cable car, or you can climb up the 408 steps. The Citadelle can be reached by road via Rue St. Jacques, the N936 in the direction of Sorinnes.

The attractive collegiate Church of Notre Dame with its bulbous spire dominates the street, or river level, of the town. The only other attraction of note in Dinant is the Grotto "La Merveilleuse" on the west bank of the Meuse. The grotto is famous for its white stalactite formations (open daily March–November).

Dinant is the starting point for kayaking trips on the River Lesse, as well as boat trips on the Meuse. There are several outfits offering these excursions. Check with the tourist office.

Tourist Information
Rue Grande 37. Phone 082 22 28 70.

Accommodations
Hotel le Plateau, Plateau de la Citadelle 15. Phone 082 22 28 34. BEF 1,500 Dbl.

Hotel de la Couronne, Rue Adolphe Sax 1. Phone 082 22 27 31. BEF 1,600 plus Dbl.
Camping de Bouvignes sur Meuse, Chaussée d'Yvoir. Phone 082 22 28 70.
    Two kilometers from center.
There are two campgrounds in Anhée and one in Profondeville, both en route
    from Namur to Dinant.

Where to Eat
    There is a nice selection of restaurants and cafés; however, due to the
many day-trippers, some tend to be touristy and pricey.

Bicycle Shops/Rentals
Dinant Railway Station. Phone 082 22 28 60.

Dinant to Han-sur-Lesse via Rochefort: 42 Kilometers
    Leave Dinant on the eastern bank of the Meuse River on the N95 in the
direction of Beauraing. Go under the freeway viaduct and in 300 meters take
a half left up the hill to Dréhance. You will ride up 2 kilometers of steady incline to reach Dréhance. Go right as you enter the town in the direction of Forfooz. After approximately 2 kilometers you will reach Forfooz. Go left in the
direction of Vêves and Celles. In 3 kilometers you will reach the magnificent,
fairy-tale-like fifteenth-century Château de Vêves which is perched on a hill
to your right. The well-maintained interior is replete with family mementos
and classic French furniture (open daily between Easter and October). Just beyond the château, go left on the N910 in the direction of Celles. You will reach
Celles in 2 kilometers.
    Celles is in a pretty setting. The village was the farthest point of the Ger-
man advance in 1944. The Romanesque Church of St. Hadelin was built in
1035 and has some interesting features plus two underground crypts dating
from the eleventh century. There are three small hotels in Celles, all in the BEF
1,600–2,700 Dbl range.
    At the intersection of the N910 and N94, go right on the N94 in the di-
rection of Neufchâteau and Rochefort. Stay on the N94 for about 10 kilometers until you cross the A4/E411 freeway. After 500 meters, turn left to
Rochefort onto the N911. Continue cycling with steady climbs and descents
for 12 kilometers until you reach Rochefort.
    To reach Han-sur-Lesse from Rochefort, go back the way you entered on
the N911 and cross the bridge over the Lomme River, turning at the first left
after you cross the bridge in the direction of Eprave. You will begin on Rue
d'Austerlitz, which becomes Rue du Tige. At first you will follow the river,
and in 5 kilometers you will reach Eprave. Go straight through town to Han-
sur-Lesse, turning right after another kilometer, following the river which is
on your right as you enter Han-sur-Lesse. The distance between Rochefort
and Han-sur-Lesse is approximately 6 kilometers.

Rochefort Information
    Rochefort, on the Lomme River, is a popular base for exploring the sur-
rounding area, namely Lesse and Lomme National Park. The small town
can become quite crowded in the summer and on weekends. The main
street, Rue de Behogne, is a long street running the length of the town and
can get quite congested as most of the town's facilities are found on this
street.

Rochefort's appeal is its location and proximity to outdoor activities, but the town's main draw is the Grotto, a couple of kilometers out of town along Drève de Lorette. These wild and rugged caves cut by the Lomme River were discovered in 1865. The massive Salle de Sabbat (Hall of the Sabbath) is the most impressive feature with dimensions of 65 meters (213 feet) by 125 meters (410 feet) with a height of 85 meters (278 feet). To demonstrate its height to visitors, a balloon is allowed to float to the ceiling (open daily April to mid-November).

Two other attractions, both within a couple of kilometers of the town, are the ruins of Château Comtal, Avenue de Lorette 22, and north of town, the Abbey of St. Rémy, where the monks make a local Trappist beer.

Tourist Information
Rue de Behogne 5. Phone 084 21 25 37.

Accommodations
There are several hotels and bed and breakfasts in town. The tourist office has a free listing.

Hotel La Fayette, Rue Jacquet 87. Phone 084 21 42 73. BEF 1,300 plus Dbl.
    Cheapest in town.
La Malle Poste, Rue de Behogne 46. Phone 084 21 09 86. BEF 2,500 Dbl. Former coach stop, dating to eighteenth century. Old architecture.
Youth Hostel (unofficial): Gite d'Etape, Le Vieux Moulin, Rue de Hableau 25.
    Phone 084 21 46 04.
Camping Communal, Rue de Hableau. Phone 084 21 19 00.

Where to Eat
Due to the "tourist" nature of the town, there are several restaurants and cafés. Some are connected to hotels.

Bicycle Shops/Rentals
The tourist office rents bicycles, and there is a bicycle shop on the main street just as you enter the main part of town on your left on Rue de Behogne.

Han-sur-Lesse Information

About a fifth the size of Rochefort, this very small town is a real tourist destination, servicing over a quarter of a million tourists annually. The town itself does not hold much of interest. The main attraction is the millenniums-old limestone grotto. Visitors also come to kayak on the Lesse River and to hike, rock climb, and cycle in the vicinity. As with Rochefort, the town is a gateway to the Lesse and Lomme National Park.

The Grotto of Han is just out of town and can be reached, as part of the tour, by a special tram. Visitors have been coming to the caves since the 1850s. The length of the cave system is about 8 kilometers; however, only a couple of kilometers are covered in the tour, part of which is by boat. The caves have an abundance of limestone formations and huge chambers (open daily March to December).

To appreciate the caves, you can visit the Musée du Monde Souterrain (Museum of the Underground World) located beside the tourist office. The museum is devoted to the geology of the caves and has displays of archaeological objects found both in the caves and the local area (open daily April to

November). Han also has a Wild Animal Reserve with many animals native to the Ardennes such as bison, wild boar, tarpans (small wild horses), and chamois roaming in a 250-hectare (618-acre) area. (It is open the same hours as the Grotto. If you intend to visit the Grotto and the Reserve, check on the combination ticket which may be more economical.)

A pleasant excursion from Han is to the Château Lavaux Ste. Anne, approximately 7 kilometers west. This superb feudal castle constructed in the fourteenth and fifteenth centuries is everybody's vision of a castle. It is surrounded by a moat, flanked by four towers, has formal gardens, and is a magnificent structure (open daily, all year).

Tourist Information
Place Théo Lannoy. Phone 084 37 75 76.

Accommodations
Fewer hotels than Rochefort. Some bed and breakfasts available.

Hotel Henri IV, Rue des Chasseurs Ardennais 59. Phone 084 37 72 21. BEF 2,000 Dbl.
Hotel des Voyageurs, Rue des Chasseurs Ardennais 1. Phone 084 37 72 37. BEF 1,900 Dbl.
Youth Hostel (unofficial): Gite d'Etape, Rue Gite d'Etape 10. Phone 084 37 74 41. Hostel style accommodation.
Camping de la Lesse, Rue du Grand Hy. Phone 084 37 72 90.
Camping Le Pirot, Route de Charleville. Phone 084 37 75 96.

Bicycle Shops/Rentals
Kayaks Lesse and Lomme, Le Plan d'Eau. Phone 084 37 72 30.

Han-sur-Lesse to St. Hubert: 20 Kilometers

Leave west on the main street until you cross the River Lesse. Two hundred meters after you cross the river, turn left. You will ascend and descend until you reach Belvaux. At Belvaux, at the T-intersection, go left, then over the bridge, then turn right and immediately left in the direction of Tellin and Bure.

Cross the N899 and continue straight to Bure, and after 5.5 kilometers, turn left into town at the T and onto the N846. Descend to the N803 and turn right in the direction of St. Hubert, going through Grupont (Auberge) and continuing until you arrive in St. Hubert. Turn left and continue another 500 meters to the center.

St. Hubert stands on a plateau in the heart of one of the most heavily forested areas of the Ardennes. The town is named after the patron saint of hunters. It is said that in 683 St. Hubert had his conversion in the woods near here. Today there is a chapel on the spot. He became a monk at Stavelot Abbey and was later canonized.

This pretty town is centered around the beautiful and huge Basilique St. Hubert which is visible from anywhere in town. The houses and buildings seem to flow down the slope from the basilica. The current basilica has renovations dating from the eighteenth century, the original being built in 1526. The interior, among other features, has some lovely brickwork, an altarpiece with Limoges enamels from the sixteenth century, a Romanesque crypt, and stalls with panels depicting the stories of St. Hubert and St. Benedict. Next door are the Abbey's oldest buildings, dating from 1728 and now housing the province's Cultural Affairs offices and the Tourist Office.

Tourist Information
Next to (left-hand side) Basilique St. Hubert. Phone 061 61 30 10 or 061 61 20 70. Open June to September only.

Accommodations
Hotel de l'Abbaye, Place du Marché 18. Phone 061 61 10 23. BEF 1,600 Dbl.
Hotel de Luxembourg, Place du Marché 7. Phone 061 10 93. BEF 2,250 Dbl.
Camping Europacamp, Rue de Martelange. Phone 061 61 12 69.

Where to Eat
There are a few restaurants centered around the main square, and some of the hotels have good menus.

St. Hubert to La Roche-en-Ardenne: 34 Kilometers

Leave St. Hubert on the N848 in the direction of Bastogne. In 5 kilometers turn left onto a smaller road in the direction of Lavacherie. This takes you into the Forêt de Freÿr, the largest intact forest in Belgium. You will soon pass a military airport on your left. About 10 kilometers from the turnoff you will reach the town of Lavacherie. Turn left in the direction of Tenneville. Follow this road for about 4 kilometers until you reach the larger N4 at Tenneville. Turn left on the N4 in the direction of Champlon for several hundred meters, then turn right onto a smaller road, which takes you through the villages of Wimbay, Beaulieu, and Hives en route to La Roche.

It is not difficult to see why the pretty town of La Roche, nestled in a bend in the Ourthe River, swells with visitors in the summer months. The town cascades down the hillside from the ruins of the eleventh-century castle that overlooks the town and looks as if it might spill into the river itself. The castle is the main attraction in the town other than the views and surrounding area. To reach the castle, which is open daily, take the set of stairs opposite the town hall,

On a more somber note La Roche was under German occupation for most of the war, and as a reminder of this on Rue Châmont 5 is Musée de la Bataille des Ardennes (Battle of Ardennes Museum). This small museum displays uniforms, vehicles, weapons, and other remnants of this war-torn area (open daily).

The next stage of our route to Barvaux takes you west along the Ourthe Valley, but it is worth spending some time in La Roche to explore the Ourthe River Valley to the east of the town, which is the most impressive section. The surrounding area, both the valley and the hills, offers good hiking and biking. The best view in the area is from the tower Belvedères des Six Ourthes, accessible on some very steep roads. Hiking in this area is prime, and there are several trails, including part of the Grande Rondonnée #57 that winds its way through the valley.

Tourist Office
Place du Marché 15. Phone 084 41 13 42.

Accommodations
For a town of 4,000 people, you can see the role of tourism with no less than 14 hotels in town.

Hotel de Liège, Rue de la Gare 16. Phone 084 41 11 64. BEF 1,200 Dbl. Cheapest in town.

Hotel du Luxembourg, Avenue du Hadja 1a. Phone 084 41 14 15. BEF 1,500 Dbl.

Hotel du Midi, Rue de Beausaint 6. Phone 084 41 11 38. BEF 2,000 Dbl.

By the number of campgrounds in the area, approximately 10, it is obvious that the area is popular for all sorts of outdoor activities. Some campground suggestions are:

Camping Floréal, Route d'Houffalize 18. Phone 084 21 94 67.

Camping Benelux, Rue de Harzé 14. Phone 084 41 15 59.

Camping Les Nymphes, Rue de Harzé 18. Phone 084 41 19 58.

Youth Hostel. The closest youth hostel to the route is in Champlon, a few kilometers from Tenneville—Youth Hostel Barrière de Champlon, Rue de la Gendarmerie 4. Phone 084 45 52 94.

There are also three small hotels in Champlon and a campground at Tenneville.

Where to Eat

There are numerous restaurants. Try the smoked ham, a local specialty.

Bicycle Shops/Rentals

M. Hennebert, Place du Bronze 13. Phone 084 41 16 13.

Kayakski, Le Pont du Tram. Phone 084 41 10 35.

La Roche-en-Ardenne to Barvaux-sur-Ourthe: 30 Kilometers

Leave La Roche in the direction of Marche and Hotton on the N833. In 7.5 kilometers you will reach the town of Marcourt. Turn right as you enter town, crossing the bridge over the Ourthe River in the direction of Beffe. You will begin this stretch with a steep but short climb. Veer left at the top of the hill and continue on a gentler climb to Beffe. Continue on to Soy through the tiny communities of Trinal and Melines. At Melines, veer right for 1 more kilometer up to Soy.

Side Trip

From Soy it is only a short distance of 5 kilometers on the N807 to the town of Hotton where the Grottes de Hotton (Hotton Caves) are located. The caves are worth a visit, but if you spent time in the caves at Rochefort or Han, you may want to just pass them by.

To continue on to Barvaux, enter the town of Soy and turn right on the main street (N807) in the direction of Erezée. Then, in approximately 300 meters, veer left in the direction of Oppagne, taking an immediate half right past an old service station, passing an electrical substation in 500 meters. Continue on this farm road for 2.5 kilometers. At the T-intersection, turn left to Barvaux on the N841. You will have nice gentle terrain between Soy and Barvaux. Barvaux is a tourist center with a lovely setting in the Ourthe River Valley.

Accommodations

Le Grillon, En Charlotte 33. Phone 086 21 15 37. BEF 2,000 Dbl.

Le Cor de Chasse, Petit Barvaux 97. Phone 086 21 14 96. BEF 2,200 Dbl.

Camping: there are five campgrounds in the vicinity of Barvaux.

Bicycle Shops/Rentals

M. Tassigny, Grand'Rue 9. Phone 086 21 27 08.

Barvaux-sur-Ourthe to Namur: 48 Kilometers

Leave Barvaux to the west on the N983 in the direction of Durbuy. About 1 kilometer out of town, cut off on a small road to the right, in the direction of Bohon. In the minute center of Bohon, turn left in the direction of Durbuy. In a few meters you will reach a roundabout. Turn right. Continue until you reach a T-intersection. Turn right, following directions to Durbuy. You will descend, go round a hairpin bend in the road, and keep descending with the valley and the town of Durbuy visible below.

Durbuy has the honor of being billed as the smallest town in Belgium. This tiny medieval town is set in a picturesque valley on a bend in the Ourthe River and is all that the Belgian tourist brochures make it out to be. It has maintained its character with a maze of narrow, winding streets lined with charming stone houses. This tiny town even has a seventeenth-century castle to call its own. Walking through the streets is like taking a step back in time. The one thing that all the tourist brochures forget to mention are the hoards of tourists that descend upon this well-publicized spot, especially in the summer and on weekends. Should you decide to stay in Durbuy, this small town of 700 inhabitants has no less than 11 hotels, 2 campgrounds, and plenty of places for visitors to eat. The tourist office is located in Halle Aux Blés, the sixteenth-century corn market, phone 086 21 14 28.

Leave Durbuy along the river on the N833 to the southwest. A walking path is an alternative to riding on the road. You can try cycling this to avoid traffic on the road, which can be heavy, especially on weekends. At the T-intersection, turn right in the direction of Liège on the N983. In a couple of kilometers you will see above and to the right, a château. If you wish to take a closer look, go past it and take the next right onto a side road. Backtrack the 700 meters to the château. This impressive structure is the Château de Petite Somme, now a Hare Krishna establishment with a vegetarian restaurant.

Return to the N983 and continue on to Havelange, crossing the large N63 freeway and riding through the small town of Maffe. Continue straight through Havelange in the direction of Ohey and Andenne. You will still be on the N983. This part of the N983 is gentle rolling hills and farmland. The terrain is much milder now, as you are exiting the Ardennes. Just before you reach Ohey, at the large intersection that is the junction of the N983 and N921, turn right, joining the N921 through Ohey in the direction of Andenne.

Continue on the N921 for 4 kilometers, then turn left in the direction of Haltinne. You will arrive in Haltinne in 1 kilometer. Continue straight. Go past the big moated château, veering left, then right just past the church. Continue another kilometer or so to the town of Strud. Go through town, veering left to Bonneville. Continue 3 kilometers to Bonneville. When you arrive in Bonneville, turn left in the direction of Thon-Samson. Peek in the château gate on your left as you ride past. In approximately 100 meters, veer left at the Y-intersection, then in another few hundred meters, turn right; both turns are signposted in the direction of Thon. When you arrive in Thon, wind your way through the village, always descending. When you reach the main road, turn right. Follow the signs for Nameche, which will take you over the bridge crossing the Meuse River. Once over the bridge, turn left in the direction of Gelbressée. When you come to a Y-intersection, veer left in the direction of

Namur. You will follow the N959 along the Meuse River to Namur, the river being on your left.

Namur to Leuven: 68 Kilometers

To return to Leuven, the starting point of this route and connection to the Northern Belgium Route, use the Leuven to Namur stage, in reverse.

Connections to and from Luxembourg

Belgium to Luxembourg—St. Hubert to Eischen (Grand Duchy of Luxembourg) via Arlon: 72 kilometers

Note: This is a long stretch with little possibility of accommodation except camping en route. Take lunch and be prepared to complete this segment in one day if you are not camping. If you feel it necessary to break the journey, there is a small six-room hotel at Neufchâteau as well as camping. Neufchâteau is a little way off the route, approximately 8 kilometers from Ebly. In Habay-la-Neuve, just 14 kilometers before Arlon, there are a couple

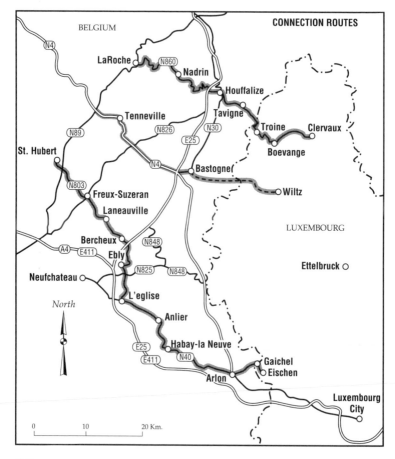

of hotels, but they are on the expensive side. Arlon is a lodging option if you don't want to cycle the last 6 kilometers into Luxembourg.

Leave St. Hubert, ascending in the direction of Vesqueville, crossing the N89. Go through town, veering right in the direction of Freux, turning right soon after the church. Cross the N826 at Freux-Suzeran in the direction of Bougnimont. Approximately 1 kilometer after crossing the N826, notice the superb avenue of trees. Continue straight through Remaux and Laneuville. Go to the village of Wideumont and on to Berchaux where you cross the N85. From where you cross the N85, continue straight to Juseret, going under the A26 about 1.5 kilometers before entering town.

At the fork entering town, veer right, then left at the T through town past the church on the right and continue to Chêne. Then turn right in the direction of Ebly; go into town and turn left in the direction of Léglise. Cross the N825 and continue straight to Léglise, passing through Wittimont. At the N40, turn left in the direction of Habay-la-Neuve, continuing along the N40 through Behême and Anlier to Habay-la-Neuve. From Habay-la-Neuve continue on the N40 to Arlon.

The ancient town of Arlon, sitting atop a hill, is the capital of the province of Luxembourg. It dates back to Roman times, and there is much evidence of the third-century remnants throughout the town. The center of the town is not the Grand'Place as one would expect, but Place Leopold. The Grand'Place is a few minutes from here. To get a view of the town and its slate roofs, visit the seventeenth-century Eglise St. Donat (St. Donat's Church). On a clear day you can see four countries—Belgium, France, Luxembourg, and Germany.

In Place Leopold a World War II tank commemorates the liberation of Arlon in September 1944. Visiting the Grand'Place you will see evidence of the town's age, namely, the Tour Romaine (Roman Tower), which was once part of the third-century ramparts. For more Roman remains, head to the archaeological park on Rue des Thermes Romains where there are remains of the first-century Roman baths as well as foundations of a fifth-century basilica, said to be the oldest church in Belgium (open daily May to September)

An impressive archaeological museum to visit is the Musée Luxembourgeois (Luxembourg Museum) on Rue des Martyrs 13. It has a collection of Roman discoveries from Arlon and the surrounding area including objects found in the excavations of the baths and basilica discussed above plus other sculptures, tools, and pieces giving this museum the largest Roman collection in Belgium (open daily mid-June to mid-September).

To continue into Luxembourg, leave Arlon on the N844 in the direction of Mersch. After 4 kilometers you will reach the Luxembourg border at the village of Gaichel with its cluster of hotels and restaurants. Turn right in the direction of Eischen. Go to Eischen. Then join the Eischen to Luxembourg City stage (see Luxembourg Route).

Arlon Tourist Information
Place Leopold. Phone 063 21 63 60.

Accommodations
Hotel A L'Ecu de Bourgogne, Place Leopold 10. Phone 063 22 02 22. BEF 2,500
    Dbl. Right in the center.
Hotel des Druides, Rue Neufchâteau 106. Phone 063 22 04 89. BEF 1,500 Dbl.
    Cheapest in town but farther from center.
Nearest camping is in Bonnert, 4 kilometers north of Arlon. Route de Bastogne 304. Phone 063 22 65 82.

Where to Eat

There are many eateries around the Grand'Place. Try a *maitrank* (means May drink), an Arlon specialty. It is an aperitif made from Moselle wine flavored with woodruff and served cold with a slice of orange.

Luxembourg to Belgium
Clervaux to La Roche-en-Ardenne: 52 Kilometers

Leave Clervaux in the direction of Eselborn, which is a left turn shortly after the railway station, following the signs to the abbey. The road to Eselborn is approximately 2 kilometers, then you are on the CR332. In Eselborn, veer right in the direction of Weicherdange, where you will ascend for 2 kilometers. Turn left in the direction of Donnange/Weicherdange and descend a little, go up and down and past the golf course on your left, veering right to Donnange. Descend into Donnange and ascend as you leave in the direction of Lullange still on CR332. Continue on to Bovange, and then veer right to Wincrange and continue through Wincrange and veer left until the N12. Cross the N12 and continue straight in the direction of Crendal, still on CR332. Go through Crendal in the direction of Troine; continue through Troine, veering left at the Y in the direction of Houffalize, still on CR332.

Enter Belgium 14.7 kilometers after leaving Clervaux.

Here, for several kilometers after you enter Belgium, the terrain is relatively flat. Go through Buret, then veer left in the direction of Houffalize. Go through Tavigny and Vissoule. Note that between Vissoule and Houffalize the road you will climb is quite narrow, so use caution. Veer right at the T-intersection. In 2 kilometers you will reach Houffalize, a pleasant town with half a dozen hotels and two campgrounds.

At the base of Houffalize, take the N860 in the direction of La Roche and Nadrin. You will follow the river out of town, and go under the huge E25/A26 freeway bridge that looms high above you. With the river on your left, you will pass several campgrounds. The road continues to follow the river, so the gradient is quite gentle; however, unfortunately, this is a winding road with no shoulder.

About 1 kilometer before you reach the town of Mormont, the road becomes steeper. Continue on the N860 to Nadrin. From Mormont to just before Berismenil, the terrain is gentle; then there are rolling hills. Soon you will have a huge 4-kilometer descent from Berismenil to Maboge. At Maboge you rejoin the river and will have a long, but more gentle, 4-kilometer climb. Continue on into the town of La Roche. In La Roche, join the Southern Belgium Route.

Luxembourg to Belgium
Wiltz to Tenneville via Bastogne: 37 Kilometers

Another alternative for leaving Luxembourg is to use the cycle route from Wiltz to Bastogne. The route leaves Wiltz through the wooded Wiltz valley and goes through the town of Winseler, a typical Ardennes village on the Wiltz River. Continue through the peaceful countryside and through a tunnel to arrive at Schleif. Continue, passing through three tunnels to Schimpach, located on the Belgian border. The route along a former railway track leads you to the Belgian town of Bastogne where there is lodging and restaurants.

From Bastogne, follow the N4 highway for 17 kilometers to Tenneville. In Tenneville join the Southern Belgium Route.

Chapter 11

Luxembourg Route

Total Distance:	237 kilometers (147 miles)
Terrain:	Flat along eastern border, hilly throughout the country, plus extended inclines in the north.
Maps:	Michelin Map 215 (1:150,000), or Michelin Map 214 (1:200,000)
Connecting Route:	Route 4—Southern Belgium

Luxembourg is a tiny country, but within its boundaries it offers a great number of sights and attractions. For the cyclist, this compact country provides plenty of interest within short distances.

As well as its own cosmopolitan and very international capital, Luxembourg boasts its own mountains, the Ardennes; a wine-growing region along the Moselle; gentle farmlands; several museums; impressive castles; dramatic river valleys, such as the Sûre Valley; great hiking possibilities; picturesque villages; spectacular gorges; and more. The people are very proud of their country and the splendid opportunities and diversity it offers visitors.

The country is a cyclist's paradise, offering easy cycling along river valleys and the challenge of hefty inclines in the mountains of the north. To encourage the cyclist, Luxembourg is in the midst of an ambitious program to create 600 kilometers of segregated bicycle paths by the year 2000. At the time of writing, over 300 kilometers of these were completed, many using old railway lines. These paths lead the cyclist through serene forests, along babbling brooks, and through idyllic villages. Even when there is no segregated path, the roads in Luxembourg seem to be designed for the cyclist. With a population of less than 400,000, most of that concentrated in the capital and the industrial south, Luxembourg is for the most part very rural. The backroads see little traffic, and the drivers are very aware of cyclists. Even the highways in most of the country are quiet.

173

Luxembourg City (La Ville de Luxembourg)

The name of the 1,000-year-old capital city of the Grand Duchy may not be very imaginative, but never judge a city by its name. Luxembourg City is one of the most enchanting cities in Europe. It is small, with a population of only 75,000, yet has a cosmopolitan and international feel. It is the home of many European political organizations (see Kirchberg below). Its setting is quite stunning with views from many sides. The gorges cutting through the city lend themselves to dramatic views of the bridges and the city's outer areas. For a small city one has to wonder how they managed to build amongst so many hills, which actually add a charm as you climb through the winding streets to the center, which has an abundance of shops, restaurants, historic buildings, and plenty of atmosphere.

Luxembourg City has several bicycle lanes, and it is not difficult to get around by bicycle, but the best way to explore the city is definitely by walking. The city is compact, and sights are not too far apart, so take a day and amble through the city on foot.

As you would expect, Luxembourg City has the typical tourist sights of museums and churches. However, one of the most interesting sights in this city is the Bock Casemates (open daily), the remains of a huge complex of tunnels and fortresses built by the Austrians as a defense against the French in the mid-eighteenth century. More recently, they were used as bomb shelters in the last two World Wars. There are 22 kilometers (14 miles) of tunnels, although only parts are open to the public. You can also visit the Pétrusse Casemates, a smaller fortification on the south side of the city center.

The Place D'Armes is the central square of the city, a bustle of outdoor cafés, restaurants, and shops. The Palais Municipal, where the tourist office is housed, is on one corner of the square. Head to the Grand Ducal Palace, formerly the town hall, and now the residence of the Grand Duke on Rue du Marché-aux-Herbes. The original building, elegantly decorated, dates to the sixteenth century, although there have been additions. It is not open to the public, except when the Duke is away in July/August (check with tourist office for tour information). Continue on to the Cathédrale Notre Dame on Rue Notre Dame whose spires dominate the city's skyline. The seventeenth-century Jesuit church is a mix of Gothic and Renaissance. There is also an interesting crypt with tombs and artwork.

The Musée Nationale (National Museum of History and Art), entrance on Rue Wiltheim, contains ancient and modern art, a Gallo-Roman collection, ceramics, jewelry, and Luxembourg history displays (closed Monday).

For scenic views, take a walk along Promenade de la Corniche, the old ramparts and fortifications of the city. At the south Citadelle du St. Esprit (Citadel of the Holy Spirit), a seventeenth-century citadel built by Vauban, offers more views over the valleys of the Pétrusse and Alzette Rivers.

For a quiet alternative venture to the Vallée de la Pétrusse, a beautiful city park full of willows and cherry trees with cliffs on both sides. Stairways lead down to the valley floor.

Tourist Information

There are two tourist offices in Luxembourg City. The one located in the center at Place d'Armes, phone 22 28 09, is geared specifically to providing information on Luxembourg City. The other tourist office is at the railway station, 9 place de la Gare, phone 48 11 99, and offers information on both the city and the whole country. Be sure to stop here at some point to pick up the free *Luxembourg Accommodation/Restaurant Guide* and other information you might need plus, most importantly, the brochure *Cycle Tracks* detailing bicycle routes throughout the entire country and on which we have based segments of some of our routes.

Luxembourg Airport

Findel Airport is 6 kilometers northeast of Luxembourg City. Unfortunately, at the time of writing, the only form of public transport into town was buses (which do not accommodate bicycles). However, it is not a difficult process to cycle into Luxembourg City or join the route to Echternach.

From the terminal, follow the N1 highway northeast for 2 kilometers to the town of Senningerberg. Once in Senningerberg, you will join the Luxembourg City-Echternach stage of the route (see below) and either turn west for Luxembourg City or east in the direction of Echternach.

Note: There is a larger town of Senninger about a kilometer away from Senningerberg. Be sure to go to Senningerberg, a small village where you will have no trouble finding the bicycle route signs.

Accommodations

Luxembourg City has an abundance of hotels. Check with the tourist office. Here are a few to begin with:

Hotel-Restaurant Français, 14 Place d'Armes. Phone 47 45 34. LUF 3,600 Dbl. A splurge if you want to be right in the center.

Hotel-Restaurant San Remo, 10 Place Guillaume. Phone 46 04 31. LUF 3,200 Dbl. Centrally located in heart of the city.

Hotel Carlton, 9 Rue de Strasbourg. Phone 48 48 02. LUF 1,500 Dbl. For the budget conscious, plain, clean rooms. Near the station. (There are a few more budget hotels in this area, e.g., The Bristol next door.)

Youth Hostel Auberge de Jeunesse Luxembourg, 2 Rue de Fort Olisy. Phone 22 68 89. Just below the casemates.

Camping Kockelscheuer, 22 Route de Bettembourg. Phone 47 18 15.

Where to Eat/Markets

There are a host of restaurants and eateries in Luxembourg City in all price ranges. On Wednesday and Saturday mornings there is an open air market in Place Guillaume selling produce and wares. On the second and fourth Saturday of the month, Place D'Armes is the site of a lively flea market.

Book Shops

English language books are available from Magasin Anglais, 19 Allée Scheffer, and Librarie Ernster, 27 Rue du Fosse, phone 22 50 77.

Bicycle Shop/Rentals

Vélo en Ville, 8 Rue de Bisserwé. Phone 47 96 23 83.

Luxembourg City to Echternach: 40 Kilometers

Leave Luxembourg City via the Rond-point (roundabout) Robert Schuman, where you will find the first sign for the Luxembourg City-Echternach bicycle route. The route first takes you across the Pont Grande Duchesse Charlotte, the high red bridge, to the Kirchberg Plateau. This is a new suburb of Luxembourg City still being developed with unique futuristic architecture. It houses several offices of the European Community and the European Court of Justice.

Once through this suburb, the bicycle trail heads off into the Grengewald Forest. Soon you will pass through the town of Senningerberg, using residential

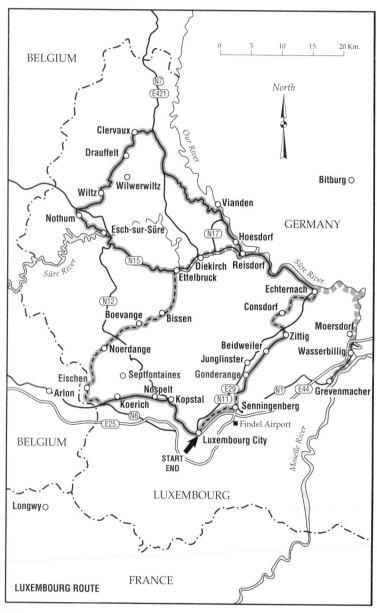

LUXEMBOURG ROUTE

streets. Follow the route signs through the town before rejoining the bicycle path through the forest again. Just past Senningerberg you will have a fairly long descent with great views of the valley and the town of Hostert below. The route does a good job of smoothing out the ups and downs, but some hefty climbs are inevitable in Luxembourg, and one of those follows this long descent. You will then have another long descent, veering right at the bottom along the valley floor.

Follow the trail through the town of Ernster and continue on to Gonderange. Here you will join the CR132 for several kilometers past the town of Junglinster, dominated by the tall transmitter towers of Radio-Télé-Luxembourg (RTL), a European media giant.

From Junglinster, you will continue through beautiful farmland (mainly corn, apple orchards, and cows) with great views, touching on the towns of Beidweiler and Rippig. You will go through an old railway tunnel, and you will see the old train station, now the office of a campground, shortly thereafter.

After a climb of several kilometers and crossing the N11 highway, you will reach the town of Consdorf, a pleasant town with several small hotels. From here on to Echternach it's all downhill—literally. The next 5.5 kilometers are pure cycling heaven, a gentle downhill through a beautiful forest on a well-maintained cycle path. There is a stretch where you will go through a narrow gorge with unique rock formations. Someone has spray painted the words *Gran Canon* on the pavement at both ends. You will then join the N11 for a short while before you rejoin a path off the road to town, which is another 2 kilometers away. Just before you reach Echternach you will come to Echternach Lake. The trail goes all the way around the lake, so you can detour around it or continue on past it into town about 1 kilometer farther on.

Echternach is known for its many historical buildings, including the fifteenth-century town hall located on the picturesque central Place du Marché (Market Place), eighteenth-century patricians' houses, and most importantly, its abbey. The abbey includes the eleventh-century basilica Basilique de St. Willibrord, which was rebuilt after suffering severe damage in World War II. The crypt of the basilica houses the remains of St. Willibrord, the patron saint of Luxembourg. The Abbey Museum (open daily Easter through October, weekends November through Easter) has an excellent display of illuminated manuscripts from the abbey dating from the ninth to eleventh centuries, including examples of the famous *Codex Aureus*, one of the most famous such works in the world. The original is now housed at the German National Museum in Nuremburg. The museum also includes some eighth-century monks' tombs, complete with skeletons.

Eglise Sts.-Pierre-et-Paul is in the center of town. Parts date back to the seventh century and also to the Roman era when a palace stood on the site, but it has been reconstructed many times over the centuries.

You can still see some of the old town walls and towers from the thirteenth century and visit the ruins of an old Roman villa, Palais Romain, dating from the first century, near the lake, which you will pass on your right as you enter Echternach.

Petite Suisse Luxembourgeoise (Little Switzerland) is the tiny enclave of gorges, rushing streams, rock formations, and tranquil wooded areas to the west of Echternach. Although the last portion of the Luxembourg City to Echternach stage takes you through this area, which has some of the most perfect cycling you'll ever experience, it's worth spending some extra time in the area and exploring some of the other bicycle routes, as well as some of the hiking trails, such as the Gorge du Loup. The Gorge du Loup is the most popular hike in the area. It can be reached by using the trail identified as Promenade B-1, which begins near the bus station. It is just over a half hour walk from there.

Tourist Information

Porte St. Willibord at the Basilica. Phone 7 22 30. For a change of pace you may want to consider some hiking in this area. You are at the base of the Petite Suisse (see above). The tourist office has maps and information on area hiking trails. Also the town hosts one of the most well-attended arts events in Luxembourg, the Echternach Festival (classical music) weekends during May/June when accommodations may be tight.

Accommodations

Hotel and restaurant row is Rue de la Gare.

Hotel Bon Acceuil, 3 Rue des Merciers. Phone 7 20 52. LUF 1500 Dbl. Excellent value and atmosphere, plus good food. Run by a friendly Portuguese family.
Hotel Aigle Noir, 54 Rue de la Gare. Phone 7 23 83. LUF 1,500 Dbl.
Youth Hostel, 9 Rue André Duchscher. Phone 7 21 58.
Camping Officiel, Route de Diekirch. Phone 7 22 72.
Camping Alferweiher, 1 Alferweiher. Phone 7 22 21.

Where to Eat

Several restaurants are scattered through the town. Many are around the square or along Rue de la Gare. Try the restaurant at Hotel Bon Acceuil for good value and well-prepared meals.

Bicycle Shops/Rentals

Trisport, 31 Route de Luxembourg. Phone 7 20 86.

Optional Day Trip: Echternach to Grevenmacher
Round Trip: 60 Kilometers

Join the cycle path along the Sûre River just south of the Echternacherbruecke. The bridge across the river is just a couple blocks from the abbey and the center of town. The bridge is the connection with Germany, as the Sûre forms the border between the two countries at this point. You'll actually see the small stone building at this end of the bridge that says *Douane* and *Zoll*; this is the old customs and immigration building. Since the start of the open border policy and the United Europe, it is completely unused.

Just south of the bridge, the path starts in the city park along the river, and you will share the path with pedestrians for the first couple of kilometers. At this point you are at the same level as the river. Farther on the path climbs above the river for brief periods giving you some nice views of the river valley. Most of what you see is actually Germany, the other side of the river. The cycle path you will follow is the Route de Basse Sûre, or "Lower Sûre River Route." From Echternach it follows the river, sometimes right alongside, sometimes on the other side of the road. The first part, from Echternach to Moersdorf, is a cycle track separated from the road. It takes you through the towns of

Rosport (famous for its mineral water) and Born. In between is lovely farm-land and forest. Since you are following the river the whole way, there are no large hills to deal with.

At the town of Moersdorf 17 kilometers south of Echternach, you will come to a wooden pedestrian and bicycle bridge over the Sûre. The Basse Sûre route sign directs you over the bridge telling you that Wasserbillig is 7 kilometers via BRD (Bundesrepublik Deutschland-Germany). Cross the bridge and continue on the German side of the Sûre, following the green and white bicycle signs, which now direct you along the Sauertal route. *Sauer* is the German word for Sûre, and *tal* means valley. This gives you a chance to look across at the Luxembourg side of the valley. In about 5 kilometers you will come to another small bridge over the river, and the sign directs you back to Luxembourg. Cross the bridge, then follow the road south another 2 kilometers to the town of Wasserbillig.

At Wasserbillig the Sûre River flows into the larger Moselle River. As you come to the church, continue straight down one of the smaller side streets rather than turning right and following the car signs to Grevenmacher. This will take you down to the Moselle River. Turn right and follow the Promenade de Moselle for 2 kilometers to the town of Mertert. Here the Promenade ends, and you must veer right through the town and to the main road where you turn left and follow the road south 4 kilometers to Grevenmacher. Notice the vineyards along the river as you continue south.

Grevenmacher, a small village, is the center of the Luxembourg wine region. There are both cooperative and private wine producers with tasting rooms where you can sample and buy the local wines. Some of the local wines to try are Ebling, a very dry white, Rivaner, a pleasant fruity wine, and Pinot Gris, a full bodied white. The tourist office is near the river just below the pedestrian shopping zone. Grevenmacher also has a butterfly garden that you pass on your way into town.

Tourist Information
10 Route du Vin. Phone 75 82 75. Check for wine festivals in the area, espe-cially in August/September when it is harvest time.

Accommodations
Hotel-Restaurant Mosellan. 35 Route de Trèves. Phone 7 51 57. LUF 1,800 Dbl. Youth Hostel, Gruewereck 15. Phone 7 52 22.

Bicycle Shops/Rentals
Maison Schwall, 23 Rue de Thionville. Phone 7 52 45. No rentals.

Return to Echternach using exactly the same route, heading back to Mertert and on to Wasserbillig. Then we suggest you skip the Germany de-tour and head straight up the main road to Moersdorf. This cuts about a kilo-meter and a couple of small hills off the return trip.

Echternach to Reisdorf: 17 Kilometers
Begin at the bus station at the west end of Rue de la Gare. The cycle path begins in town, where in the initial stage you will share the path with pedes-trians. The path follows the Sûre River, going northwest, weaving through the woods alongside the riverbank, sometimes following the bank and at other

times the road, the N10, but never crossing the N10. You will always have a bicycle path.

After a couple of kilometers, you will pass through the village of Weilerbach. Just beyond the village, at a covered wooden bridge, is a memorial to the 5th U.S. Infantry Division, which crossed the river on February 7, 1945, during the Battle of the Bulge. It's a reminder that this part of the world has not always been this peaceful. Continuing on, the next town you pass through is Bollendorf-Pont, then Grundhof, and Dillingen. In Dillingen the bicycle path veers right and goes through the Campground Bon Accueil, rejoining the road at the west end of the campground.

Continue on through the town of Wallendorf-Pont and on to Reisdorf.

Reisdorf has numerous camping possibilities, but there it is not much of interest in the village.

Side Trip

From Dillingen it is a 4-kilometer detour up to Beaufort. Note: This road, the CR364, climbs up to Beaufort. (From Reisdorf it is 5 kilometers and also a climb.) Beaufort is home to the ruins of a twelfth-century castle. It is lots of fun to climb around and explore the keep, the dungeon, the remains of the kitchen, and so on. It is located on a steep wooded slope, and there are some fine walks in the area (open daily, April to October). The tiny village of Beaufort is known for its *cassero*, a black currant liqueur similar to the French cassis. If you decide to stay here, there are a few small hotels, a youth hostel, and a couple of campgrounds.

Accommodations

Reckinger Hotel/Restaurant de la Sûre, 17 Rue de la Sûre. Phone 8 62 10. Only open during peak season.
Camping de la Rivière, 21 Rue de la Sûre. Phone 8 63 98.
Camping de la Sûre, 23 Rue de la Sûre. Phone 8 62 46.

Reisdorf to Vianden: 13 Kilometers

In Reisdorf, cross the bridge over the Sûre River, following the bicycle sign for Vianden, veering right just across the bridge. Notice the cute little stone church on your left as you cross the bridge. You will begin on the CR358, and you'll have beautiful valley views with several picnic benches. At 2.2 kilometers, just before the bridge that crosses into Germany, turn left at the yellow bicycle sign onto a small farm road, where you will immediately deal with about 600 meters of a hefty uphill grade. After this you will have some gentler ups and downs through orchards and cow pastures with beautiful views of the Our River valley. Approaching the town of Hoesdorf, you will have great views of the pretty village with its unique church belfry, a former defense tower.

In Hoesdorf, join the N10 for about 4.5 kilometers to Bettel. Along this stretch you will start high above the Our River, but by the time you reach Bettel you will be at river level. Arriving in Bettel, notice the onion-domed church. Just past the church, watch for the cycle path veering off to the left. This takes you up through a beautiful forest. As you climb the hill, watch for a tricky hairpin right, which is marked not by a sign but a white bicycle and an arrow painted on the road itself. Just as you make this turn, you will reach a great picnic area with several tables. Then you will descend back down to the river, where, just before reaching Vianden you will cross the N10 and then the river. Take the cycle path through the campground Camping de Moulin and on to the stunning town of Vianden. You will arrive at the bottom end of town, and your toughest climb of this segment is through town up to the castle at the top.

Vianden is one of the most picturesque villages in Luxembourg or, for that matter, in all of Europe. It is the epitome of the fairy-tale village, set with a backdrop of hills, surrounded by forests. You will enter the village along a pretty section of the Our River and climb up through cobblestone streets to the crowning glory of the village, the Château de Vianden (open daily). The Château, a twelfth-century castle, was restored through government efforts in the early 1980s. Visit the colorfully painted chapel and the Count's Hall complete with tapestries.

Victor Hugo lived in Vianden several times during his life, including 1871 when he lived here in exile. His house was rebuilt after sustaining damage during World War II and is now a small museum housing some of the author's letters and belongings, as well as the tourist office.

On the Grand'Rue is Eglise des Trinitaires (Trinitarians Church), one of the oldest religious buildings in Luxembourg, its nave dating back to 1248. Visit the fourteenth-century cloister behind the church. Across the road is the Musée d'Art Rustique (Folklore Museum) with crafts, antiques, dolls, and other items on display (open daily except Monday in off season).

Tourist Information
Victor Hugo House, 37 Rue de la Gare. Phone 8 42 57.

Accommodations
Several hotels along Grand'Rue and Rue de la Gare. Plus the tourist office has information on bed and breakfasts in town.

Auberge-Restaurant de L'Our, 35 Rue de la Gare. Phone 8 46 75. LUF 1,900 Dbl.
Auberge-Restaurant Aal Veinen, 114 Grand'Rue. Phone 8 43 68; LUF 2,000 Dbl.
Hotel-Restaurant Heintz, 55 Grand'Rue. Phone 8 41 55. LUF 1,700–2,800 Dbl.
    Former monastery.
Youth Hostel, 3 Montée du Château. Phone 8 41 77. Beautifully located in the
    shadow of the château.
Camping du Moulin. This is the campground you ride through as you enter
    Vianden. Phone 8 45 01.
Camping op dëm Deich, on the river as you enter town. Phone 8 43 75.

Where to Eat
Lots of restaurants, especially on Rue de la Gare or Grand'Rue.

Bicycle Shops/Rentals
In the Pavillion next to the bus station. Rental and minor repairs.

Vianden to Clervaux: 29 Kilometers
Leaving Vianden, walk or ride to the top of the town. Ascend on the road to Fouhren. After 1 kilometer turn right in the direction of Clervaux on the CR322. You will have a spectacular view back down on Vianden and the château. There is just enough of a shoulder along this road to make it a comfortable ride.

A separated bicycle path leaving Dillingen en route to Grundhof.

Continue for 3.5 kilometers, gradually climbing up. On the left side of the road, a walking path begins approximately at the top of the climb and continues for about 2 kilometers. Use this with caution if you would prefer to get off the road for a bit. This stage starts with a total of 7 kilometers going uphill, the first 3.5 kilometers fairly steep.

Follow the CR322 until you reach the N7, take a right and continue in the direction of Clervaux. This is a fairly busy road, but you will have no other options to get to Clervaux. You will be on this road for approximately 8 kilometers until you turn left at Manach onto the N18. Follow the N18 west for 5 kilometers until you reach Clervaux.

Clervaux is a pretty village, and you will get a great view from above as you descend. The main attraction is the twelfth-century feudal castle which is right in the center. In the peace of the moment, you will notice the tank at the entrance to the castle, a stark reminder of the battles of the Ardennes. The castle was damaged in December of 1944 and is now restored. It houses several exhibits, the most visited of which is Edward Steichen's permanent exhibit, *Family of Man*, with 503 photos from all over the world. The theme is "human solidarity"; it is a moving presentation in black and white. There is also a Battle of the Bulge Museum. The castle is open daily from June to September, Sundays the other months, and is closed January and February.

There is a walking trail marked "Abbaye" leading up to the red brick turreted Benedictine Abbey St. Maurice which sits in the forest above the village. The Abbey was built in neo-Romanesque style in 1910 by monks who moved here from France. There is an exhibit of monastic life in the crypt.

Tourist Information
Inside the castle. Phone 9 20 72.

Accommodations
There are four hotels in town.

Hotel/Auberge-Restaurant des Ardennes, 22 Grand Rue. Phone 92 02 54. LUF 2,300 Dbl. In center of town.
Hotel du Parc, 2 Rue du Parc. Phone 9 10 68 or 92 06 50. Even if you don't stay here, ride past this elegant former château set in the lovely park setting across from the castle.
Camping Officiel. 33 Klatzewé. Phone 9 20 42.

Clervaux to Wiltz: 19 Kilometers
Following the CR325 toward Wiltz, descend on the narrow road out of Clervaux. At 6.2 kilometers, cross the bridge by turning right into Drauffelt in the direction of Wiltz, still on the CR325. Climb out of Drauffelt, continuing in

the direction of Wiltz, then descend for several kilometers. At 11 kilometers, turn right toward Wiltz, still on CR325. Climb for 1 kilometer, then continue with some hefty ups and downs to Wiltz, passing through Erpeldange and Weidingen, with excellent views of Wiltz as you approach it from above.

Built into the side of a small plateau, Wiltz seems to flow down the slope. The town is divided into Ville Haute (Upper Town) and Ville Basse (Lower Town). The town's twelfth-century château, with additions in 1631 and 1722, is at the top of the Ville Haute. There is a small museum in town, Musée Arts et Métiers (Museum of Arts and Trades), with antique displays from local bakers, tanners, and distillers (open late May to mid-September).

Tourist Information
In the castle. Phone 95 74 44.

Accommodations
Hotel/Auberge-Restaurant Michel Rodange, 11 Rue Michel Rodange. Phone 95 82 35. LUF 1,700 Dbl. In center of town.
Hotel-Restaurant Beau-Séjour, 21 Rue du 10 September. Phone 95 82 50. LUF 2,000 Dbl. Rustic setting in lovely gardens.
Youth Hostel, 6 Rue de la Montagne. Phone 95 80 39.
Camping Kaul, Rue Jos Simon. Phone 95 00 79.

Bicycle Rentals
At the youth hostel.

Wiltz to Esch-sur-Sûre: 12 Kilometers

From the parking area for the château, take the Route de Bastogne in the direction of Roullinger. Turn right and climb 1 kilometer to the village of Roullinger. Go through the village and continue on the CR318. At 4 kilometers, join the N26 for about 500 meters. Cross the N15 and turn left into Nothum next to the Hotel Schuman. Go through Nothum and on to Kaundorf on the CR318, another 4.5 kilometers. Leave Kaundorf on the CR316 and climb a bit before starting a long steep descent. You will cross the dam over the River Sûre. This dam was built as part of a hydroelectric project in 1937 that created the 10-kilometer-long lake, the Lac de la Haute Sûre, above it. Veer left at the end of the dam and descend farther into the town of Esch.

The setting of Esch-sur-Sûre, a village of 240 inhabitants, has to be seen to be believed. The entire village is tucked inside an elbow loop in the river which is almost a full circle, leaving only a tiny piece of land. The imposing ruins of a tenth-century castle tower over the village, and a climb up to them offers a fine view.

Tourist Information
6 Rue de L'Eglise. Phone 89 93 67. Open only in summer.

Hotels and Restaurants
It is not cheap to stay in Esch-sur-Sûre. All the restaurants are attached to hotels.

Hotel-Restaurant Le Postillon, 1 Rue de l'Eglise. Phone 89 90 33. LUF 3,000 Dbl. Located on the bank of the Sûre River.
Auberge-Restaurant de la Sûre, 1 Rue du Pont. Phone 89 91 10. LUF 2,400 Dbl.

Esch-sur-Sûre to Ettelbruck: 35 Kilometers

To leave Esch, go through the tunnel and proceed on the N27 in the direction of Diekirch/Ettelbruck. Stop for a moment in the parking area on the left for a great view of the château. Follow the N27. The Sûre River will be on your right. At 1.4 kilometers, after the second tunnel, turn right onto the N15 in the direction of Göbelsmühle, then left in about 500 meters, back onto the N27. Wind up and down the 11 kilometers to Göbelsmühle following the Sûre River below you on the right. There are beautiful views of the valley below.

Bourscheid Moulin is located in the big bend in the river with the town and camping below. As you come around the bend, note the château on the hill in the distance. This is Bourscheid Castle, another castle in ruins. The castle is accessible by a steep road, but as a cyclist you may just want to take in the view from here. There are a couple of campgrounds right on the river at the village of Bourscheid Moulin. Continue 13 kilometers to Erpeldange and turn right in the direction of Ettelbruck, then at the E421, turn right to Ettelbruck.

Ettelbruck to Eischen: 32 Kilometers

Note: The bicycle path that was, at the time of this writing, completed from Colmar-Berg to Eischen was scheduled to be extended to Ettelbruck. Check with the tourist office to see if it is completed.

Leave Ettelbruck to the south, passing through the town of Schieren after about 2 kilometers, continuing another 3 kilometers to the twin towns of Colmar-Berg. Stay on the main street through Colmar-Berg. At the far end of town you will pass the big Goodyear factory on your left. Just past the factory, as the main road starts up a big hill, you will see a bicycle route sign indicating a right turn onto the bicycle path. The route you will follow from this point all the way to Eischen is the Piste Cyclable de l'Attert and is signposted.

The route takes you through lovely forest and farmland with rolling hills. There are no difficult hills, although there is an ascent of over a kilometer after you pass through the village of Bissen. You then descend through the town of Boevange and continue on to the town of Useldange, which is very much dominated by the ruins of the old feudal castle. The castle is currently being partially restored, and you can climb up the hill and wander around the old walls and visit the cemetery next to the ruins of the old chapel.

The route then continues through forest and farmland to the town of Eischen. About 3 kilometers before you reach Eischen, you will pass through an old train tunnel that has been carved through the mountain. It is about 700 meters long and is lighted and straight, so it is not difficult, but it is a bit spooky. Continue to Eischen.

Eischen Vicinity Accommodations

There are no hotels or campgrounds in Eischen itself, but the tiny border town of Gaichel, just over 1 kilometer to the northwest, offers hotel alternatives. Camping is nearby in Septfontaines and Steinfort. There is one restaurant in Eischen.

Hotel/Restaurant La Bonne Auberge, Maison 7, Gaichel. Phone 39 01 40. LUF 2,500 Dbl.

Hotel/Restaurant La Gaichel, Maison 5, Gaichel. Phone 31 01 29. LUF 3,750 Dbl.

Camp An der Hô, Route de Mersch, Septfontaines. Phone 30 60 48.

Camp Simmerschmelz, Septfontaines. Phone 30 70 72.
Camping Steinfort, 72 Route de Luxembourg, Steinfort. Phone 39 88 27.

Eischen to Luxembourg City: 30 Kilometers

If you are joining this route from Belgium, you will enter Eischen from Arlon via Gaichel. Cross the river from the main part of town, following the direction to Steinfort. Just as you start up the hill, you will see the bicycle route signs leading off to your right.

Continue on the bicycle route from Eischen to Steinfort (Piste Cyclable de l'Attert). The path skirts around the town of Steinfort, going down a hill with an S-curve at the bottom. Just after the curve, turn left at the intersection, leaving the bicycle route which continues straight up the hill to the south. You will now join the CR109 up a slight incline lined with trees ringed with white paint. Follow this road over the hill into the town of Koerich. You will come to a T-intersection.

Side Trip: Vallée des Sept Châteaux (Valley of Seven Castles)

If you go left at the T onto the CR110 in the direction of Hobscheid and Septfontaines, you can visit the Vallée des Sept Châteaux. The castles, in various stages of repair and restoration, are scattered through the forests and farmlands of the Eisch Valley. From here Hobscheid is 4 kilometers and Septfontaines is 6 kilometers. Should you wish to see more of the valley, go on the CR110 in the direction of Septfontaines (note the seven-mouthed fountain), then follow the CR105, veering off a road on the left, to Ansembourg, Hollenfels, and then back onto the CR105 and conclude in the town of Mersch.

Continuing on the route to Luxembourg City from Koerich, turn right in the direction of Goeblange, still on the CR109. This takes you past the ruins of the Château Grevenschloss, built in 1585. Koerich is the southernmost town of the Valley of Seven Castles. Next to the ruins, the pink building is the Mairie (town hall), dating from 1798 and still in use. Above and behind the ruins is the impressive seventeenth-century deanery church with its bulb-like steeple and beautiful Baroque altar.

Continue past the ruins and on up the hill to the almost adjoining village of Goeblange. Turn left in the direction of Simmerschmelz and Septfontaines, then in another couple hundred meters take a right in the direction of Nospelt. Ride up the hill past the water tower with the unique spiral design, then through some lovely forest to the town of Nospelt about 3 kilometers away. Turn left in the direction of Kehlen.

In Kehlen, turn right into the center. Just before the church, turn left onto Rue de Kopstal, also the CR103. Ride up the hill out of town, and continue 3 kilometers on to Kopstal. Just before Kopstal, you will come to the N12. Turn right and follow the N12 through town, then up for over 2 kilometers to the town of Bridel. It is fairly steep for the first kilometer with only a small shoulder to ride on. If you are riding this unloaded as part of a day trip, the hill is not as bad as it looks. If you are riding this loaded, it is a difficult climb, but we found no better alternative.

Once through the town of Bridel, you will enter the Bamboesch Forest and ride down an even bigger hill than you came up; it is about a 3-kilometer descent. At the bottom of the hill you are on the outskirts of Luxembourg City. Turn right at the intersection and follow the signs to the center of town.

Reisdorf to Ettelbruck via Diekirch: 15 Kilometers

This short stage is an alternative connection between Reisdorf and Ettelbruck and enables you to either shorten the route or select Ettelbruck or Diekirch (both centrally located) as a base for day trips.

In Reisdorf, stay on the south side of the Sûre and leave to the west following the sign in the direction of Diekirch. Soon you will join the bicycle path, which follows the old railroad line along the river. This takes you away from the road and into the lovely, quiet forest. In a couple of kilometers you will pass through the village of Moesdorf, then in a couple more you will come to Bettendorf. Notice the small park with the monument to the 10th Infantry Regiment of the U.S. Army, erected by the citizens of Bettendorf. Most of the town is on the other side of the river, but you actually turn left as you come to the bridge, staying on this side of the Sûre.

At the 9.6-kilometer mark, follow the yellow bicycle signs up from the river and across the pedestrian/cycle bridge into the town of Diekirch. (See below if you wish to visit or stay here.) If you want to continue on to Ettelbruck, turn left just across the bridge, continuing in the same direction along the Sûre but now on the other side. In about 1 kilometer you will come to a wooden bridge across the river. At this point, the bicycle path takes you away from the river and follows the main road for less than a kilometer. Then, following a yellow bicycle sign, you veer left onto a bicycle/pedestrian path and are along the river once again.

At 13 kilometers you will cross the Sûre another time, traveling over a covered wooden bridge. Continue along the river for another 2 kilometers until you come to a T-intersection. Turn right; this takes you under the railroad bridge. You will then curl up and around, crossing the same bridge, which has a bicycle/pedestrian lane on one side. This takes you to the Ettelbruck train station. The town's information office is located in the station building, and the main part of town is just a few blocks away.

Diekirch Information

Inhabited since before Roman times, Roman remains are still visible in town today. Two museums of note are the Diekirch Historical and Battle of the Bulge Museum at 10 Bamertal, containing dioramas of the battle (open daily Easter to October), and Musée Mosaïques Romaines (Municipal Museum) at Place Guillaume, housing beautiful Roman mosaics from the fourth century, found in Diekirch, as well as other local relics.

Vieille Eglise St. Laurent (Old St. Laurent's Church) at Place de la Libération is a small church that had its origins in the fifth century. The old crypt, discovered in 1961, dates from the time of the Franks and, during excavations, about 30 sarcophagi were found, some with intact skeletons.

Heading out of town on hiking path D from Route de Larochette in the south of town, you can hike for 15 minutes or so to the Dieweiselter, a dolmen (a rock mound). It is believed by some to be a Celtic sacrificial altar. Its origins are uncertain, and the forest setting gives it a mysterious feel.

Tourist Information

1 Esplanade. Across road from newer Eglise St. Laurent, not to be mistaken for the older one tucked away in houses. Phone 80 30 23.

Accommodations

There are a few hotels in town:

Hotel-Restaurant Ernzbach. 4 Avenue de la Gare. Phone 80 36 36. LUF 1,500 Dbl.
Camping de la Sûre, Route de Gilsdorf. Phone 80 94 25.
Camping du Cercle Nautique, 21 Route d'Ettelbruck. Phone 80 39 39.

Where to Eat

There are a few restaurants in town. Check restaurants in hotels. Hotel Ernzbach has a good restaurant.

Bicycle Shops/Rentals

Speicher Sports, 56 Rue Claire Fontaine, Diekirch. Phone 80 84 38. No rentals.
Camping de la Sûre, Route de Gilsdorf. Phone 80 94 25. Rentals in season only.

Ettelbruck Information

Ettelbruck is the gateway to the Ardennes. It is conveniently located in the heart of the country where the Alzette, Sûre, and Wark rivers meet. It is not as spectacular as some towns in the country but makes a good base for exploring. It has all types of accommodations, good rail connections, and good biking and hiking in the vicinity.

About the only attraction of any note in Ettelbruck is Musée Patton at 13 Grand Rue, which houses memorabilia of the Battle of the Bulge. It is located in Patton Park, which has a 3-meter- (9-foot-) tall statue of General George Patton. A cute statue that is more fun to look at than the General is the statue of the milkmaid with animals leaping around her skirts in the square (Place de la Résistance) outside the Hotel Herckmans.

Tourist Information

At the train station. Phone 8 20 68.

Accommodations

Hotel Herckmans, 3 Place de la Résistance. Phone 81 74 28. LUF 1,500 Dbl. Excellent rooms at reasonable prices.
Auberge-Restaurant Arthur, 1 Rue Neuve. Phone 81 04 27. LUF 1,600 Dbl.
Youth Hostel, Rue Grande-Duchesse Josephine-Charlotte. Phone 8 22 69.
Camping Kalkesdelt, Rue du Camping. Phone 8 21 85.

Where to Eat

There are a few restaurants in town. Most are restaurants in hotels.

Bicycle Shop

Ferrari, 44 Ave. J. F. Kennedy Ettelbruck. Phone 81 64 64. No rentals.

Appendices

A. Glossary of Terms

Abbaye: Abbey
Abdij: Abbey
Begijnhof (Beguinage): Enclosed residential community for Beguines, an order of lay nuns; usually a group of buildings surrounding a small, peaceful courtyard
Benelux: Belgium, Netherlands, and Luxembourg
Brug: Bridge
Carillon: Church tower chimes
Casemates: Tunnels built into natural hills for military defense
Centrum: Center
Château: Castle
Cloister: Monastery, abbey, or convent
Dorp: Village
Eglise: Church
Gables (stepped): Building facades with step shape on upper level
Gracht: Canal (also Kanaal)
Grande Rondonnée: Network of European hiking paths
Guild House: Offices of the medieval trade unions, or guilds
Haven: Harbor

Hôtel de Ville: Town hall
Huis: House
Jaagpad: Towpath along canal
Kasteel: Castle
Kerk: Church (Grote and Kleine: Great and Small)
Locks: Gate mechanism in a waterway or canal to raise or lower water level of boats
Maison: House
Markt: Market Square
Molen: Windmill
Moulin: Mill
Onze Lieve Vrouw (O. L. Vrouw): Our Lady (as in Church of)
Place: Square
Place du Marché: Market Square
Plein: Square
Polder: Area of reclaimed land
Poort: Gate
Speeltoren: Bell Tower
Stadhuis: Town Hall
Veer: Ferry
Ville: Town
Vrijthof: Regional term for a church square (used in southeast of the Netherlands)
Waag: Weigh house

B. Cycling Vocabulary

English	Dutch	French
Bicycle	Fiets	Vélo/Bicyclette
Handlebars	Stuur	Guidon
Light	Licht	Feu
Brakes	Rem	Freins
Front fork	Voorvork	Fourche avant
Pump	Pomp	Pompe
Tire	Buitenband	Pneu
Spoke	Spaak	Rayon

Inner tube	Binnenband	La chambre d'air
Rim	Velg	Jante de roue
Air	Lucht	Air
Crank	Crank	Manivelle
Pedal	Pedaal	Pédale
Chain	Ketting	Chaine
Hub	Wielnaaf	Moyeu
Rack	Bagagedrager	Porte baggages
Wrench/Spanner	Moersleutel	Clef
Screwdriver	Schroevedraaier	Tournevis
Wheel	Wiel	Roue
Lock	Slot	Anti-vol
Front	Voor	Avant
Rear	Achter	Arrière
Map	Kaart	Carte
North	Noord	Nord
South	Zuid	Sud
East	Oost	Est
West	West	Ouest
Left	Links	Gauche
Right	Recht	Droite
Straight on	Rechtdoor	Tout droit
Direction	Richting	Direction/Sens
Through traffic	Doorgaand verkeer	Voie de traversée
Caution	Let Op/Pas Op	Attention
Path	Weg	Chemin
Street	Straat	Rue
Excepted	Uitgezonderd	Excepté

C. Weights and Measures

All three of the Benelux countries use the metric system of weights and measures. Basic conversion tables are as follows:

Inches to Meters: 39 inches = 1 meter
Inches to Centimeters: 1 inch = 2.54 centimeters
Miles to Kilometers: 1 mile = 1.6 kilometer
Kilometers to Miles: 1 kilometer = 0.6 mile
Pints to Liters: 2 pints = 1.1 liter
Pounds to Kilograms: 1.1 pounds = 500 grams, 2.2 pounds = 1 kilogram

Distance: To convert miles to kilometers, multiply by 1.6. To convert kilometers to miles, multiply by 0.62.

Examples: 10 miles = 16 kilometers, 10 kilometers = 6.2 miles.

Temperatures: Fahrenheit to Celsius. For an approximate conversion from Celsius to Fahrenheit, double the Celsius amount and add 30.

| Celsius | 0 | 10 | 15 | 20 | 25 | 30 | 35 |
| Fahrenheit | 32 | 50 | 59 | 68 | 77 | 86 | 95 |

Note: In Europe you will see decimal points denoted by commas.

Electricity: Current: 220 volts. Socket: two-pin type.

D. Further Reading

Your trip will be greatly enhanced by a knowledge of where you are going. Background reading before you leave and supplemental guidebooks and literature are most helpful. Some suggestions are:

Guidebooks

Insight Guides: available for Holland, Amsterdam, Belgium, and Brussels (APA Publications)
The Rough Guide: Holland (Penguin)
The Rough Guide: Belgium and Luxembourg (Penguin)
Fodor's *Netherlands, Belgium and Luxembourg* (Random House)
Frommer's *Belgium, Holland and Luxembourg* (Macmillan)
Michelin Green Guides: available for Netherlands; Belgium and Luxembourg
Michelin Red Guide: Benelux
The Blue Guides: available for Holland; Belgium and Luxembourg (Norton)
Backroads of Holland by Helen Colijn (Bicycle Books)

Other Titles of Interest

The UnDutchables by Colin White and Laurie Boucke (White-Boucke Publishing): a look at the Dutch and their culture
The Black Tulip by Alexandre Dumas: historical novel
Hans Brinker or the Silver Skates by Mary Dodge: children's literature
Anne Frank: Diary of a Young Girl: classic World War II autobiography
Mysteries set in the Benelux. Authors include Janwillem Van de Wetering, A. C. Baantjer, and Georges Simenon

Index